Fundraising for Sport and Athletics

Fundraising for Sport and Athletics

BY **RICHARD LEONARD, PHD**

Fitness Information Technology
A DIVISION OF THE INTERNATIONAL CENTER FOR PERFORMANCE EXCELLENCE

262 Coliseum, WVU-CPASS
PO Box 6116
Morgantown, WV 26506-6116

Library of Congress Card Catalog Number: 2011944717

ISBN: 978-1-935412-33-5

Production Editors: Matt Brann, Rachel Tibbs

Cover Design: 40 West Studios

Typesetter: 40 West Studios

Copyeditor: Rachel Tibbs

Proofreader: Maria E. denBoer

Indexer: David C. denBoer

Printed by: Data Reproductions Corp.

Cover image: field hockey: © Nico Smit | Dreamstime.com; calculator: © Michael Flippo | Dreamstime.com; hurdlers: © Hkratky | Dreamstime.com; money: © Vincent Giordano | Dreamstime.com; tennis: © Nick Stubbs | Dreamstime.com

10 9 8 7 6 5 4 3 2 1

Fitness Information Technology
A Division of the International Center for Performance Excellence
West Virginia University
262 Coliseum, WVU-CPASS
PO Box 6116
Morgantown, WV 26506-6116
800.477.4348 (toll free)
304.293.6888 (phone)
304.293.6658 (fax)
Email: fitcustomerservice@mail.wvu.edu
Website: www.fitinfotech.com

Contents

Acknowledgments

I want to express my sincere thanks to the administration and editorial staff of Fitness Information Technology at West Virginia University. Their support throughout the construction of this textbook has been exceptional. A special note of gratitude goes to senior editor Matt Brann, whose diligence and commitment to this book is evident in its overall depth and quality.

I am indebted to my colleagues and associates at Flagler College for all of their cooperation and encouragement. It is an honor to be connected with a group of professionals whose dedication to the learning process and the mission of the school is so evident.

Finally, I would like to convey my heartfelt thanks to my family and friends for their continued support throughout all of my professional endeavors. My wife, Shuli, has continued to be my inspiration and has shown unconditional support for all of my work.

Preface

The primary rationale behind the construction of this textbook relates to today's drastically shifting local, regional, and national economic conditions. Recent events have made fundraising a vital necessity at all echelons of amateur and collegiate athletic administration and coaching, as well as in sports management education. While the obligation of fundraising has been an indispensable component of many athletic organizations in the past, the uncertainty of future philanthropic donations and support compels all athletic organizations to consider implementing aggressive fundraising plans and activities. In basic terms, athletic programs can no longer be passive about fundraising. There is fierce competition for the limited charitable dollars available, and that rivalry will only intensify in the future.

Another salient motive for the development of this text is the direct relationship that the athletic world has with the business world. In business, strategic initiatives can only be created, implemented, and controlled with the proper allocation of resources. Underfunding a corporate strategy will most likely guarantee its breakdown and ultimately its failure. The exact same scenario faces athletic organizations. Current and projected strategic goals and activities will unquestionably fall short of anticipated results without proper funding. Will having the appropriate funding assure an athletic organization's success? No. There are other extraneous variables like administrative proficiency, coaching expertise, and athletic ability that are also fundamental for athletic organization accomplishments. However, having the proper resources through adept fundraising can provide a sustainable competitive advantage over otherwise equally capable athletic programs.

Two core themes of this textbook revolve around the concepts of (1) strategic planning and preparation and (2) operational organization and efficiency of fundraising activities and programs. The text examines exploiting external fundraising opportunities while addressing internal organizational concerns associated with fundraising. This strategic premise furnishes the fundraiser with the ability to examine the external operating environment, assess the organization's capabilities in conducting successful fundraising activities, and construct viable programs that will yield positive cash flows and beneficial public perceptions. Efficiency is displayed through the delineation of focused administrative processes. This emphasis on administrative competency will reduce the wasting of resources and time that can often happen in fundraising.

Because the formation and execution of fundraising programs can be overwhelming, this text will be designed to be logical and user friendly. Section I will introduce the subject of fundraising and present an exhaustive examination into all administrative functions associated with fundraising. Section II will examine tangible fundraising events/activities/programs that can be structured and used by athletic fundraising administrators, coaches, and students. The concluding chapter in Section II will take a comprehensive look into the operation of summer instructional sports camp fundraisers. Additionally, this textbook incorporates the following:

- short-term (terminal) fundraising programs as well as long-term (perpetual) fundraising systems;
- fundraising skills and competencies for a diverse audience of readers;
- proven fundraising events and activities with detailed time frames, limitations, and financial expectations; and
- a broad blending of capital and annual fundraising endeavors.

THE ADMINISTRATION OF FUNDRAISING PROGRAMS

Introduction to Fundraising

INTRODUCTION

This initial chapter of the text will provide a foundational overview and tactics for athletic organization fundraising. These concepts will supply fundraising administrators and team members with a philosophical foundation prior to the tangible administration components (e.g., planning, staffing, and marketing) of the fundraising program. Conceptualizations discussed in this chapter include:

- describing program fundraising;
- presenting several basic guidelines for fundraising events/activities/ programs;
- distinguishing the underlying difference between annual and capital fundraising;
- examining situational leadership concepts for fundraising programs;
- elaborating on fundraising ethical operations and concerns; and
- furnishing a delineated list of essential rights for all athletic program patrons/donors.

Fundraising Defined

Fundraising Tip

The choice of fundraising events/activities/programs relates to the long-term vision and growth potential of the fundraising program as a whole. Some fundraising events and activities take multiple applications over years of operation to reach their maximum financial potential.

The importance of fundraising is determined by the financial position of the organization. If the existing monetary (and resource) status of the program warrants fundraising, the athletic organization's uses for the contributions, gifts, and donations can be unlimited. Fundraising can supplement salaries as well as furnish the means to procure additional equipment, expand travel regions, and amplify promotional activities. Whatever the uses, to generate supplemental athletic organization finances, a fundraising administrator, athletic organization manager, or program coach must apply the systematic foundations of management as they relate to and are focused on the endeavor of fundraising.

Merriam-Webster's Online Dictionary characterizes fundraising as "the organized activity of raising funds (as for an institution or political cause)" and a fundraiser as "a person employed to raise funds...[or] a social event (as a cocktail party) held for the purpose of raising funds." From this definition, to have a lucrative fundraising program, one must first delineate some basic foundations for the fundraising program.

BASIC GUIDELINES TO FUNDRAISING

A special note relating to all fundraising events/activities/programs—there are indispensable guiding principles that must be discussed and imparted to anyone associated with the athletic organization's fundraising. While these guidelines will be discussed many times throughout the text, it is important to introduce them at this point:

1. *No amount is too small.* A minor contributor today could be a generous benefactor tomorrow.

2. *Always personalize the 'thank-you' for the donation, participation, or support of an individual.* The thank-you should present the accomplishments of the event or activity as well as reiterate the individual's worth in reaching the athletic program's fundraising objectives. Thank-you notes should be sent to all volunteers, donors, key players, board members, and community officials. The intrinsic reward realized by each of the individuals receiving a thank-you note is immeasurable.

3. *The fundraising activity or event needs to be selected based on its capacity to correspond with the organization's goals, target market, image, and operational capabilities.* The choice of an inappropriate fundraising event/activity/program could deal permanent damage to the fundraising program and its parent athletic organization.

4. *The fundraising program's databases need persistent updating and accuracy.* Information on current donors, volunteers, and potential new patrons should be a program priority. In the simplest terms, these listings can be the 'lifeblood' of the operation.

5. If a fundraising program is small and unable to put resources into its own autonomous event/activity/program, *the opportunity of 'piggy-backing' on another organization's fundraising effort is a distinct possibility* and should be considered. The key to this arrangement is the cooperation between the fundraising program and the external organization. Both parties must experience a mutually beneficial relationship and should in no way encounter a conflict of interest.

6. *Contingency planning is an imperative function for all fundraising activities/events/programs.* Back-up plans could encompass arrangements for inclement weather, unforeseen community conflicts, pull-outs by financial supporters, and many other possible circumstances that could negatively affect fundraising endeavors.

7. *All athletic program fundraising should be approved through the athletic organization's administration and fall within the guidelines of the athletic organization's governing body of regulations.* The avoidance of any impropriety and regulatory violations should be paramount. Additionally, detailed financial records must be maintained for review and audit by all parties in the athletic organization.

ANNUAL AND CAPITAL FUNDRAISING

There are two distinct and separate categories of fundraising. The first and most consequential is annual fundraising. The ultimate objective of an annual program is the maintenance and fortification of ongoing operations for the current athletic season and fiscal year. Annual fundraising programs should fill the deficit between revenues

© Stock.XCHNG/studioBob

generated and expenditures incurred. If the existing athletic program is functioning at a profit (surplus funds or 'in the black'), the primary purpose of an annual program may be to upgrade and diversify services to the staff and athletes, as well as to enlarge the volume of spectators through increased promotion.

In most nonprofit ventures, annual fundraising is used to underscore sizable endowment campaigns. This fundraising effort concentrates on large philanthropic donations from a small number of individuals. While this approach is the most straightforward to track, it is also a tremendous gamble. For example, if a fundraising program has five principal benefactors and one or two of these individuals or organizations are unable to match their annual projected contributions, the fundraising program could immediately experience up to a 20-40% reduction in operational funds. From a risk-averse perspective, a program that cultivates a broad base of donors and fundraising activities will experience far less financial impact from smaller abstaining donations. This is not to argue in support of abandoning the large donors and sponsors, but rather to stress the monetary stability of a broad-based fundraising philosophy.

The principal difference between capital and annual fundraising is that annual is considered to be more of a perpetual, unending activity while capital is an assignment-specific endeavor. In capital fundraising, the bigger the 'one-time' donation to the program, the better. Most capital fundraising programs have multimillion dollar goals, characteristically within two to five years.

FUNDRAISING LEADERSHIP

As with all fundraising undertakings, the operational aspect of leadership is a critical and decisive factor in whether a fundraising program is successful. The selection of fundraising programs' main administrators goes far beyond their ability to run the 'nuts and bolts' of a fundraising event, activity, or program. They must inspire their people to go beyond the basic criteria of the project. They must use their charisma to influence volunteers to give of their time freely. They must have the vision to see beyond the day-to-day functions of the job. Most importantly, they must lead by example in all elements of the fundraising program. The right person can take the athletic organization to new heights, while the wrong person can inflict irreparable damage from which the athletic organization might not be able to recover.

The first step in recruiting outstanding fundraising leadership is to describe the qualities one wants for the athletic organization. A partial list includes:

1. Integrity

2. Humility

3. Ability to think on the spot

4. Willingness to listen and learn

5. Willingness to grow and stretch

6. Trust in the group process

Fundraising Tip

Fundraisers must appraise the limitations of the overall fundraising program as a guiding element in choosing a fundraising event, activity, or program. Utilize fundraising events/activities/programs that have the greatest promise within the resource restrictions of the program.

© iStockphoto.com/4774344sean

7. Ability to develop new people

8. A goal-oriented nature

9. A sense of humor (Flanagan, 1993, pp. 35-36)

Situational Leadership

Once a fundraising leader is appointed, he/she will need to understand the critical and often multifarious circumstances in which he/she must lead. Because of the dynamic nature of fundraising programs, fundraising leaders/administrators must consciously avoid having a stagnant leadership style. The concept of one style and approach for all circumstances is outdated and will lead to ineffectual group leadership. Fundraising administrators need to be situational evaluators of internal and external environments as well as of people. In other words, fundraising administrators need to assess situations and choose an appropriate leadership response. This underlying foundation of situational leadership can be applied to all fundraising programs.

Situational leaders are uniquely flexible in their observations of their surroundings. They look at every person, event, and environment as a distinct, exclusive challenge and understand that each challenge requires an individual response instead of a formatted reaction. In the simplest terms, for fundraising administrators to become successful situational leaders, they need to actively assess their surroundings and choose appropriate, definitive responses to maximize the fundraising program's potential. There are some major components to becoming an effective situational leader for fundraising programs.

First, never forget that the administrator is the leader and decision maker for the fundraising program. This is easier said than done. Fundraising involves emotions that might not be associated with, or as intense as, business management and leadership. Emotions can cloud decision making and, more importantly, behavior. In most of a fundraising program's administrative circumstances, fundraising administrators can control their emotions, which, in turn, can make situational leadership easy. However, in actual real-world, real-time situations, emotions can run high, making recognition of the appropriate leadership tactic more difficult. To alleviate emotional debilitation, fundraising administrators should try to consciously recognize their emotional states and use internal speech to reiterate their leadership role in the fundraising program. This will help them assess the situation and choose the right leadership tactic.

Second, the administrator must be true to him/herself. Each person, through his/her idiosyncratic background, has certain personality traits and leadership styles. Fundraising program administrators must recognize these traits and become consciously aware of them in specific fundraising leadership situations. There are numerous leadership theories and test instruments that can objectively examine an administrator's personality and leadership base. Administrators can confirm the findings by asking family, friends, and even fundraising staff members if the assumptions and conclusions about their personality are correct. Once a confirmed dominant style is identified, the information should be locked away. It will be the leadership base from which to work in the fundraising program.

Third, the administrator should be true to the board of directors, volunteers, and fundraising program staff. Fundraising administrators should be up front about what type of leadership base they have and how they will handle certain fundraising situations. The fewer the number of surprises, the less apprehension and greater the focus on the message and task. For example, communicate to the fundraising board of directors, volunteers, and staff that there will be a democratic and participative approach to setting individual and project goals. Conversely, tell them that in a real time operational situation, the adoption of a more autocratic and authoritarian approach might be necessary. Also, communicate to the board of directors, volunteers, and staff that each fundraising situation that arises will be evaluated individually and an appropriate leadership approach will be chosen accordingly.

Fourth, the fundraising administrator must listen to people, but he/she should also listen to the environment in which the fundraising program operates. The administrator should also be equipped to handle a fundraising event/activity/program crisis or difficult situation. Whether in the office or at a fundraising activity, a fundraising administrator will sometimes need to lead quickly in a situation that requires a confident, 'take-charge' attitude. Self-confidence emanates from a person and is immediately recognized by a group. The administrator's confidence will help the group to believe in its own abilities. Use the group's positive concept as an influencer in many fundraising situations. The higher the level of an administrator's positive concept, the more a fundraising group will be accepting of that person's leadership. Unfortunately, the opposite is also true. If a fundraising program administrator has a lack of self-confidence, his/her leadership will be minimized (or even rejected) and the fundraising group will fail to perform.

Finally, no matter what the situation or what decision must be made, every leadership action taken must be positive and in line with the fundraising program's pre-

Fundraising Tip

Learn more about leadership. There are countless textbooks, case studies, and self-help books that embrace the subject. Then, look inside the profession of fundraising to discover and benchmark other successful fundraising leaders.

established goals and mission. See Chapter 2 for more information on this component.

In the 1997 publication *The Leadership Challenge*, Kouzes and Posner discuss tactics and approaches to leadership that can be adapted by a situational fundraising administrator. In every instance, the underlying theme is optimism and positive actions. For example, one of their major leadership approaches deals with attracting people to a common purpose. The common purpose is accomplished through an encouraging step-by-step process:

a. Develop a shared sense of destiny.

b. Discover a common purpose.

c. Give life to a vision.

d. Demonstrate personal conviction.

e. Commit to the challenge.
    (Kouzes & Posner, 1997, pp. 123-147)

ETHICS AND FUNDRAISING

From the onset, it must be emphatically stated that this section of the chapter is not written to lecture or to righteously pronounce what behaviors are right or wrong in a particular fundraising or administrative situation. Additionally, this section is not designed to state that everyone should conform to certain professed norms of behavior. The purpose of this component is to 'lay the groundwork' for understanding business ethics (and ethical behavior) as it relates to fundraising program administration. As will become evident, business and personal ethics are extremely complex and subjective elements in the lives of those involved in fundraising.

Fundraising Tip
In making decisions of an ethical nature regarding fundraising program types, administrators must think through all the potential ramifications of their actions.

Influences on Ethics

Ethics is a multidimensional concept that can be examined from an individual, organizational, or cultural perspective. The amount of philosophical literature devoted to the subjects of ethics and values is staggering. However, for the purposes of this fundraising text, start by considering what factors influence ethical behavior and conscience. Dienhart, in his text *Business, Institutions, and Ethics*, examines individual influences on ethical behavior from certain personality traits:

> Low self-esteem is not generally associated with successful executives. Executives need confidence, intelligence, and moral strength to make difficult, possibly unpopular decisions. However, when these traits are not tempered with modesty, openness, and an accurate appraisal of talents, ethical problems can arise. In other words, if executives' theories about themselves are seriously flawed, they are courting disaster ... several ways in which people's theories of themselves tend to get flawed ... illusion of superiority, self-serving fairness bias, and overconfidence. (Dienhart, 2000, pp. 49-50)

In the text *Ethics, the Heart of Leadership,* Ciulla looks at ethical behavior from leadership and relational interactions:

> Morality of leadership depends on the particulars of the relationship between people. It matters who the leaders and followers are and how well they understand and feel about themselves and each other. It depends on whether leaders and followers are honest and trustworthy, and most importantly what they do and what they value. (Ciulla, 2004, p. xix)

DiMauro and Grant, in *Ethics: Opposing Viewpoints,* look at ethical influences from a societal standpoint:

> People are impelled to act ethically simply because others in society do so. When faced with difficult decisions, this theory postulates, people tend to make choices based on what others do in similar situations. (diMauro & Grant, 2006, p. 19)

Fundraising Tip

The stance a fundraising program takes with regard to social/ethical choices sets the tone for the fundraising program's in-house operations and external program perceptions. Try to avoid fundraising programs that may be perceived as socially dubious or unethical.

Which of the ethical perspectives is correct? Simply put, because of the dynamic nature of the subject, they all are. From an individual ethical development point of view, nearly all ethical theorists proclaim that the personality elements of (1) family upbringing and interaction, (2) moral teachings, (3) individual life experiences, and (4) personal circumstances and environmental pressure are fundamental in an individual's ethical decision making. A key observation to note is that while each of these factors is more dominant in different life stages, they are all interrelated and continual throughout the life process. In an individual's formative years, family and peers are the most potent influences in developing an ethical foundation. During this period, most ethical judgments are supported, guided, and monitored by family members and friends. As the individual becomes more autonomous, personal life incidences and environments dominate his/her ethical development. Finally, morals, which are either influenced by a particular profession, organization, or culture/subculture group, affect the choices and beliefs in what behavior should be adopted. Through these elements, every person develops a unique perception of reality. This is why introspective values and ethics vary enormously from individual to individual.

Business Ethics and Fundraising Administration

Fundraising administrators are managers in the business of athletics. No matter at what level the fundraising program operates, the fundraising administrator is bound by the indispensable concepts of sound business practices. Nearly all the rationale that applies to traditionally conceived business ventures also applies to the profession of fundraising. Belief in this concept is crucial to developing a successful and ethical program.

With that in mind, it is important to recognize how today's businesses confront and tackle the growing subject (and often dilemma) of ethical behavior. Ethics and business ethics are defined as the following:

Ethics – the study of right and wrong and of the morality of the choices individuals make.

Business ethics – the application of moral standards to business situations. (Pride, Hughes, & Kapoor, 2002, p. 37)

So how do fundraising programs and their people make determinations in difficult (sometimes near-impossible) situations? There is a remarkable similarity between the ethical circumstances with which traditional business ventures and fundraising administrators both deal.

Four Social/Ethical Choices for a Fundraising Administrator

There are four social/ethical choices that fundraising administrators can adopt from ethical situations:

Obstructionist Stance – approach to social responsibility that involves doing as little as possible and that may involve attempts to deny or cover up violations.

Defensive Stance – approach to social responsibility by which a company meets only minimum legal requirements in its commitments to groups and individuals in its social environment.

Accommodative Stance – approach to social responsibility by which a company, if specifically asked to do so, exceeds legal minimums in its commitments to social groups and individuals in its social environment.

Proactive Stance – approach to social responsibility by which a company actively seeks opportunities to contribute to the well-being of groups and individuals in its social environment. (Griffin & Ebert, 2004, pp. 148-149)

> **Fundraising Tip**
> A fundraising program that endorses proactive social/ethical response tactics has visible side benefits. The program atmosphere will be optimistic, honest, altruistic, and healthy.

Of the above four choices, the most socially ethical method is the proactive stance. If an administrator is to implement this anticipatory methodology for confronting ethical situations, the best tools to utilize are an ethical program plan and fundraising code of ethics.

Development of an Ethical Program Plan for Fundraising

A fundraising program developing an ethical program plan and code of ethics must first explore and scrutinize its values. Values and ethics, though analogous and interrelated, are two separate concepts. The relationship between values and ethics is that "values are stable and enduring beliefs about what an individual considers to be important. Values provide basis for meaning" (Lussier & Achua, 2007, p. 361). "Ethics are standards of right and wrong that influence behavior. Right behavior is considered ethical, and wrong behavior is considered unethical" (Lussier & Achua, 2007, p. 55). In other words, values are the introspective elements that each of us accept as true, while ethics convert those beliefs into actions.

From these essential abstractions, Rue and Byars, in their 2009 text *Management: Skills and Application,* expound on areas of values and their ethical actions that are typically universal to all organizations (including fundraising operations):

- Honesty
- Adherence to the law
- Product safety and quality
- Health and safety at the workplace
- Conflicts of interest
- Employment practices
- Selling and marketing and marketing practices
- Financial reporting
- Pricing, billing, and contracting
- Using confidential information
- Acquiring and using information about competitors
- Security
- Payments to obtain business
- Political activities
- Protection of the environment (Rue & Byars, 2009, p. 93)

Fundraising Tip

The core values of a fundraising program are the side effects of a fundraising administrator's outlook toward ethical choices. All ethical decisions from the top will be noted and continuously dissected as they flow down to the fundraising program's board of directors, volunteer core, and staff.

The depth and magnitude of these subjective core values and ethical actions depend on what the fundraising program deems intrinsically desirable. Once an administrator has examined the fundraising program's philosophical base, then he/she can develop and implement an ethical program plan.

An ethical program plan is a written document that clarifies a fundraising program's values and gives miscellaneous rules that guide actions in as many foreseeable operational conditions as possible. According to Hall (1993), there are eight ingredients that must be present in fostering and employing an ethical fundraising program plan:

(1) Statement of Values is the ethical equivalent to a business mission statement. This statement is a comprehensive narrative that is a broad basis for the fundraising program's ethical plan.

(2) Corporate Tradition and Values and **(3) Tone at the Top** are historical overviews of the past fundraising program ethical actions and values as well as the current overall atmosphere in the profession of fundraising.

(4) A Code of Conduct, (5) Established Procedures, and **(6) Ethical Training Programs** are the determined, tangible codes and procedures for ethical action in the fundraising program. The more circumscribed and tangible an administrator can be with each definitive procedure, the better.

(7) Hot Line/Open-Door Policy and **(8) Oversight/Control** are the overseeing and monitoring directives in a fundraising ethical program plan.

When writing an individual and specific ethical code of conduct, there are some relevant directives that should be followed:

1. Be clear about the objectives the code is intending to accomplish.

2. Get support and ideas for the code from all levels of the organization.

3. Be aware of the latest developments in the laws and regulations that affect your industry.

4. Write as simply and clearly as possible. Avoid legal jargon and empty generalities.

5. Respond to real-life questions and situations.

6. Provide resources for further information and guidance.

7. In all its forms, make it user-friendly because ultimately a code fails if it is not used. (Hartman & DesJardins, 2008, p. 126)

Because athletic programs and their fundraising programs are visible organizations in society, each fundraising administrator, when constructing singular ethical codes, must examine the ramifications of each ethical code from a public relations standpoint, as well as from a right-or-wrong perspective. The more public an issue, the more detail a fundraising administrator needs to use in spelling out the ethical actions expected. All code of conduct elements must be continuously communicated to the board of directors, volunteer core, and fundraising staff. Ethical conversations should be a focal part of a fundraising program's 'kickoff' orientation. When it comes to ethical behavior and expectations, a good maxim is 'leave nothing to chance.'

SUMMARY

The aggregate number of fundraising programs accessible to an athletic program is restricted only by the resourcefulness and enthusiasm of the people involved. If the fundraising program's leader and/or fundraising director has 'bought into' the fundraising program and is committed, the rest of the stakeholders will be committed. While fundraising activities can be difficult and a tremendous amount of hard work, they can have both extrinsic and intrinsic rewards. The extrinsic rewards from fundraising are simple—increased cash flow and operational funds. The intrinsic rewards from a successful fundraiser can range from providing others with enjoyment to the satisfaction of knowing that the athletic organization is being funded.

REVIEW AND DISCUSSION QUESTIONS

1. What is the difference between capital and annual fundraising campaigns?

2. List the basic guidelines to fundraising events and program activities.

3. What are the factors of situational leadership?

4. What are eight ingredients for an ethical program plan?

5. What are some salient elements when writing a fundraising program's ethical code of conduct?

CHAPTER

2

Fundraising Program Planning

INTRODUCTION TO FUNDRAISING PROGRAM PLANNING

An essential concept of fundraising is to acquire additional resources to augment and support an athletic organization's future operations. The planning process in fundraising proactively takes charge of the future. Instead of hoping for additional resources, fundraising plans actively seek them out. Fundraising plans also provide an athletic organization with a tangible shared vision that all stakeholders (people involved with the athletic organization) can reference and follow. This collective focus reduces the unproductive use of time, materials, manpower, and finances. In other words, fundraising plans are critical for not wasting valuable resources in an attempt to raise valuable resources.

Who Is Responsible for the Fundraising Planning Process?

The strategic levels of a fundraising plan for sports and athletic organizations parallel the three central levels in the corporate world. "The three strategic levels (for the corporate environment) are corporate, business, and functional... corporate level is the plan for managing multiple lines of businesses...business level is the plan for managing one line of business...functional level is the plan for managing one

area of business" (Lussier, 2006, p. 151). One example of how these three echelons of planning equate to fundraising plans is found in college/university fundraising. The corporate level plan would be the college/university institution-wide fundraising plan. These plans would be done by top-level personnel of the college/university (presidents, provost, VPs) and would target large philanthropic donations, both corporate and private. The business level plan would consist of each division in the college/university (e.g. medical, business, education, athletic). The athletic division fundraising efforts would be spearheaded up by the executive staff (athletic director, associate/assistant athletic directors, and fundraising administrators/external development directors) and would target not only large philanthropic donations but also more pragmatic activities and events. The functional level plan would be the individual athletic programs/teams within the business level athletic department plan. This type of fundraising plan would be constructed and implemented by individual coaches and program associates. Fundraising plans at the functional level would focus on sports-specific activities, as well as general philanthropic donations.

No matter what the level of fundraising plan, the utilization of individuals in a team concept is critical in developing a cohesive and achievable plan. The adage 'you are only as strong as your weakest link' directly applies to the process of planning. For fundraising plans to be developed and successfully implemented in athletic organizations, all administrators and indeed all staff members in athletic departments need to engage in planning to some degree; some larger departments develop a planning committee or staff. Organizations set up such a planning group for one or more of the following reasons:

1. *Planning takes time.* A planning group can reduce the workload of individual staff within the department.

2. *Planning takes coordination.* A planning group can help integrate and coordinate the planning activities of individual staff.

3. *Planning takes expertise.* A planning group can bring more tools and techniques to a particular program than any single individual in the athletic department.

4. *Planning takes objectivity.* A planning group can take a broader view than one individual and go beyond specific projects and particular athletic department units. (Yow, Migliore, Bowden, Stevens, & Loudon, 2007, p. 8)

There is an additional side benefit of involving multiple internal stakeholders in the planning process for fundraising. No matter how adept one is at planning, the collective group (in our case fundraising program) may have difficulty embracing and working toward executing that plan. Most people are intrinsically motivated by being included and involved. They have a vested interest in the results. A fundraising plan that has group input can have a more concentrated effort toward a common accepted goal.

FUNDRAISING PLANS: ADVANTAGES AND DISADVANTAGES

The following lists detail the benefits as well as the drawbacks of fundraising planning.

Advantages of Fundraising Plans

- Formalized fundraising plans provide a framework for looking strategically into the future. Fundraising strategic prioritization will lead to developing more diverse (and hopefully steady) revenue sources.

- Fundraising plans furnish a structure for future resource allocation and financial stability.

- Fundraising plans can enhance the fundraising program's internal operational focus as well as enhance fundraising efficiency. Each member of the fundraising team will have definitive tasks and empowered responsibilities along with accountability criteria.

- A well-constructed fundraising plan can develop strong inter-organizational cooperation between various departments and divisions. Teamwork will develop and the fundraising program's effort will be targeted toward the benefits of all departments, divisions, and sports.

- Fundraising plans can be used as strong control elements; the fundraising administrator can compare how well a fundraising activity, event, or program is doing in comparison to how it was projected to do. This control factor associated with planning will make it possible to have midcourse corrections which, in turn, can save resources and generate more revenue.

- Fundraising plans can generate an optimistic belief concerning the future of the entire athletic organization. This optimism can augment athletic organization citizenship, teamwork, and loyalty.

- With all other things being equal, formalized fundraising plans can present a sustainable competitive advantage over athletic organizations that do not have a fundraising planning system in place.

- A solid fundraising plan conveys a sense of professionalism and legitimacy for internal athletic organization staff and administrators as well as external supporters and potential contributors.

Disadvantages of Fundraising Plans

- Accurate fundraising plans take a substantial amount of time and energy to develop. With salaries typically being an athletic organization's largest expense, time spent is money spent. While these opportunity costs are typically recovered, they are still a serious consideration.

- Fundraising administrators may consider completed fundraising plans as inflexible documents—a serious misconception. This rigidity creates 'tunnel vision' on fundraising goals and actions that may have become irrelevant or even counterproductive.

- Designing fundraising plans involves demanding and often difficult choices. The selection of some of these alternatives can profoundly influence (either positively or negatively) a fundraising activity, event, or program.

- Fundraising planning deals with the indeterminate future. This uncertainty can trigger athletic organization-wide apprehension and anxiety.

TYPES OF FUNDRAISING PLANS

The planning process for fundraising programs can go from wide-ranging and all-inclusive to distinct and specific. Plans can be generated by top level administrators, fundraising teams, or by individual fundraising program members. As a fundraising administrator, one's task is to determine which plan is the most appropriate for the athletic organization and its needs.

The two primary types of plans are single use plans and stand alone plans. "Single use plans are developed to achieve a set of goals unlikely to be repeated in the future. Standing plans are ongoing plans used to provide guidance for task performance repeated within the organization" (Daft & Marcic, 2006, p. 169). From a fundraising vantage, standing plans need to be established for long-term fundraising goals. Single use plans are project specific (activity or event) with terminal time frames. It should be noted that the depth of a single use fundraising plan will be determined by the importance of the activity/event to the athletic organization and fundraising program. Additionally, all external and unique fundraising projects outside the fundraising standing plan need some type of single use plan (from a one-page synopsis to a detailed step-by-step blueprint) that all individuals in the fundraising program can utilize.

ATHLETIC PROGRAM FUNDRAISING PLANS

The fundraising program planning process can simplify planning into these basic factors:

- Set goals
- Develop commitment to goals
- Develop effective action plans
- Track progress toward goal achievement
- Maintain flexibility in planning. (Williams, 2000, p. 127)

These five components are found in virtually every type of fundraising planning process. The configuration and interpretation of each of these items, as well as their utilization, change from athletic organization to athletic organization. The most logical way to structure these five factors of planning is through an instrument called an athletic organization fundraising plan. Table 2.1 is an illustration demonstrating how to arrange a fundraising plan.

Section 1: Fundraising Plan Summary

The fundraising plan summary is an abridgment of the entire athletic organization's fundraising plan. This overview accentuates key sections of the fundraising plan to provide readers with a summation (characteristically one or two pages) of the plan's core components. The fundraising plan summary can be composed of:

- a condensed description of the athletic organization's proposed fundraising events/activities/programs;
- an abstract view of the proposed marketing tactics for the fundraising program;
- a run-down of the fundraising management team (administrators, board of directors, volunteers, and staff) and their duties and responsibilities;
- an encapsulated picture of the financial condition of the overall athletic organization, new projected expenditures, and budgets and projected revenues from fundraising activities and events.

Table 2.1. Athletic Organization Fundraising Plan Sectional Breakdown

Section 1: Fundraising Plan Summary

Section 2: Program Vision and Fundraising Mission Statement

Section 3: Athletic Organization and Fundraising History

Section 4: Long-Term Fundraising Goals (3-5 Years)

Section 5: Short-Term Fundraising Goals (1-2 Year Actions)

Section 6: Fundraising S.W.O.T. Analysis

Section 7: Fundraising Policies, Procedures, and Ethical Obligations

Section 8: Fundraising Human Resource Management

Section 9: Fundraising Marketing and Promotion

Section 10: Fundraising Budgets and Financial Projections

Section 11: Appendix

Section 2: Program Vision and Fundraising Mission Statement

The fundraising plan starts with a coherent vision for the fundraising program and a defined mission statement. A strategic vision for business operations (which can easily be adapted for an athletic organization's fundraising program) is described as "the route a company intends to take in developing and strengthening its business. It lays out the company's strategic course in preparing for the future" (Thompson, Strickland, & Gamble, 2010, p. 25). A critical point regarding vision development is that the more focused one's fundraising vision, the better chance a fundraising program has of achieving it.

From the athletic organization's vision stems the fundraising plan's mission statement. A mission statement is defined as "a broad declaration of an organization's purpose that identifies the organization's products and customers and distinguishes the organization from its competitors" (Jones & George, 2004, p. 177). From a fundraising perspective, a mission statement is an all-encompassing declaration/affirmation that defines the overall purpose, philosophy, and vision of the athletic organization's fundraising program. "The mission is a clear and concise expression of the basic purpose

Fundraising Tip

Because the fundraising plan summary is a narrative synopsis of the entire fundraising plan, it is completed after all other plan components are finalized. Additionally, the quality of this section's writing should be exemplary because the summary is typically the first component external stakeholders will review, and it should 'grab' their interest by telling the fundraising program's story.

of the organization. It describes what the organization does, who it does it for, its basic good or service, and its values" (Bateman & Snell, 2011, p. 136). All objectives, policies, procedures, and actions emanate from the mission statement.

There are countless books and related literature on business planning and the development of a mission statement. Each has its own style and design criteria for a mission statement. The format and wording used is a matter of individual preference and style, as well as the intended audience who will read the mission statement. However, in writing the fundraising program's mission statement, answer the following broad but indispensable questions:

- What is the athletic program about?
- What is the principal purpose of the fundraising program?
- What is the overriding philosophy in running the fundraising program?
- What is the operational environment for fundraising?
- What are the future objectives of the athletic program, and how is fundraising going to help achieve these objectives?

A mission statement for an athletic organization's fundraising plan can be as succinct as a few sentences or as lengthy as a multi-paged elaboration. A short, straightforward mission statement could be advantageous if the fundraising plan is to be utilized by external stakeholders. A multi-page mission statement could be useful to motivate internal fundraising team members by providing a comprehensive operational rationale and a philosophical course of action.

Section 3: Athletic Organization and Fundraising History

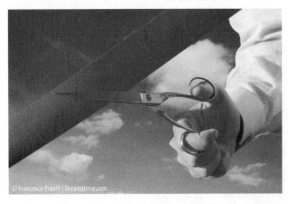

© Francesco Ridolfi | Dreamstime.com

This section of the fundraising plan is actually two sections in one—the athletic organization's history and the fundraising program's history. Developing a program history section in a fundraising plan might seem unproductive to some administrators. In actuality, this segment furnishes internal and external stakeholders with a point of reference and a clear picture of where the athletic organization and its fundraising efforts currently are. The question to ask when developing this section is: Who are the people who have any type of existing or future interest in the fundraising program? Internal stakeholders are fundraising team members and staff, and external stakeholders are outside administrators and, hopefully, future sponsors. The fundraising history component of this segment directly relates to previous fundraising plans and goals, as well as what was actually achieved from past fundraising programs and activities.

There are many ways to arrange this section. It can be in narrative form, outline, or even in a timeline style. More importantly, it should be in ascending chronological order from beginning to the present. The justification for compiling both the athletic organization's and fundraising program's history this way is that the fundraising plan is futuristic in nature. The segment should reflect where the program was, where it is, and where it needs to go.

Sections 4 and 5: Long-Term and Short-Term Fundraising Goals

The following sections of the fundraising plan deal with substantial, tangible goals and objectives. Long-term goals are the fundraising program's aspirations while short-term goals are the sequence of specific actions to achieve those aspirations.

> A goal, also known as an objective, is a specific commitment to achieve a measurable result within a dated period of time. The goal should be followed by the action plan, which defines the course of action needed to achieve the stated goal. (Kinicki & Williams, 2003, p. 153)

In essence, these two sections are the substance and heart of the fundraising program plan. Obviously, long-term goals (three- to five-year projections) will be broader in outlook. Short-term goals will be decisive actions that will be utilized to reach long-term objectives.

The actual makeup of each unique fundraising goal is up to the program administrator, board of directors, fundraising team, and other internal and external stakeholders associated with the fundraising program. However, there are some integral parameters and rules that should be placed on establishing fundraising goals. They are as follows:

1. All fundraising goals should ultimately emanate from the fundraising vision and mission statement.

2. When formulating fundraising goals, long-term objectives should be defined first. Subsequently, short-term actions should be formulated regarding how to accomplish each long-term goal.

3. It is critical to base all fundraising goals in reality. It is necessary to ask the following questions:
   - Do we currently have the internal resources to achieve the projected fundraising goals?
   - Do we have the future potential to acquire the essential resources to accomplish fundraising goals?
   - Do we have the staff or the likelihood of acquiring the staff to attain fundraising goals?
   - Is the timeframe for executing fundraising goals practical?
   - Will there be any internal or external resistance or confrontations to fundraising goals? If so, can they be overcome or will they be debilitating to the objective?

Fundraising Tip

Because of the generalized nature and enormity of long-term fundraising goals, as well as the limited resources of most athletic organizations, no more than four or five long-term fundraising goals should be attempted. It may, however, take a few short-term goals and immediate actions to reach a long-term fundraising goal.

4. Fundraising goals should be easily comprehensible to everyone in the organization. They should be straightforward, concise, and written in common language.

5. Each fundraising goal should be distinctive and salient. In other words, are the fundraising goals repetitive or are they unique in origin?

6. Each fundraising goal should have the unconditional endorsement and focus of everyone on the fundraising team and in the athletic organization. In the overall athletic organization setting, the athletes, coaches, administrators, and concerned stakeholders should be knowledgeable as to the fundraising goal-setting process. Without everyone's input, key stakeholders might not take an active interest in the fundraising program, which may in turn leave some, if not all, fundraising goals unattained.

7. Each fundraising goal should be as precise and measurable as possible. The advantage of quantifying objectives is to supply all concerned with concrete numbers to compare projected fundraising goals with actual fundraising results.

8. Fundraising goals should be challenging but realistic. Setting fundraising goals 'beyond the reach' of current resources and capabilities could be profoundly discouraging to all who are involved in the fundraising program. Conversely, setting fundraising goals that are too easily achieved will depreciate the critical value of goal setting and achievement. A fundraising administrator and team must balance these two factors to maximize the fundraising program's potential.

9. In order to be effective, fundraising goals need individual and/or team accountability. Simply stated, a fundraising goal without individual and/or team accountability will fail because assumptions will be made about who is to work on and accomplish the goal.

10. Fundraising goals need to be time exact. While the word 'deadline' has a negative connotation in our society, in goal setting and achievement it is tremendously appropriate. Once again, the time frame to achieve a particular fundraising goal must be challenging but realistic.

Section 6: Fundraising S.W.O.T. Analysis

A fundraising S.W.O.T. (Strengths, Weaknesses, Opportunities, Threats) analysis, which is the evaluation of an organization's internal strengths and weaknesses and external opportunities and threats, is an essential part of establishing the future direction of the fundraising program. "The elements of S.W.O.T. analysis are included in the general planning model, and in using strategic inventory to size up the environment. Given S.W.O.T.'s straight forward appeal, it has become a popular framework for strategic planning" (DuBrin, 2006, p. 148). From an athletic organizational and fundraising perspective, the analysis supplies a comprehensive, contemporary picture of the organization's capabilities.

The first step is to assess the prevailing fundraising situation from an internal and external perspective. An internal strength and weakness evaluation, which is very similar to a pro and con assessment, looks critically at the athletic organization's fundraising operations (or future operations) and contemplates if each component of the fundraising program is an operational strength/asset or an operational weakness/liability. It is advisable to start the fundraising strength and weakness evaluation process by prioritizing the factors of the fundraising program's operation from most critical to least consequential. Hopefully, when the assessment is completed, the most notable and significant fundraising elements will be predominantly considered strengths. The fundraising team, in converting the internal analysis to strategizing, should always focus on maximizing strengths and minimizing weaknesses (or, even better, converting the weaknesses to strengths).

The second step in comparing where the fundraising program is to where it needs to be is an external analysis or an opportunity/threat study. This process essentially audits all of the external environmental factors that affect the fundraising program's operation to determine if they are possibilities for growth and competitive fundraising advantage, or threats to the program. Once again, prioritize the environmental elements from the most significant to the least notable. If one is fortunate, fundraising opportunities will outweigh threats. A fundraising team's philosophy in this external analysis should be to exploit opportunities and to fortify the fundraising program against any current or future threats.

Fundraising Tip

Another way to conceptualize a S.W.O.T. analysis is to (1) maximize the program's internal strengths, (2) minimize the internal weaknesses, (3) exploit the external opportunities, and (4) defend against the external threats.

The true value in a fundraising S.W.O.T. analysis is when the fundraising administrator and planning teams take the internal elements of strength and weakness and combine them with the external elements of opportunity and threat. This is called a scenario analysis.

To strategize from the strengths/weaknesses and opportunities/threats evaluation (S.W.O.T. analysis) is straightforward logic. The best-case scenario is that the fundraising program has a distinct internal strength that can be used to exploit an external opportunity. At the other end of the spectrum, the program might have a prominent internal weakness that coincides with an external threat. As the fundraising program administrator, one's obligation is to look at each external element as it relates to the internal operational strengths/weaknesses. There are four primary scenarios.

Strength--------------Opportunity

Take advantage of the fundraising program's internal resource and capability strengths to exploit the external fundraising opportunity.

Strength--------------Threat

In this circumstance, the fundraising program should be able to counteract this particular danger.

Weakness------------Opportunity

This condition needs a resolution. Does the fundraising program bolster the weakness to take advantage of the circumstance or does it pass on the opportunity? Remember, this fundraising predicament is potentially dangerous. If the fundraising program passes on the opportunity and the program's competition takes advantage of the contingency, it might later become a distinct fundraising threat.

Weakness------------Threat

This condition typically requires prompt action to be taken. The more hazardous and powerful the fundraising threat, the more immediate and decisive is the need to respond to it.

Section 7: Fundraising Policies, Procedures, and Ethical Obligations

In their 2010 text Crafting and Executing Strategy: A Quest for Competitive Advantage, Thompson, Strickland, and Gamble highlight the acute importance of developing fundraising program policies and procedures by stating that new policies and operating procedures act to facilitate strategy execution in three ways:

1. Instituting new policies and procedures provides top-down guidance regarding how certain things now need to be done.

2. Policies and procedures help enforce needed consistency in how particular strategy critical activities are performed.

3. Well-conceived policies and procedures promote the creation of a work climate that facilitates good strategy execution. (Thompson, Strickland, & Gamble, 2010, pp. 359-360)

Fundraising Tip

Policy and procedure manuals are only beneficial if they are acknowledged, established, and applied. Either through formal meetings or informal exchanges, constantly re-emphasize the fundraising program's commitment to its policies and procedures.

While policies and procedures are ordinarily listed together in a fundraising program plan, they are two autonomous elements that help facilitate an organization's fundraising achievements. In straightforward terms, policies are more in line with program rules that guide behavior (people-oriented) while procedures are narrow-scope steps/methods that explain how to perform fundraising functions (task-oriented).

The most consequential aspect for the development and use of policies would be dealing with the board of directors, team members, and staff. The different areas in policy formulation and implementation concerning these groups would encompass all types of behavioral expectations. The concentration and range of policy items within a fundraising plan are determined by the athletic organization's philosophies, position, operational environment, history, and ethical traditions.

Fundraising procedures are step-by-step actions taken to perform specific fundraising tasks. One of the biggest dividends in determining fundraising procedures for administrative functions is uniformity. Uniformity saves time, coordinates activities, and minimizes frustration and stress that arise from a disorganized fundraising program.

Section 8: Fundraising Human Resource Management

The human resource segment of the fundraising plan is essentially a plan within a plan. The human resource planning process in a fundraising plan consists of four basic steps:

1. Determine the impact of the organization's objectives on specific organizational units.

2. Define skills, expertise, and total number of employees (demand for human resources) required to achieve the organizational and departmental objectives.

3. Determine the additional (net) human resource requirements in light of the organization's current human resource.

4. Develop an action plan to meet the anticipated human resource needs. (Byars & Rue, 2008, p. 90)

As stated, the human resource section needs to delineate action plan systems that will be used to reach fundraising goals. Action plan systems can consist of, but are not limited to, the following:

- Equal Employment Opportunity compliance systems;
- new fundraising staff recruitment and selection systems;
- internal promotional systems;
- information processing systems;
- new fundraising staff orientation systems;
- fundraising training and design systems;
- performance appraisal systems;
- compensation systems for fundraising staff (e.g. wage, benefit, incentives);
- disciplinary systems (which should be in line with athletic program systems); and
- safety and health systems.

The human resource section of the fundraising plan will selectively 'pick and choose' human resource areas that will have the greatest impact on fundraising goals. The human resource function will be described in more detail in Assembling an Effective Fundraising Department (Chapter 4) and Development of a Fundraising Board of Directors and Volunteers (Chapter 5).

Section 9: Fundraising Marketing and Promotion

While the Marketing Fundraising Programs chapter of this text (Chapter 6) will be devoted to marketing concepts, it is meaningful to discuss them as a component of the fundraising program plan. The business discipline of marketing (which can be

directly applied to fundraising) is broken down into four factors known as the 4 Ps of marketing, or the marketing mix. The 4 Ps are *Product, Price, Place,* and *Promotion.*

Product: The first of the 4 Ps, product, is the component that fundraising administrators and team members spend the greatest effort in developing. All other marketing activities stem from it. The product is a quality fundraising event, activity, solicitation, camp, etc. In the most elementary terms, if a fundraising activity/event/program is not good, the public will stay away no matter what marketing communication strategies are employed. Conversely, if a fundraising activity/event/program is targeted toward a community's interest, it will attract patrons and supporters.

Price: The second of the 4 Ps, price, is derived from the same logic. The more in demand a fundraising activity/event/program, the more flexibility the fundraising program will have in pricing that activity/event/program. The more dynamic and community-centered an activity/event, the more supporters (or potential supporters) will contribute.

Place: The third of the 4 Ps, place, relates to the distribution of the fundraising activity/event/program. For some fundraising items such as direct mail, phone campaigns, and publications, the choice of location is not a consideration. Other events and activities such as carnivals, camps, and luncheons depend greatly on the selection of a central and convenient location. The more in-demand an activity/event, the more flexibility the fundraising team will have in selecting its location.

Promotion: The final component of the 4 Ps, promotion, is the one facet on which fundraising administrators and teams can, if properly directed, have the most effect. It is the one area of the marketing mix that needs to be expressly spelled out in the fundraising program plan. If an athletic program has a competent, quality fundraising product at an acceptable price and locale, then it is up to the fundraising team's own resourcefulness, creativity, and effort to promote it. Are monetary resources consequential in promotion? They are significant but not imperative. Any advertising executive will communicate that the ultimate aspiration of any promotional campaign is to secure and enlarge positive word-of-mouth about the product. Can a fundraising program achieve this without major monetary resources? Yes. Would it be easier to implement fundraising promotion strategies with relevant resources? Undoubtedly. Yet fundraising teams cannot let money be the stumbling block of promotion.

It should be restated that marketing will be presented in more detail later in the text. However, from a fundraising plan perspective, the fundraising team will need to distinguish what resources are going to be available for marketing, then formulate a strategy to augment every dollar allotted. For fundraising programs with minimal dollars, concepts such as utilizing athletes (and families), developing distinct logos, composing and distributing flyers, and verbally publicizing fundraising activities, events, and programs is pivotal. Additionally, a fundraising team can persuade student groups, participate and attend other organizations' charitable functions, make publicity speeches, utilize alumni groups and former players, build a rapport with local media, and develop a news release system. These are all cost-effective techniques for fundraising promotion. Once again, fundraising administrators and team members must be enterprising and imaginative.

After the foundations of the fundraising program's marketing mix have been developed, the marketing component of the fundraising program plan needs to be assembled. The fundraising team has two choices. The marketing section of a fundraising plan can:

1. Embody and incorporate the entire comprehensive marketing plan of a fundraising program. These detailed documents break down the marketing mix:
   a. Target marketing and demographics
   b. Evaluation of fundraising competition
   c. Donors/supporters profiles
   d. Detailed elaboration of the marketing mix of the fundraising plan

2. Summarize the marketing component of the fundraising plan. This strategy provides a broad overview of the marketing objectives, tactics, and projected results.

Section 10: Fundraising Budgets and Financial Projections

Financial projecting is budgeting. There are two direct ways of budgeting for fundraising programs:

Method 1 – Assess and evaluate all of the fundraising program's expected expenditures, total the amount, and that result is the targeted income (break-even) amount.

Method 2 – Estimate the realizable income (or total revenue generated from a fundraising program), then attempt to adapt an acceptable percentage of expenditures within that amount.

The budgeting concept is that simple. The quandary comes from how to arrive at one's conclusions and how precise one can be at predicting the future. For a lucky few, they just know how to 'guesstimate' and their approximations are, in general, accurate. The majority of fundraising teams need to budget through concrete formulas and calculations. There are some basic rules for deriving calculations and formulating budgets:

1. Base beginning projections in recorded facts. Usually the amount spent or received in previous fundraising years is a good starting point.

Fundraising Tip

Never blindly leap into a marketing and promotions campaign for a fundraising program. It is the fastest way to squander a fundraising program's limited and most precious resource of money. Learn as much as possible about marketing theories and enlist people with backgrounds in marketing to 'lend a hand' to the program.

2. Always forecast high on projected expenditures and low on projected income/revenue.

3. Get solid dollar amounts on all fundraising expenditures whenever possible. This might mean additional phone calls and leg work, but the effort will provide substantially more dependable projections. Furthermore, whenever conceivably possible, get all expense quotes in writing.

4. Always anticipate miscellaneous expenses in all fundraising events/ activities/programs. The amount of miscellaneous/float dollars should be projected at 5-10% of the total estimated expenditure amount.

5. Take time to contemplate all fundraising budget line items before computing total dollar amounts. Attempt to incorporate every realistic fundraising expense and income source.

6. Triple check all calculations.

7. Keep organized fundraising files for back-up and confirmation of budget amounts.

The fundraising plan should not only include the budget and projections, but also a short narrative explanation of each item and how those estimates were derived. While financial projections are future oriented, financial statements are historic records of what actually was received and expensed from previous fiscal periods. The importance of including this type of information in the fundraising plan is in the validation of the current budget projections. Additionally, the quantitative comparison of what happened during the fundraising program's last fiscal period(s) and what is predicted to happen in the fundraising program's future fiscal period provides the fundraising team an opportunity to analyze and explain variances.

The extent to which a fundraising program budgets depends greatly on the type and size of the program as well as the level of expertise team members have in budgeting and financial statement accounting. The explanation of all of the different possible financial statements and quantitative forecasting techniques moves beyond the parameters of this manuscript. However, a fundamental working knowledge of budgeting is critical for all coaches and program administrators.

Section 11: Appendix

The appendix section of a fundraising program plan can be just as important in providing significant information to fundraising administrators, team members, and stakeholders as the other sections. Information such as event itineraries, training programs, timetables and schedules, booster club criteria, and legal documentation are just some of the items that can be included in a fundraising plan's appendix section. Once again, the extent of information provided in the appendix depends on numerous variables that are fundraising program specific.

Fundraising Tip

Knowing and recognizing one's distinctive limitations when it comes to financial administration will help a fundraising program. If one is not detail-oriented, delegate the financial task to someone with the appropriate background who is. The importance of financial accuracy in a fundraising program should never be underestimated.

OTHER ELEMENTS OF A FUNDRAISING PROGRAM PLAN

Title Page

The title page/cover to the fundraising program plan is a considerable informative ingredient as well as a relevant presentation component. Features can include:

- Athletic organization name (school, university, club name);
- Operational address, phone, emails, website;
- Date of fundraising plan;
- Athletic organization logo;
- Primary fundraising administrators and team members; and
- Copy numbers (which is essential for tracking copies).

Table of Contents

Because of the extensive dimensions of a fundraising program plan, a table of contents is an indispensable component. A table of contents provides readers with an easy way to access specific information without going through the entire document.

Key Team Members/Organizational Chart

The fundraising plan segment titled Key Team Members/Organizational Chart has two independent, but closely interconnected, elements. The subsection of key team members is a conventional job description behind each team/staff position in the fundraising program. The second subsection is a standard organizational chart. The diagram should display the hierarchical structure of the entire fundraising program, who is accountable to whom, and who is answerable for each division below (chain of command). When combined together, these elements furnish everyone in the fundraising program with clearly defined roles, positions, and structure.

FUNDRAISING PLANS: FINAL POINTS

The following list provides generic fundraising plan tips for consideration prior to implementing the plan:

- Fundraising plans should have a purpose beyond just planning for planning's sake.

- Fundraising plans should blend seamlessly into the athletic organization's overall program plan. The fundraising plan's vision/mission, goals, and specific action must be strategically in line with the overall direction and aspirations of the athletic organization (a concept known as unity of strategies).

- Fundraising planning is a continuous process. Plans need periodic revisiting to evaluate and adjust or they become stagnant and irrelevant.

Fundraising Tip

The appendix segment of a fundraising program plan is not a 'junk drawer' section. Keep only salient information in it and maintain its organization.

- The smaller the athletic program, the more targeted the plan should be on legitimate potential donors/supporters. If not, the plan could waste valuable time and limited resources.

- Fundraising plans need to have definitive long-term goals as well as concentrated short-term actions.

- Contingency planning should be strongly considered if the fundraising program's operating environment is considered volatile. A contingency plan is best described as "an alternate plan to be used if the original plan can not be implemented or a crisis develops" (DuBrin, 2003, p.116).

- Stringent financial controls should be adopted throughout the entire fundraising process (including the planning stage).

- A fundraising plan is only as good as its execution.

SUMMARY

There are distinct benefits and applications associated with developing a fundraising program plan. The most predominant are:

1. To furnish fundraising team members and stakeholders with a concrete, tangible focus for the future;

2. To project professionalism to external groups and potential supporters;

3. To provide a valuable and useful tool for enlisting future team members, board of directors, and volunteers;

4. To give fundraising team members a sense of continuity; and

5. To provide the fundraising team with a real foundation. In other words, it simply distinguishes what can or cannot be accomplished.

Once again, the fundraising plan is not a stagnant document. It should be considered an alterable and flexible athletic organization component that needs constant progressive updates and amendments. While most revisions to the fundraising plan will be minor modifications, they are indispensable in maintaining the plan's ongoing benefits. The ability to adapt and amend the fundraising plan to the changing external environment could mean the difference between a fundraising program's success and failure.

REVIEW AND DISCUSSION QUESTIONS

1. What does the function of planning provide for a fundraising program?

2. What are the four reasons to establish a fundraising planning team?

3. Define single-use fundraising plans. Define standing fundraising plans.

4. List (in sequential order) the primary sections of a fundraising program plan.

5. List the 10 parameters and rules on establishing fundraising goals.

3

Fundraising Program Organization

INTRODUCTION TO FUNDRAISING PROGRAM ORGANIZATION

To be successful, a program administrator should consider the fundraising program, no matter how large or small, a business. To think of it as anything else would be to restrict its capacity for revenue generation and ultimate success. From a management standpoint, planning is the initial and foremost priority in establishing the fundraising program. To reiterate, planning is the future-oriented function of determining strategic goals for the program's operation. From this plan, the fundraising team must mold and configure the enterprise to achieve the stated planning mission and goals. This is the underlying thought behind organizational development and design.

FUNDRAISING STRUCTURING PROCESS

Hiring a strong fundraising team (through sound human resource practices and strategies discussed in Chapter 4 and 5) goes hand-in-hand with the structuring of a fundraising program. The structural design of the fundraising program (like other athletic organization departments) is dependent upon numerous variables. Some of the variables can encompass the following:

- Personnel size of the fundraising program;
- Resources available to the fundraising program;
- Strategic importance the fundraising program has in relation to other athletic organization departments/functions;

- Number of specific committees, volunteers, and board of directors members along with their incorporation and authority;
- Philosophical position of the fundraising program's administration toward delegation, empowerment, and accountability;
- Organizational policies associated with fundraising program structuring (or re-structuring).

With this being said, no two fundraising programs are going to be alike. Each situation and program will have its own distinctive structure. For example, two comparative university athletic departments with similar fundraising goals can have two totally different fundraising department structures. One university might emphasize committees and volunteers while the other might rely heavily on an administrative driven departmental structure. These two diverse structures might be equally successful at reaching their fundraising program objectives.

While fundraising program configuration cannot be standardized, there is a logical step-by-step process to structuring one's fundraising program. While uncomplicated in concept, the construction and application can be, at times, tedious and demanding. It is crucial that the process be followed and a fundraising program structure established (or re-established if re-organizing an already existing fundraising program). Without a sound organizational structure, a fundraising program will most likely never realize its potential and achieve success. The step-by-step process is as follows:

Step 1: Lay out and re-visit all of the fundraising program's goals created in the fundraising program plan. The principal rationale for this is to concentrate the structure on the objectives that are directly related to the fundraising program's achievement.

Step 2: From the goals (both long-term and short-term actions), assemble a detailed inventory of all the major fundraising jobs and action-oriented tasks/assignments to accomplish each specific goal.

Step 3: This is the extracting and grouping of fundraising tasks stage. Individually or in a collective session with fundraising program team members, craft job positions (job designing) from items grouped. First and foremost in constructing these fundraising positions should be effectiveness and the ability of these positions to achieve fundraising goals.

Step 4: The fourth step in the progression is taking each fundraising position and building hierarchical departments. Additionally, this stage should have profound emphasis on resource allocation, span of control for each fundraising department and job position, and accountability.

Step 5: This stage encompasses the formulization of the structure. A well-defined hierarchical chart as well as complete position/job descriptions should be composed. The fundraising administrator and team will need to meet with all fundraising program personnel (both in-house and board of directors and volunteers) to illuminate positional responsibilities and to define the fundraising program's reporting chain of command. It is imperative that every individual in the fundraising program completely understand his/her status and duties, along with the resources available and supervisory authority in the fundraising program.

Step 6: The final step in the process is monitoring and adjusting the fundraising program structure for goal realization. In most cases, if the first five steps in the process are followed, this stage will have some positional 'tweaking' of obligations and assignments. However, a substantial environmental change (or changes) will need scrutinizing as to the current and future effects on the fundraising program's structure and the projected goals. If in these cases the external circumstance has a profound influence on the fundraising program, the re-structuring process (steps one through five) will need to be addressed.

JOB DESCRIPTIONS

As stated in step three of the six-step fundraising program organizational process, individual job descriptions/positions need to be constructed prior to departmentalizing positions. In other words, each internal fundraising position, from strictly a fundraising program viewpoint, needs a detailed and precise job description. In this job description, list

1. the official title of the fundraising position and summarize its placement in the fundraising program;

2. the functions of the fundraising position in order of the most significant to the least;

3. if feasible, an approximate range of time, in percentage form, of each function (50% of the position is activity/event planning, 25% is program implementation, etc.);

4. the empowerment of the fundraising position (e.g. the sanctioned authority delegated by the program's fundraising team for the position);

5. the accountability of the fundraising position; and

6. the reward system for the fundraising position (if applicable).

DEPARTMENTALIZATION

Step four in the six-step process for fundraising program structuring is to group the fundraising positions into departments. A fundraising administrator and team should assemble these departments with a desire to put together the best possible cross-functional work units. There are four key ways businesses establish departments which can easily be adapted to fundraising programs.

Today the most common bases for organizing a business into effective departments are by function, by product, by location, and by type of customer.

Departmentalization by function – grouping jobs that relate to the same organizational activity

Departmentalization by product – grouping activities related to a particular product or service

Departmentalization by location – grouping activities according to the defined geographic area in which they are performed

Departmentalization by customer – grouping activities according to the needs of various customer populations. (Pride, Hughes, & Kapoor, 2002, pp. 214-215)

Smaller fundraising programs might find that one departmentalization method (customarily by function) is more than sufficient to structure their fundraising programs. Larger fundraising programs with numerous locations, activities, and events may employ more departmentalization groupings under an all-encompassing fundraising program structure.

ORGANIZATIONAL CHARTS

Organizational charts help employees understand how their work fits within the overall operation of the firm…it is a visual representation of a firm's structure that illustrates job position and functions…an organizational chart depicts the division of a firm into departments that meet organizational needs. (Boone & Kurtz, 2006, p. 284)

The types of organizational charts in today's businesses are numerous. For a majority of fundraising programs, an uncomplicated classical method with direct lines of command will be more than adequate. This traditional format (or vertical hierarchical chart) has distinct advantages even as it has some limitations. Its advantages include being a top-down blueprint that has clear lines of authority and communication, minimization of formal jurisdiction power struggles between different fundraising team members, and the provision of status to primary areas necessary for fundraising program survival and prosperity. Its disadvantages include minimal coordination and interaction between nonaligned fundraising positions, lack of horizontal training (which promotes well-rounded team members), potential for informal power friction between fundraising positions of the same level, and reduction of the ability of the fundraising team to progress and advance in the fundraising program because all occupational promotions are on the vertical axis.

Organizational structure clarification should be a top priority for fundraising administrators. Team members will perform better if they know the expectations of the job, their fundraising duties, the importance of their assignments in the hierarchical design, and their fundraising position's compensation and rewards.

Job descriptions, along with hierarchical charts, should be readily accessible and always utilized in fundraising team evaluations. Take time to create them. In the long run, it will save countless hours of miscommunication, supervision, and frustration. The aggregate total of all of the fundraising job descriptions should encompass every known element of the operation. Regard them as adaptable documents that can be molded to fit the fundraising program's needs if the situational environment changes.

CENTRALIZED VERSUS DECENTRALIZED MANAGEMENT/STRUCTURE

Another fundraising program structural concern relates to the concept of centralized or decentralized management. The philosophies are easy to understand. Centralized management is when a fundraising administrator (at the top of the hierarchal chain of command) retains the greater part of the fundraising program's authority, decision making, and power. Centralized management is a top-down theory in which prominent decisions are controlled by top-level administrators while routine, day-to-day actions are completed by lower-level personnel. Decentralized management is diametrically opposite. Formal authority, decision making, and power is 'pushed down' or 'spread out' to the fundraising positions in the lower level of the fundraising program's structure.

Centralized versus decentralized management and structure is a philosophical outlook as well as an operational situation. If the fundraising program's primary administrator believes he/she has a capably trained, loyal, and mature fundraising team, he/she might choose to, during the construction of job positions and duties, assign tasks to fundraising program positions that have an elevated deal of autonomy and program authority. Conversely, a new and inexperienced fundraising team could need a centralized management structure until they acquire fundraising program experience and maturity.

Special Note: A miscalculation in constructing fundraising jobs and structure could have disastrous consequences. For example, if a fundraising administrator chooses a centralized management structure with a mature and experienced fundraising team, there is a strong chance that some (if not all) fundraising program members will be dissatisfied and unmotivated. This, in turn, will contribute to fundraising goal breakdown. However, if a fundraising administrator chooses a decentralized power structure and bestows critical job responsibilities and influence to inexperienced team members, there is also a strong chance that fundraising jobs will be inadequately completed and that this will contribute to fundraising program goal breakdown.

Some salient terms that need to be included in a discussion about centralized and decentralized structures are job

Fundraising Tip

Make sure all internal stakeholders know precisely where they are positioned in the fundraising program. If a fundraising administrator takes for granted and assumes that the internal team members know their power and structural position, he/she is exposing the fundraising program to destructive interpersonal conflicts within its operations.

scope, job depth, and empowerment. Each of these elements interacts with the individual fundraising team member's authority and job dynamics inside the fundraising program's structure. Job scope and job depth can best be defined by the following:

> *Job Scope* – Refers to the number of different types of operations performed on the job.

> *Job Depth* – Refers to the freedom of employees to plan and organize their own work, work at their own pace, and move around and communicate as desired. (Rue & Byers, 2009, p. 162)

Finally, empowerment in specific fundraising positions is defined as how much autonomy and authority the position in the fundraising program's structure has to make decisions. Will the position (and the individual in the position) have total control over the delineated job responsibilities or will there be systematic reporting duties related to all of the major operational functions?

The topic of centralized and decentralized structure, along with job scope, job depth, and empowerment becomes problematic when discussing fundraising programs. Fundraising programs have paid employees (program administrators and staff) along with volunteers (board members, fundraising specialists, and general committee and core volunteers). Administrative personnel inside a fundraising program's structure are motivated to accomplish goals because their livelihood is on the line. Volunteers are a totally different component of a fundraising program's structure. Simply stated, they can walk away from the fundraising program at any time, without any notice, leaving major gaps in the structure. It is strongly recommended that volunteers have structural limitations in critical job scope elements so that through contingency planning, an administrative staff member can quickly absorb the volunteer's structural duties into their responsibilities until a suitable volunteer replacement can be incorporated into the program. Hopefully, the absorption of responsibilities will be temporary. If a suitable replacement cannot be found, a departmental restructuring might be necessary to reorganize and share the vacated position's work responsibilities.

No matter what the concentration and complexity, design and construction, or centralized or decentralized style, a fundraising program's structure will not facilitate the achievement of program goals without accountability. In the 2007 text *Introduction to Business*, Madura succinctly summarizes the magnitude of accountability in organizational structure by stating:

> While organizational structure indicates job descriptions and the responsibilities of employees and managers, the firm also needs to ensure that its employees and managers are accountable. One of the important duties of the firm's managers is to evaluate employees and make them accountable for fulfilling their responsibilities. The job descriptions provide direction for the positions, but the managers above the positions must determine whether the employees performed according to their job descriptions. (Madura, 2007, p. 282)

ADDITIONAL CONSIDERATIONS WHEN STRUCTURING A FUNDRAISING PROGRAM

The following are additional considerations when designing a fundraising program's structure.

Outsourcing

Outsourcing is "the practice of hiring an individual or another company outside the organization to perform work" (Dubrin, 2003, p. 231). In other words, outsourcing is the process of subcontracting services, operational activities, and supplies that become an ingredient of the production process and/or final product (in our case fundraising event, activity, or program). There are some questions to ask when considering outsourcing for a fundraising program: Can this outsourcing individual or company do the function more inexpensively, faster, and better than us? Can the energy and time that we conserve with outsourcing provide the fundraising program with a competitive advantage? The rationale behind outsourcing is to ensure that the program will not rely on outside entities for core fundraising activities that have an impact on success and survival.

From the standpoint of program structure and organization, if an outsourced job/position is a temporary fix, then few or no structural changes will be needed. However, if the outsourcing is a long-term or permanent situation, it should be included as a structural component with clear lines of authority and accountability.

Mechanical Versus Organic Concepts in Structures

Mechanical structures in organizations relate to the concept of flexibility in operations. Most mechanical structures are traditional and rigid in cross-functional work. Conversely, organic structures in relation to mechanical structures can best be described by the following:

> Organizational structure in which the boundaries between jobs continually shift and people pitch in wherever their contributions are needed... a rigid structure is rarely suitable for a very small organization...a top challenge to this approach is that employees may become confused about the details of their roles and responsibilities. (Certo, 2008, p. 178)

If the athletic organization's fundraising program is small, then a more organic structure and philosophy could be adopted. As a fundraising administrator, communication would be essential. Each fundraising team member would need to know what primary responsibilities he/she has as well as what program duties have an 'all hands on deck' status.

Self-Managed Cross-Functional Teams

Another possible structural component that fundraising programs could construct is a self-managed cross-functional team structure. While the title of this type of organizational structure can be confusing, its application is easily understandable. A self-managed cross-functional team structure is a project-oriented organic format where the fundraising program is flexibly structured on specific fundraising activities/events/programs. Once these activities/events/programs are completed, a new team structure is put in place. People and job responsibilities are adaptable for the explicit tasks being accomplished. For example, a specific event in Year 1 could have certain personnel in various positions, and in Year 2 the same or similar event could have totally new personnel or the same personnel with different job responsibilities (based on the ability to complete those responsibilities). The self-managed and cross-functional aspect of this structure relates to the team's delegated authority as well as the distribution of expertise inside the team. Self-managed teams are ones in which "workers are trained to do all or most of the jobs in a work unit, have no direct supervision, and do their own day-to-day supervision" (Kinicki & Williams, 2003, p. 424). True self-managed teams will have their own hierarchical structure, individualized policies and procedures, and the authority to self-discipline non-performance toward goals and non-compliance toward team operations.

The benefits to a self-managed team structure inside a fundraising program are tremendous. The team's productivity will be enhanced through the team members' vested interest in the results. This vested interest comes from the fact that it is their fundraising project and their responsibility (through empowered authority) that it succeeds. The primary danger in the use of self-managed teams relates to the selection of team members. Each team member must have an intrinsically strong desire to control his/her work or volunteer destiny. It is crucial for a self-managed, cross-functional team to 'weed out' individuals who do not seek or want authority (known in the business world as 'clock punchers'). Does this mean that these individuals have no value in a fundraising program? Absolutely not. There are always tasks that need to be done by staff and volunteers that do not need a high level of authority or autonomy. However, it is critical that these individuals not be put into a high performance culture of self-managed teams.

No matter what team structure the fundraising program selects (from self-governing to directly supervised and controlled), the cross-functional aspect will be essential for success. Cross-functional teams are comprised of individuals with different areas of operational expertise who focus on a common goal. Each of these individuals will complement the rest of the group and 'bring to the table' vital skills and competencies. For example, if a fundraising administrator was constructing a self-managed team for a specific fundraising event or activity with a terminal time frame, he/she could:

1. Bring in an individual with a strong background in management and administration to be the project leader;

2. Acquire an individual with a concentrated financial background to oversee budgeting and accounting;

3. Place in the team an individual with a high level of expertise in marketing and promotion;

4. Incorporate individuals with expertise in personal selling (depending on the activity, event, or program); and

5. Add any other business-competent individuals to augment the team's ability to reach its collective goals.

The advantages are obvious with cross-functionality. All of the team's operational elements will have an individual (or individuals) with proficiency. As with any team structure, the key will be to have those individuals focused on collective group and program objectives.

© Jonathan Ross | Dreamstime.com

Virtual Team Structure

A final consideration in how a fundraising program is structured concerns technology and virtual work teams. Technology is changing the dynamics of fundraising program administration. Williams, in his text *Management,* describes virtual teams (and their advantages and drawbacks) as the following:

> Virtual teams are teams composed of geographically and/or organizationally dispersed co-workers who use telecommunication and information technologies to accomplish tasks…virtual teams can be employee involvement teams, self-managed teams, or nearly any kind of team…the principle advantage of virtual teams is that they are flexible. Employees can work with each other, regardless of physical location, time zone, organizational affiliation…a drawback of virtual teams is that team members must learn to express themselves in a new context. (Williams, 2000, p. 516)

From a fundraising standpoint, instead of having the fundraising program limited to one location, technology is allowing fundraising committees, activities and events, and alumni groups to form and contribute from multiple locations. Because of the benefits from this level of involvement, virtual teams should be a strong fundraising program consideration.

SUMMARY

Professional fundraising program organization is an essential operational component for successful fundraising programs. Through organization, one can reasonably employ all personal and program resources in the fundraising program's vision/mission and its achievement of operational goals. The fundraising program will be able to effectively utilize personal and program power as well as control and develop external patrons and followers. A properly ordered professional fundraising environment can do several positive things:

1. Convey professionalism that, in turn, inspires confidence.

2. Minimize stakeholder and influencer apprehension about the fundraising operation.

3. Provide a competitive edge in fundraising by furnishing the fundraising administrators and team members with more time to concentrate efforts on improving activities and events rather than catching up on a disorganized workload.

REVIEW AND DISCUSSION QUESTIONS

1. What is the step-by-step process for structuring a fundraising program?

2. What are the six components of a job description?

3. What is the difference between centralized and decentralized management/structure?

4. Describe job scope. Describe job depth.

5. What are mechanical structures? What are organic structures?

4

Assembling an Effective Fundraising Department

INTRODUCTION

This chapter will examine the fundamentals of human resource management as it relates to fundraising personnel and the construction of the fundraising program. The chapter's human resource strategies and applications can be adapted for any size athletic organization and its fundraising program. The depth of adaptation of these human resource strategies will depend on the importance the organization places on fundraising and its subsequent commitment of resources toward fundraising objectives. Inside a particular fundraising program in an athletic organization, the supply of human resources can come from program staff/employees, board of directors, volunteers, and athletic administrators. The following tactics can be utilized throughout program operations to support these internal stakeholder groups.

Strategic human resource management is defined as "the pattern of human resource deployments and activities that enable an organization to achieve its strategic goals" (Bohlander & Snell, 2007, p. 50). In other words, human resource administration is a hands-on, people-oriented function. It directly correlates to the productivity of the fundraising program. Productivity can be thought of as the acquisition and effective utilization of resources to maximize a fundraising program's worth. Undoubtedly, the most indispensable resources in any athletic organization (and its fundraising program) are its human resources.

LEGAL ASPECTS OF HUMAN RESOURCE MANAGEMENT

Before one can examine the business models and applications involved in human resource management for fundraising programs, it is first essential for fundraising administrators to recognize, comprehend, and appreciate the basic legal aspects and responsibilities that go along with this managerial function. While the field of human resource management law is considerably beyond the capacity of this text, it is important that all stakeholders involved with the fundraising program (especially program administrators) be cognizant of the legal foundations and ramifications of proper human resource management. As with all specialized fields, it is advisable to discuss any and all legal concerns with trained experts. For fundraising programs operating within educational institutions, the human resource department is characteristically a knowledgeable informational and advisory asset. For individual, autonomous athletic programs, contacting/retaining a lawyer (or lawyers) with a solid emphasis in employment law can provide indispensable value.

Table 4.1 is a synopsis of some of the key human resource-related laws and acts that can affect an athletic organization's fundraising program.

It is imperative that a fundraising administrator know that there are specific state and local employment laws and regulations in addition to the federal laws/acts listed in Table 4.1. Once again, consult with human resource managers and/or legal counsel to review these particular laws and regulations and how they could affect the athletic organization's fundraising program.

HUMAN SYSTEMS IN FUNDRAISING PROGRAMS

In today's business world, organizational philosophies and obligations toward the human element have gone beyond the simple duties of hiring, firing, and filling gaps. Modern human resource management systems embrace concepts such as employee enhancement and satisfaction, increased productivity though empowerment, and providing positive social environments for long-term commitment. This new perspective on developing and maximizing human potential should be a part of each fundraising program's agenda and operation. Fundraising administrators need to perceive that each fundraising program (no matter what the extent or competitive level) is a business and that staff/team members are employee stakeholders. Program administrators need to commit to this basic premise. From there, they will need to construct a system that comprises six vital human resource operations:

- *Staffing* – Recruiting, selection, and placement.
- *Orientation* – New hire athletic organization and fundraising program orientation.
- *Training and development* – Training activities, counseling, and career planning for fundraising staff.
- *Performance evaluations* – Analysis of fundraising performance expectations and accomplishments.

Table 4.1. Summary of Equal Employment Opportunity Laws and Executive Orders

Law/Acts/Year	Purpose or Intent/Coverage
Equal Pay Act (1963)	Purpose: Prohibits sex-based discrimination in rates of pay for men and women working in the same or similar jobs.
	Coverage: Private employers engaged in commerce or in the production of goods for commerce and with two or more employees; labor organizations.
Title VII, Civil Rights Act (1964/1972)	Purpose: Prohibits discrimination based on race, sex, color, religion, or national origin.
	Coverage: Private employers with 15 or more employees for 20 or more weeks per year, institutions, state and local governments, employment agencies, labor unions, and joint labor-management committees.
Age Discrimination in Employment Act (1967)	Purpose: Prohibits discrimination against individuals who are at least 40 years of age but less than 70. An amendment eliminates mandatory retirement at age 70 for employees of companies with 20 or more employees.
	Coverage: Private employers with 20 or more employees for 20 or more weeks per year, labor organizations, employment agencies, state and local governments and federal agencies, with some exceptions.
Pregnancy Discrimination Act (1978)	Purpose: Requires employers to treat pregnancy just like any other medical condition with regard to fringe benefits and leave policies.
	Coverage: Same as Title VII, Civil Rights Act.
Immigration Reform and Control Act (1986)	Purpose: Prohibits hiring of illegal aliens.
	Coverage: Any individual or company.
Americans with Disabilities Act (1990)	Purpose: Increase access to services and jobs for disabled workers.
	Coverage: Private employers with 15 or more employees.
Older Workers Benefit Protection Act (1990)	Purpose: Protects employees over 40 years of age in regard to fringe benefits and gives employees time to consider an early retirement offer.
	Coverage: Same as Age Discrimination Employment Act.
Civil Rights Act (1991)	Purpose: Permits women, persons with disabilities, and persons who are religious minorities to have a jury trial and sue for punitive damages if they can prove intentional hiring and work place discrimination. Also requires companies to provide evidence that the business practice that led to the discrimination was not discriminatory but was job-related for the position in question and consistent with business necessity.
	Coverage: Private employers with 15 or more employees.
Family and Medical Leave Act (1993)	Purpose: Enables qualified employees to take prolonged unpaid leave for family and health related reasons without fear of losing their jobs.
	Coverage: Private employers with 15 or more employees.

- *Rewards, compensation, and benefits* – Wages, performance incentives, and miscellaneous benefits for applicable staff and fundraising team members.
- *Disciplinary procedures* – Disciplinary processes and grievance procedures.

STAFFING SYSTEMS

Fundraising Tip

Think of the fundraising program's staffing system as a living person. It requires unremitting attention and monitoring.

From the standpoint of fundraising program administration, one's skillful use of staffing systems is related to acquiring the precise number of and the best-qualified staff/team members. This segment of the chapter analyzes the human resource concepts of demand-shift analysis, manpower planning, and recruitment and selection.

Demand Shift Analysis

When initiating a discussion on staffing, one must first examine the internal fundraising program demand for human resources and the external factors that affect that demand. External factor questions that can affect human resource demand in a fundraising program can encompass the following:

- How will a fundamental shift in our local, regional, or national economic condition affect our fundraising program? Since fundraising relies on disposable income for support, will an economic change in the operating community result in a financial change in our internal operating system? In turn, will this shift the fundraising program's financial situation, affecting our fundraising staff? Some athletic administrators would see an economic downturn as a factor in decreasing resources given to a fundraising program. Conversely, other athletic administrators would perceive the importance of increasing fundraising efforts and expand resources for fundraising efforts.

- How do EEOC, Affirmative Action, the Disabilities Act, and other governmental regulations affect the fundraising program? Are the athletic organization's fundraising efforts considered socially responsible in its staff/team member recruitment? What does our governing athletic association state about fundraising staff/team member recruitment?

- Will we be able to increase our fundraising program's staffing and operational efficiency through effective use of technology?

- What are our competitors doing in terms of staff recruitment? Are they growing or downsizing? Are they focusing their human resource efforts on certain individuals with particular fundraising strengths and areas of expertise?

These are just a few of the questions that could be asked when examining the external factors that can affect a fundraising program's staffing demands. It should be noted that when examining any external environmental element that could affect the fundraising program (not only from a human resource perspective, but from the perspectives of all areas of the fundraising operation), it is helpful to look at each factor as an opportunity or a threat. If it is an opportunity, strategize how to exploit it. If the environmental element is a threat to the athletic organization's fundraising program, minimize it.

Internal elements that might shift a fundraising program's demand for human resources are organizational forces and workforce. These internal factors need continuous oversight and management. Organizational elements such as changes in a fundraising program's strategic plan, budget and forecasted projections, new fundraising activities and events, and job designs are all explicit elements that have a direct relationship to the human resource needs of the fundraising program.

Budgeting and forecasting are the most obvious and immediate determinants for fundraising staff/team member solicitation. Budgeting and forecasting delineate and place into focus what an athletic organization can spend fiscally on its fundraising program and what it projects to spend and earn in the future. They determine the fundraising program's size, operational limits, equipment and facilities, and human resource limitations.

Another organizational planned strategy is new fundraising activities and events. If planned properly, not only will these new ventures have goals and structure, but they will also have human resource demands within specific timeframes. New fundraising activities and events are directly related to the fundraising program plan and should be included within that document.

The last of the internal organizational elements that affect human resource demand in a fundraising program is job design. Job design refers to the initial development of positions in a fundraising program or the restructuring of fundraising positions in an ongoing operation. Either way, new job designs and descriptions typically mean a fundamental change in internal human resource demand for a fundraising program.

An internal element that might shift human resource demand is the fundraising program's current workforce. Program administrators should see the fundraising program's staff/team members as a workforceprogram's staff/team members as a workforce. This workforce must be thought of as a flexible, flowing component of a fundraising operation that could change daily. Some changes can be anticipated in advance and planned for, such as a scheduled retirement or an anticipated leave of absence. However, other changes might not be so easy to predict. Sudden and critical demand can arise from resignation, employment termination, or severe illness and injury. To compensate for abrupt shifts in a fundraising program's human resource demands, a program will need to have in place a well-defined staffing system.

Once a need for human resources has been determined, program administrators must apply a systematic staffing strategy. Staffing strategies for fundraising programs can be isolated into three types: manpower planning, recruiting, and selection.

Fundraising Tip

The fundraising program's size will determine its demand shift analysis. The smaller the staff base, the less analytical thought and structure need go into a demand shift analysis. Conversely, the smaller the staff foundation, the more important replacement becomes.

Manpower Planning

Manpower planning (which is similar to human resource demand planning but more specific and narrowly defined) is

> the process of anticipating and making provisions for the movement of people into, within, and out of an organization. Its purpose is to deploy these resources as effectively as possible, where and when they are needed, in order to accomplish the organization's goals. (Bohlander, Snell, & Sherman, 2001, p. 122)

Table 4.2. **Manpower/Human Resource Planning for Fundraising Programs**

Step 1

From the fundraising program plan, lay out and revisit all of the projected goals and actions for the entire fundraising program.

Step 2

Lay out and revisit all of the job positions in the fundraising program structure. Each job should have a comprehensive listing of all current and future fundraising duties and responsibilities.

Step 3

From each individual job listing of fundraising duties and responsibilities, analyze what human resource skills, education, and experience each duty and responsibility requires (both now and in the future). This is commonly known as the job analysis process.

Step 4

Complete a current skills inventory for each person in those job positions. The skills inventory will examine the individual's ability to fulfill the job's fundraising duties and responsibilities based on Step 3's analysis of the skills, education, and experience required to perform the program's job duties and responsibilities.

Step 5

The concluding step is to construct an action plan. This action plan is used to align the goals and objectives of the fundraising program with the current human resource asset of the fundraising program.

From a fundraising program outlook, the fundraising administrators need to carefully analyze both long-term goals, which are future-oriented by nature, as well as short-term objectives, which call for more immediate actions. One must prioritize which of these goals (short and action-oriented or long and future-oriented) are critical and in need of quality staff/team members. Two scenarios may emerge from this process. The first is that the existing manpower position is deemed sufficient for the fundraising program's future goals and direction. In this case, the fundraising administrator might need to do some adjusting of job responsibilities and workloads, but the staff/team members will remain essentially the same. The second scenario is that the fundraising program's manpower needs are deemed insufficient and will require additional human resource to attain the future fundraising program projections.

The one inherent constant in all athletic and fundraising programs is that there will always be turnover. Manpower planning for athletic programs can be accomplished simply through a diagram known as a depth chart. A depth chart is a versatile diagram that lists the positions in the fundraising program and the people in each position. How the fundraising administrator delineates and designs the graph is entirely subjective. One possible design is as follows:

1. Across the topmost section of the chart, list the fundraising positions in the program.

2. Arrange the program staff/team members under each category in order of significance and value. If there are individuals who are multi-skilled, classify and index them under their primary area.

3. After placing individuals in descending order, color code them for staff/team member position along with other program-specific critical criteria. For example, all office/administrative staff could be highlighted in one color, all sales in another, and so forth.

This diagram will furnish a visual picture of future recruiting requirements as well as where each individual is currently situated in the fundraising program. Always consider this document a flexible chart. Staff/team members can move up the chart as their value and importance to the fundraising program increases and (unfortunately) down the chart as their worth and usefulness to the program decreases. Staff/team members can progress up the diagram and (unfortunately) down as their abilities and worth increase or decrease.

Fundraising Tip

Depth charts can have two valuable purposes in a fundraising program. They evaluate the functional turnover of the fundraising program and they can be used as motivational tools. Some staff members might not be content with where they lie in the fundraising program's depth chart. This could encourage them to increase their tangible productivity levels as well as intensify their intangible commitment to the fundraising program.

Recruitment and Selection

After manpower planning assessments have been outlined and there is a definite internal human resource need in the fundraising program, the next logical procedure in staffing is recruiting. "Recruiting is the process of developing a pool of qualified applicants who are interested in working for the organization and from which the organization might reasonably select the best individual or individuals to hire for employment" (DeNisi & Griffin, 2001, p. 170).

Sources of Fundraising Personnel
There are two principal resources for attaining a pool of competent applicants—internal sources (known as promotion within) and external sources. Internal sources for a fundraising program can include:

- current employees already in the fundraising program;
- prospective employees recommended by current fundraising program members/staff, volunteers, board of directors members, or alumni; and
- former re-hirable fundraising staff members.

External sources can include:

- media advertising in wide-ranging or targeted mediums (newspapers, trade publications, radio, TV, governing athletic bodies);
- college/university graduates with a focused degree and coursework in sport management, non-profit management, and/or fundraising;
- networking sources in a particular sport or conference in which the athletic program competes; and
- other external sources.

Which source a fundraising administrator selects hinges upon the recruiting situation as well as the benefits and drawbacks of each method. The following list is an itemization of the benefits and drawbacks of internal and external recruiting.

Internal Recruiting Benefits

Internal recruiting (promotion within) is a persuasive motivational tool for current fundraising program members and staff. For example, an assistant external developmental director is going to execute his/her current position to the best of his/her ability if he/she knows that the developmental director position is attainable. Promotion within leads to a cascading outcome throughout the entire fundraising program.

There is also a considerably reduced amount of risk with internal sources. Simply put, a fundraising administrator is already familiar with, through a working relationship, the aptitude and potential of a present staff/team member. That individual is an established quantity. Additionally, the learning curve (the time a fundraising staff member takes to become proficient at his/her position) is significantly less for a current fundraising program staff member. While the individual being promoted will need to cultivate additional skills and learning in the new fundraising position, he/she is already familiar with and accustomed to the overall fundraising program's operating systems as well as internal operational policies and procedures.

Internal Recruiting Drawbacks

The first negative aspect associated with internal recruiting for a fundraising program relates to what most human resource theorists call 'inbreeding.' A staff/team member who is promoted within a fundraising program could either be 'set in their ways' or so 'programmed' (from long-term habit) that he/she does not recognize that there are innovative and more resourceful methods of completing fundraising tasks.

If there is more than one eligible candidate for an open fundraising position, promotion within can lead to an exceptionally competitive work environment. Some would argue that this internal competitiveness drives individuals to function better, while others would say that it fractures the cohesiveness of the 'team' atmosphere. If a fundraising program has an open position with several qualified candidates, the individual members not acquiring the open position could have irreparable morale- and employment-related issues in the future.

Other internal source recruiting obstacles include:

- Employees who are promoted only because they've worked with the organization a long time.

- Pressure from someone inside the organization to see a favored, but unqualified individual promoted.

- In the case of a supervisory position, a promotion that is based upon skill alone, without consideration of leadership abilities.

- 'Popular' people who are promoted because they get along well with people even though they are not necessarily qualified. (Hacker, 1996, p. 9)

External Recruiting Benefits

With a suitable pool of candidates, external recruiting (bringing someone in from the outside) can legitimize and bring attention to a fundraising program. External recruiting has an overriding benefit of infusing the fundraising program with innovative ideas, new fundraising processes and procedures, novel talents and skills, and fresh energy. An external recruit is also not embroiled and entangled in the internal political/bureaucratic structure of a fundraising program. He/she can bring about more substantive change by being involved less.

External Recruiting Drawbacks

The first obstacle (and possibly the most internally damaging) from external recruiting is the existing personnel's perception of how they were 'stepped over' or given false hope of being promoted. This scenario can be exceptionally detrimental with long-term fundraising program members who have been steadily productive and dedicated to the fundraising program.

External recruiting not only has a positional learning curve but an organizational and fundraising program learning curve. This organizational and fundraising program learning curve adds time and a shortfall of productivity until the newly hired staff/team member understands the organization's operating systems. There is also substantially more risk in external recruiting of fundraising personnel than internal. While recruiting and selection have logical step-by-step processes to follow, there are no assurances that the selection of an external recruit will be successful.

In terms of cost, the financial expenditures associated with external recruiting are a great deal higher than those associated with an internal promotion. Additionally, while internal promotion can take literally days or even minutes, external recruiting of fundraising staff/team members can take weeks or even months.

Selection Process

Now that the sources of fundraising talent have been clarified, the next stage is the selection process. The selection process of a fundraising team member (which can be terminated at any time) customarily proceeds as follows:

Phase 1 – Phase one consists of an *informal preliminary evaluation.* In other words, it is the assessment of the talent of a potential fundraising staff/team member.

It can be as informal as the fundraising administrator and other team members verbally assessing a candidate's qualifications or as formal as charting detailed selection criteria and quantifying the results.

Phase 2 – Phase two consists of *applications/questionnaires* and a *review of résumés* for prospective fundraising program employees. These two types of instruments are accepted and recognized techniques for gathering pertinent information regarding a specific individual. The design of application and questionnaire instruments is limited by legal boundaries. For fundraising employees and staff members, employment applications must conform to all Equal Employment Opportunity Commission and Privacy Information Act provisos and stipulations.

When discussing types of applications,

> some organizations have developed weighted application blanks, in which responses to questions on the application form are compared to measures of job performance…thus, certain items [are] found to be more important than others in regards to performance. The important or "predictive" items are then weighted and used to help select future employees. (Anthony, Perrewe, & Kacmar, 1993, p. 283)

Phase 3 – Phase three consists of *face-to-face* conferences with potential fundraising staff and team members. Program administrators initiate this meeting through a conventional interview process. The intensity and format of the interview is determined by the significance and gravity of the position in the fundraising program's operating scheme.

There is characteristically one way for a fundraising administrator to become a skillful and adept interviewer—by doing legitimate interviews. Time and practice are needed to become skilled as an interviewer. However, there are some fundamental steps that can be taken to assist a fundraising administrator with becoming a more accomplished interviewer.

Step 1: A fundraising administrator must conscientiously *prepare for each and every interview.* Interview preparation is a mental state as well as a logistical structure. The mental preparation for an interview correlates to 'clearing one's mind' of other distractions so absolute attention can be given to the fundraising program candidate being interviewed. Logistical interviewing components can encompass times and locations, a thorough examination of each individual candidate's credentials and history, and pre-established questions related to fundraising program goals.

Step 2: The second step in the interviewing progression is the *actual interview.* Actual interviewing is the

> core of the hiring process. No matter how long the interview lasts, there is still only a short period of time in which to assess the worth and value of another person and to make the decision as to whether or not you want to work side-by-side with that person for many years to come. (Curzon, 1996, p. 46)

The actual interview for fundraising personnel can have a multitude of formats and participants. A fundraising administrator can conduct the interview over a meal, with his/her supervisor, in his/her office, or in a separate conference area. Additionally, a fundraising administrator can ask pre-established fundraising-specific questions that have pre-determined answers or he/she can use open-ended questions that elicit more probing reactions/responses to fundraising issues and scenarios.

Special Note: It is imperative that a fundraising administrator circumvent questions that are illegal or discriminatory. Prior to interviewing, it is strongly advised to analyze areas and questions that can or cannot be asked during an interview. Sources for this type of information are human resource departments, human resources texts, and legal counsel.

Step 3: *Post-interview assessment* is the last step in the interviewing process. After the conclusion of the interview (or interviews), a fundraising administrator needs to scrutinize all the facts and data gathered during the all-inclusive interview process. Items such as re-reading notes taken during interviews, annotations and comments given by other interview participants, responses to fundraising questions asked, and overall behavior of individuals are just some of the elements a fundraising administrator must evaluate.

Step 4: This step consists of *personal and professional reference checks*. This step in the selection process is habitually disregarded, but is crucial in affirming the character of the fundraising staff/team member. The fundraising administrator should have a slate of definite questions ready for all reference communications.

Step 5: This step consists of negotiations and hiring. After all the germane information has been assembled and references checked, the decision is made to offer the fundraising program position.

There are two consequential rules that must always be applied when securing additional fundraising staff/team members. The first standard is to always convey the truth in all recruiting practices no matter how much the fundraising program might desire or need a particular individual. The second principal is to never 'negative recruit' against another athletic organization. Negative recruiting is basically identifying other competitors for a potential fundraising team member and verbalizing derogatory remarks about their program, fundraising methodology, and overall organization. Violating these basic rules will always come back to 'haunt' the fundraising program one is trying to maintain and build.

FUNDRAISING PROGRAM ORIENTATION SYSTEMS

After going through the arduous recruiting and selection process for fundraising team members, the fundraising administrator has hired who he/she believes is the best-suited candidate. The new fundraising staff/team member's first organizational impressions are the most noteworthy component in determining the length and productivity of the individual's tenure with the fundraising program. The first initial weeks 'set the tone' for the individual on what work ethics, fundraising policies and

Fundraising Tip

Before interviewing, prepare a list of appropriate questions that will prioritize vital information needed to evaluate the candidate. Outline the presentation but encourage open dialog as long as the discussion remains on topic.

Fundraising Tip

A fundraising administrator needs to declare up front which items in the negotiation meeting are open for discussion and which items are deal breakers. Not only will a fundraising administrator avoid critical personnel errors by using this technique, he/she will set the tempo of the interview and have total control of the negotiation.

procedures, and overall organizational culture exists in the athletic organization and fundraising program. To achieve the right atmosphere, a professional, appropriately structured orientation program is indispensable. Conversely, a haphazard and incomplete orientation program can have a destructive and often long-term influence on the new fundraising team member.

There are two types of orientation programs for fundraising personnel: athletic organization orientation, and fundraising program and job orientation.

Athletic Organization Orientation

Athletic organization orientation (in larger athletic programs) is typically conducted by a human resource specialist. The new hire is presented with a complete picture of the entire athletic organization during this orientation session. In the text, *Keeping Your Valuable Employees*, Dibble's chapter titled "Retention Starts with Orientation" suggests what organizational orientation programs should provide new employees. Table 4.3 displays an extrapolation of her orientation points.

Table 4.3. **What Orientation Programs Should Provide to New Employees**

Overview	Personal welcome from chief executive officer; Mission statement; Annual report; Employee handbook; Tour of the facilities
Forms	Personal information; Personalized forms for benefits enrollment; I-9, W-4, direct deposit, and other forms
Getting Started	Map of organization's locations; Directions to them; Samples of products; Employee publications; Schedule of group orientation session; Organizational chart; Pictures of key leaders; Computer and other passwords; Telephone book, including locations and email addresses; Attendance expectations; Planner with pages on the organization
About the Job	Job description; Career opportunity services; Mentoring program; Individual development services; Feedback tools used to assist in development; Compensation philosophy and details; Performance management process; Training catalog
Orienting the Workplace	Flextime policies; Neighborhood features; Fitness facilities; On-site services; Opportunities for involvement with volunteer and community programs; Recreational facilities; Restaurants in the neighborhood
Fun	Video to take home and show the family; Work and family programs; T-shirt with logo; Sport leagues/team sign-up sheet; Invitation to annual picnic
Evaluation of Orientation	Evaluation process; Evaluation forms

From the opposing organizational orientation perspective, Branham in the text *Keeping the People Who Keep You in Business*, elaborates on five common mistakes employers make when welcoming new hires:

- Having assembly-line orientations during which new hires attend long lecture sessions and fill out forms.

- Not having the new employee's desk, phone, computer, and other office supplies in place prior to first day.

- Ignoring the new hire or leaving the person to read manuals without one-to-one contact.

- Making new hire orientation a strictly HR run affair with little involvement of the new hire's manager and department.

- Failing to have the new hire's manager set specific performance objectives. (Branham, 2001, p. 143)

Fundraising Program and Job Orientation

© Vladimir Kolobov | Dreamstime.com

Fundraising program and job orientation is the production-centered initiation in which the new hire acquires job-specialized knowledge and fundraising systems understanding. The important question relating to this type of orientation is "Who should conduct it?" Should it be administered by a current fundraising staff/team member in a hands-on, on-the-job configuration or should the fundraising administrator be the sole contact to review program activities and responsibilities? The answer is both. There should be a balance between the involvement of fellow staff/team members and fundraising administrators. The specific position the new hire is filling will impact job orientation interaction. Some fundraising program positions will be heavy in employee-to-employee orientation while others will stress supervisory influence in the orientation.

Regardless of who performs the fundraising program and job orientation sessions, a detailed outline (or job-related check-off list) of all of the fundraising position's tasks and obligations as well as the operating systems employed by the fundraising program should be utilized. The advantage in utilizing a pre-determined program and job outline is the avoidance of omitting/overlooking vital operational items necessary for the new hire's productivity and effectiveness in the fundraising program.

TRAINING AND DEVELOPMENT SYSTEMS

Training and development augment the fundraising program's most valuable resource—people. There is a wealth of instructional methodologies that a fundraising program administrator can utilize.

Skill Training

Skill training is the refining of specific abilities associated with fundraising. There are two primary methods that fall under the category of skill training—block training and random training.

Block training is the teaching of skills through the unremitting repetition of a particular activity. Simply put, the skill is completed over and over again until it is

Fundraising Tip

No matter what type of program or job training is being performed (skill, knowledge, attitudinal), never undervalue the influence of fun. The more a fundraising administrator can balance his/her training goals with a pleasant environment, the more productive the training sessions will be.

proficiently and adeptly displayed. It should be noted that there are no set number of repetitions to achieve competency. Human beings learn at disparate rates. As an administrator, recognize this fact and, through pragmatic observation and distinct evaluation, analyze each person's progress accordingly.

Random training is the teaching of a particular skill or action through real-world situations. In random training, the teaching techniques are scenario driven, which means that the real-world conditions are defined specifically for the individual(s), then the activity is conducted in a live-action state. Random training has some distinctive advantages in its application. Following are some of the benefits:

1. It is as close to real-world fundraising as training can be.

2. It is participative learning in unsystematic conditions.

3. It combines the whole of the fundraising skill or activity, in contrast to block training, which trains parts to make the whole.

4. It has the capacity to be dynamic and can keep cognitive focus longer.

Some areas of fundraising where skill training can be applied encompass:

- written correspondence with potential supporters;
- preparation and presentation of fundraising solicitations and meetings;
- distribution of fundraising literature to mass markets; and
- all types of diverse donor interactions.

Knowledge Training

Knowledge training guides and teaches an individual to think, which is critical for fundraising. The concept of intelligence training and development encompasses business and psychological theories such as individual cognitive analysis, preconditions of learning (acceptance and motivation), creative cognitions, and rationality among others.

Attitudinal Training

Attitudinal training is concerned with the character, disposition, and mindset of an individual. This is by far the most difficult type of training for the obvious reason that attitudes are immeasurable and are by individual perspective. However, there are ways in which fundraising administrators can instruct their staff/team members on attitudinal expectations:

1. Candidly discuss what attitudes are anticipated and expected.

2. Document the behaviors and attitudes projected so each individual has a tangible reference.

3. Lead by example.

The third component could be the most potent of the three. If a fundraising administrator displays an impoverished, pessimistic, and unenthusiastic attitude toward a fundraising activity, event, or program, then staff/team members will more than likely adopt the same stance. Conversely, if a fundraising administrator exhibits an encouraging, optimistic attitude, the staff/team members can observe, reference, and follow that behavior.

No matter what type of training (skill, knowledge, attitudinal), the instruction of a fundraising program's personnel (staff and players) can strongly enhance consistent and competent results by applying a straightforward, systematic approach. According to the text *Training for Non-Trainers*, there are three basic tasks that all training programs must follow:

> Your first task as a manager is to precisely define your employees' training needs…the second task is to figure out the best way to present the train-ing information to each employee so that only such training as is required is presented and so that it is learned in an appropriate amount of time . . . your third task as a manager is to get the right training to the right people so that the resources it uses up are an investment in productivity. (Nilson, 1990, p. 3)

The various training methods to choose from for fundraising programs include, but are not limited to, the following:

- On-the-job/real-world application training
- Supervisory consultations (one-to-one)
- Peer subordinate training
- Group collective training
- Virtual/distance training (self-directed training)
- Classroom/lecture series training
- Understudy/apprenticeship training
- Case study training
- Job simulation training

Once again, the training technique a fundraising administrator selects depends on the purpose of the training, the resources accessible for the training (e.g. time, money, training knowledge), and the productivity expectations of each technique.

Training Program Evaluation

For continuous improvement, fundraising training programs need to be objectively and subjectively scrutinized as to their value. While skills and knowledge training lend themselves toward quantitative evaluation (numerical measurements that con-trast before and after training outcomes), attitudinal training is much more challeng-ing to objectively measure. Typically, attitudinal training is evaluated by empirical observation of the fundraising team member's individual attitude/behavior before and after the training.

No matter which goal a fundraising administrator has for the fundraising program's training, the evaluation can be based on four simple steps.

Step 1:   Reaction. How well did the conferees like the program?

Step 2:   Learning. What principles, facts, and techniques were learned? What attitudes were changed?

Step 3:   Behavior. What changes in job behavior resulted from the program?

Step 4:   Results. What were the tangible results of the program in terms of reduced cost, improved quality, improved quantity, etc.? (Craig, 1996, p. 295)

It is pivotal to understand that most fundraising administrators unquestionably go straight to Step 4: Results to appraise the efficacy of a training series. While 'bottom line results' are a decisive factor in the appraisal of any training program's effectiveness, the elements in Steps 1-3 (Reaction, Learning, Behavior) are also valid measurement criteria for fundraising training programs. Simply stated, if reaction to a training program is positive, if learning from a training program increases, and if behaviors and job/work ethics are changed from a training program, there is a strong presumption that the by-product of results should increase (more supporters, donations, program interest, etc.).

PERFORMANCE EVALUATION SYSTEMS

The primary intention behind the evaluation of a fundraising program's staff/team member's productivity is to supply feedback to internal stakeholders, standardize goals, and improve productivity outcomes. There are abundant methodologies that can be employed when completing performance evaluations. One of the most contemporary practices for evaluating fundraising staff and team members is based on the concept of Management by Objective appraisals (MBOs).

© Maxexphoto | Dreamstime.com

Management by Objectives (MBO)

MBO assessments are a more cooperative, motivational, and constructive method of performance evaluations than the traditional one-way critical judgment analysis. The MBO process is as follows:

1. *Job review and agreement.* The fundraising team member and administrator review the individual's job description and the key fundraising activities comprising the employee's job. The goal is to agree on the exact make-up of the employee's job.

2. *Development of performance standards.* Specific standards of performance must be mutually developed. This phase identifies a satisfactory level of performance that is specific and measurable.

3. *Guided objective setting.* Objectives are established by the staff/team member in conjunction with, and guided by, the program administrator.

4. *Ongoing performance discussion.* The fundraising team member and administrator use the objectives as a basis for continuing discussion about the team member's performance. While a formal review session may be scheduled, the team member and administrator do not necessarily wait until the appointed time for performance discussion. Objectives are mutually modified and progress is discussed during the period. (Extrapolated from Mathis & Jackson, 1982, p. 303)

This process is a perpetual and repeating system. From the four-step process, a key term must be emphasized: mutual. This collaborative type of evaluation process is in the best interest of the staff/team member and the fundraising program. From the vantage point of the person being evaluated, the system is good because it supports individuals with clear objectives that have been established with their own input. Furthermore, fundraising administrators will find that this method bolsters staff/team members' confidence and levels of motivation, it creates strong lines of communication, and it cultivates teamwork, which is critical for all fundraising efforts.

Two other key points should be emphasized in employing MBO evaluations in fundraising programs. Remember that these evaluations are a collaborative effort. At first, the fundraising administrator might have to 'draw out' the staff/team member in the partnership aspects of clarifying objectives. It should also be clear that the staff/team member is accountable for his/her performance. The second key point is that there should be intermittent checkpoints. These checkpoints can be in the form of formal meetings or informal updates.

360-Degree Evaluations

An evaluation method that has gained momentum in the business world and can be adopted by fundraising programs is called a 360-degree performance evaluation. The concept differs from traditional one-way performance assessments in that an individual is given work-related performance evaluations from all people the individual works with and for in the fundraising program (peers, supervisors, subordinates, donors, etc.). A true 360-degree evaluation examines the individual's own perspective of how he/she performed. There are three key assumptions on which 360-degree feedback is based:

1. Multiple viewpoints from multiple sources will produce a more accurate picture of one's strengths and weaknesses than would a single reviewer's evaluation;

Fundraising Tip

Often the most difficult aspect of an MBO evaluation is drawing out the individuals to contribute to the process. To have fundraising team members collaborate in their own productivity and futures, uncover what motivates them.

2. The act of comparing one's own self-perception with others' perceptions will lead to enhanced self-awareness and greater self-awareness is a good thing;

3. People who are effective at what they do will have self-perceptions that match other's perceptions of them fairly closely. (Carson, 2006, p. 395)

All performance assessments systems have distinct drawbacks. The drawbacks of the 360-degree system are as follows:

- Personalities can be overemphasized. In other words, the individual's actual job performance could become secondary if the evaluators emphasize his/her likeability rather fundraising job skills and productivity.

- If the peer environment in a fundraising program is competitive, 360-degree evaluations will likely provide an inaccurate picture of an individual's work quality and productivity.

- 360-degree evaluation forms need to be constructed separately for each evaluation group in a fundraising program. The evaluation criteria that a supervisor might feel is important might not necessarily be what a subordinate is concerned with.

- An individual's self-assessment might not be based on reality.

- It takes time to compile 360-degree evaluations and 'number crunch' the accumulated data from all of the fundraising sources.

REWARDS, COMPENSATION, AND BENEFITS

The final human resource system in the fundraising program relates to the compensation and benefit packages proposed to potential and current staff/team members.

Intrinsic and Extrinsic Rewards

When discussing the human resource elements involved in rewards, compensation, and benefits, a fundraising administrator must understand the concepts of intrinsic and extrinsic rewards and benefits. Intrinsic rewards (or intrinsically motivated behavior)

> is performed for its own sake; the source of motivation is actually performing the behavior, and motivation comes from doing the work itself. Many managers are intrinsically motivated; they derive a sense of accomplishment and achievement from helping the organization to achieve its goals and gain a competitive advantage…extrinsically motivated behavior is behavior that is performed to acquire material or social rewards or to avoid punishment; the source of motivation is the consequences of the behavior, not the behavior itself. (Jones & George, 2006, p. 457-458)

Intrinsically motivated rewards and behavior differs among individuals. Each fundraising program member will have different feelings of accomplishment/achievement when completing a task. A major function of the interview process is to find individuals who have a strong level of intrinsic motivation to complete the fundraising position for which they are hired.

Extrinsic rewards, which are tangible rewards/compensation such as salary, benefits, and job-related 'perks' are dictated by the financial status of the athletic program, the fundraising position, and the qualifications of the individual. Fundraising staff/team members, however, can qualify for the same compensation rewards as any other business employee. Their compensations, awards, and benefits can include salaries or wages, commissions, performance bonuses, vacation and sick leave, pension and retirement, profit sharing, and worker's compensation. In other words, the level and detail of the fundraising program's employee compensation package is dictated by the operational environment and specific situation.

Performance Bonus Systems

If a fundraising program has sufficient financial and bureaucratic flexibility, strong consideration should be given to the development and implementation of a performance-based bonus system. Bonus systems can be centered on individual performance, group achievement, or a combination of both. Constructing a lucid, structured, and fair/equitable bonus (pay-for-performance) system initially takes time to develop and implement. Consideration must be given to the fact that some fundraising job performances are difficult to quantify/measure. Furthermore, a fundraising administrator must dissect job performance goals and decide which elements warrant pay-for-performance measures.

When developing a bonus/pay-for-performance system, a number of desirable preconditions have been identified and generally accepted:

1. *Trust in management.* If employees are skeptical of management, it is difficult to make a pay-for-performance program work.

2. *Absence of performance constraints.* Since pay-for-performance programs are usually based on an employee's ability and effort, the jobs must be structured so that an employee's performance is not hampered by factors beyond his/her control.

3. *Trained supervisors and managers.* The supervisor and managers must be trained in setting and measuring performance standards.

4. *Good measuring systems.* Performance should be based on criteria that are job specific and focused on results achieved.

5. *Ability to pay.* The merit portion of the salary increase budget must be large enough to get the attention of the employees.

6. *Clear distinction among cost-of-living, seniority, and merit.* In the absence of strong evidence to the contrary, employees will naturally assume a pay increase is a cost-of-living or seniority increase.

7. *Well-communicated total pay policy.* Employees must have a clear understanding of how merit pay fits into the total pay picture.

8. *Flexible rewards schedule.* It is easier to establish a credible pay-for-performance plan if all employees do not receive pay adjustments on the same date. (Byars & Rue, 2008, p. 237)

An equitable pay-for-performance bonus system not only boosts performance and tangible results in a fundraising program, but can also substantially increase employee morale. Often, the extrinsic bonus reward becomes secondary to the intrinsic feeling of recognition for a job well done.

HUMAN RESOURCE DISCIPLINARY SYSTEMS: DISCIPLINARY PROCESS

The following is an escalating, stage-by-stage disciplinary system for an athletic organization's fundraising program.

Stage 1: Oral/Verbal Warnings

Level 1 – Oral/Verbal Warning (No Documentation)
This form of warning is for lesser/minor/first-time fundraising program offenses. No follow-up or written documentation is associated with this type of warning.

Level 2 – Oral/Verbal Warning (Documentation)
This disciplinary discussion warrants some manner of supporting written documentation for referencing. It should be kept as a permanent record in the individual's fundraising program file.

Stage 2: Written Warnings

Level 1 – Written Warning (Internal Documentation)
This phase and intensity of disciplinary action includes a formal, signed form retained in the individual's fundraising program file. It should be discussed at an official meeting with other fundraising program members in attendance. All who participate (including the violator) should sign off on the document.

Level 2 – Written Warning (Internal and External Documentation)
The subsequent level of written warning is the same as Level 1 except that the written portion is maintained not only inside the staff/team member's fundraising program file, but also in the overall athletic organization's records. Because of the gravity of this violation, it is advisable to have an athletic organization administrator present to observe the meeting.

Stage 3: Suspensions/Dismissals

Level 1 – Suspensions
This critical disciplinary situation involves the individual's receiving a participative suspension from all fundraising program activities. The length of the suspension could be predetermined or could be set through an advisory meeting with the athletic

organization's administration. All suspensions must be entirely documented with the full knowledge and support of all athletic organizational administrators. The individual can bring outside counsel if so desired.

Level 2 – Dismissal

This terminal stage involves the individual's permanent discharge/release from employment in the athletic organization's fundraising program. Because of the definitive severity of this type of response to an infringement/violation, all parties should be well represented. Once again, comprehensive documentation is mandatory. It is also a prudent strategy to videotape the dismissal conference. A few noteworthy points about the workings of the disciplinary system:

1. Continued offenses move up the stage-by-stage process.

2. Major offenses skip the lower levels of disciplinary actions.

3. The program administrator should define, in writing, typical (and if possible specific) offenses in each category and level.

4. The program administrator should provide all fundraising staff/team members with a copy of the disciplinary system and discuss it with them periodically.

Grievance Policies and Procedures

All disciplinary systems should have pre-established grievance procedures to allow individuals a chance to rebut/challenge the discipline incurred. Thus, a grievance process, which should be spelled out in both the athletic organization's and fundraising program's policies and procedures manual, should be straightforward, clear, and all-inclusive.

If a fundraising program does not have a spelled-out grievance process, one could be constructed as follows:

Step 1: The individual being disciplined must (1) notify all relevant parties (e.g. human resource department, supervisor, divisional manager, fundraising administrator) in writing that he/she is contesting a disciplinary action and (2) must recount his/her side of the disciplinary issue.

Step 2: The human resource department or athletic organization administration will coordinate a timely grievance meeting with internal athletic organization and fundraising program personnel (as well as persons outside the athletic program) to review the validity of the individual's claim. Additionally, the human resource department will issue a written confirmation to the disciplined individual stating that a grievance committee meeting will convene.

Step 3: If the committee feels that the individual's situation warrants further attention, an official meeting/hearing will be called. If the committee judges the discipline to be in accordance with athletic organization and fundraising program policies and procedures, a written notification will be issued to the staff member/athlete detailing the findings/decision.

Step 4: The official meeting convenes with all relevant parties and witnesses. It is strongly recommended that the meeting be recorded by an independent third party.

Step 5: After the official meeting, the committee will make its final decision concerning the disciplinary action. The individual will be informed in writing (and in a timely manner) of the final decision.

Critical Notes

- Depending upon the severity of the disciplinary issue, legal counsel (for both the individual and the athletic organization/fundraising program) may be advisable.

- To reiterate, the athletic organization and fundraising program should include independent outside individuals on the disciplinary committee for objectivity and impartiality.

- The direct fundraising administrator (who issued the discipline) should provide the committee with all internal documents supporting his/her decision to discipline the individual. The fundraising administrator should have no contact with the committee while the process is proceeding.

- As with all human resource systems, the grievance process, prior to its inclusion in the athletic organization's and fundraising program's policy and procedure manual, must be reviewed by human resource specialists and legal counsel. This review will ensure that every step in the process is within permissible legal requirements.

SUMMARY

For a business (in this case fundraising program) to be prosperous, one truth must pervade the fundraising program's philosophy and thinking: the fundraising program is only as good as the people in it. The selection, training, evaluation, and compensation of a fundraising program's staff/team members has an absolute and unequivocal impact on all aspects of the fundraising program. The competent utilization of human resource applications can fortify this imperative resource. The deficiency of human resource management can result in complete failure of the fundraising program.

REVIEW AND DISCUSSION QUESTIONS

1. What are the six human resource operations in a fundraising program?
2. List the five phases in the selection process (in sequential order).
3. What should fundraising orientation programs provide new employees?
4. What are the steps in an MBO evaluation for a fundraising program?
5. Name the stages in a disciplinary system for athletic organizations and fundraising programs.

5

Development of a Fundraising Board of Directors and Volunteers

INTRODUCTION

No matter how you categorize them, the significance of a formidable fundraising board of directors and volunteer core cannot be overstated. Whether it is a sport-exclusive fundraising group, a department-wide booster club, or a fully functional athletic organization board of directors, these groups and individuals can collectively be the difference between obtaining the essential resources needed to be successful or falling short of funding objectives critical for continued existence. For smaller athletic organizations, the resources they generate can literally be the 'lifeblood' of the operation. For large athletic organizations, these stakeholder groups are frequently the most important reason the athletic operation maintains its prominence, reputation, and competitive advantage.

For a fundraising board of directors and volunteer core to be effective, there must be a palpable feeling of inclusion within the athletic organization's operations. In the simplest terms, a board of directors is a separate entity that has a functional as well as symbolic affiliation with the parent athletic organization. The board of directors and volunteer core must be a strategic component of both the all-encompassing athletic organization plan and the ancillary external development/fundraising program plan. As an identifiable element in the athletic organization and fundraising plans, boards of directors and volunteer groups should have:

- a prearranged operational structure with unambiguous policies and procedures, hierarchical relationships accountability, and cross functional groupings;
- a delineated human resource management progression which spells out selection standards, job descriptions, and evaluation processes;
- a leadership foundation that has a sincere and dedicated belief in the athletic organization's mission; and
- a systematic communication mechanism that facilitates exchanges of ideas between the board of directors/volunteers and the athletic organization.

Three supplementary aspects of boards of directors and volunteer core operations that should be noted are as follows:

1. While there should be an energetic, unencumbered connection between the in-house fundraising administrators and staff, and the board of directors and volunteer core, there are conspicuous differences between the two groups. Fundraising administrators and staff members are professionally trained in all facets of strategic fundraising. The achievements or failures of a fundraising program are tied directly into the fundraising professional's employment and career (e.g., extrinsic rewards). Board members and volunteers are individuals who donate their time and money generously, more often than not without any material rewards (e.g., intrinsic motivation). If their intrinsic satisfaction is not being met by their involvement in the athletic organization's fundraising activities and programs, their tenure will be tenuous at best.

2. Board members and volunteers can come from all walks of life and have a variety of demographic characteristics. The fundamental determinate for their incorporation into the athletic organization's 'family' should be their allegiance to the athletic organization and their willingness to contribute their time, money, and effort.

3. When considering board members and volunteers, these personality characteristics and qualities should be prioritized:
   - Capacity to democratically mediate issues
   - Display of social principles and expectations that reflect the athletic organization's philosophies
   - Inherent leadership, administrative, and strategic qualities
   - Affluent articulation of one's message
   - Capability to function independently or in fundraising groups/committees
   - Possession of personality strengths such as a passionate attitude, innovative thinking, and visionary cognitions

Fundraising Tip.

Have a yearly 'fundraising retreat' away from the athletic organization's standard work environment. This getaway will provide an uninterrupted fundraising focus. If acting as a fundraising administrator, be equipped to guide meeting sessions.

- Resourceful and inquisitive disposition
- Intense devotion to the athletic organization

The final characteristic, commitment to the athletic organization, cannot be emphasized enough. A haphazard, apathetic board of directors and volunteer core jeopardizes the fundraising program and, ultimately, the entire athletic organization.

This chapter will provide an examination of the two volunteer groups involved in the majority of athletic organizations—a board of directors and general volunteer core.

FUNDRAISING BOARD OF DIRECTORS

© iStockphoto.com/urbancow

In the article "How can we boost our board from good to great?" Honaman sums up the considerable importance of a current or future fundraising board of directors by stating, "as your association's most dedicated and passionate volunteers, the members of your board of directors are capable of leaving a legacy of leadership—a foundation for new growth and accomplishment for years to come" (Honaman, 2005, p. 83). To fulfill this pronouncement (that the board of directors is capable of leaving a future legacy of growth and accomplishment), board members must be actively involved in the current fundraising program's planning process. With this concentration of foundational participation, the board of directors will be far more vested in the present and impending achievements of the fundraising program's events/activities/programs. Additionally, this functional participation in planning by the board of directors will provide the fundraising program's administration with a wider range of strategic inputs and a clearer picture of the future. The fundraising plan should, therefore, be a cooperative establishment of operational and financial goals between the overall athletic organization's administration, the fundraising program's administration and staff, and the external board of directors.

Strategic Development and Structure of a Fundraising Board of Directors

Before a discussion of a board of directors' development and structure can commence, it must be emphatically stated that no two athletic organization fundraising boards of directors will have the same composition, configuration, and maturity. Each

Fundraising Tip

A preponderance of the conceptualizations discussed in detail in Chapter 4 (Assembling an Effective Fundraising Department) will, in most instances, apply or can be adapted to the development, operation, and effectiveness of a board of directors and volunteer core.

Fundraising Tip

A fundraising planning committee should incorporate fundraising administrators, key board members, operational staffers, and critical volunteers. If a fundraising planning committee is inexperienced in the strategic planning process, a managerial consultant should be employed to assist in the facilitation of the process.

will emphasize (both philosophically and operationally) distinctive situational elements. A number of fundraising board members will be more symbolic and figurative, with the majority of tasks and responsibilities being delegated to the general volunteer core and fundraising administration. Other board members will take an energetic and substantive role in overseeing fundraising events and activities (through sub-committees) as well as taking the lead in capital fundraising programs. With that being understood, there is no right or wrong formation and organization of a fundraising program's board of directors. Each must be designed based upon the athletic organization's exclusive situation and what is best for the fundraising program.

After involving the board of directors in the future of the athletic organization through the fundraising planning process, other ingredients that contribute to the board of directors being an effectual working unit can encompass the following developmental and structural elements:

- If constructing a board of directors from the ground up, a policy and procedure manual expressly created for a fundraising program's board members is a vital document. If the board of directors is already an active component of the fundraising program, a policy and procedure manual should be produced in cooperation with all current board members. Once again, the more involved a board of directors is in the development of a policy and procedure manual, the more invested they will be in its operation.

- A strong infrastructure through hierarchical positions will provide a fundraising program's board of directors with procedural criteria as well as assignments, affiliations, and accountability standards. The organization and composition of the group's personnel will also determine the general factors for resource allocation as well as the operational climate of the fundraising program's board of directors. The board of directors' personnel and hierarchical structure should be centered on goals and strategies of the fundraising program. In other words, goals and strategies should be the solidifying features when designing board of directors jobs and responsibilities inside the hierarchical arrangement. An example of board of directors structural positions is in Figure 5.1.

- Board of directors positions and responsibilities should be separated. Job descriptions (similar to fundraising administration and staff job descriptions discussed in Chapter 4) should be assembled for each board of directors position. All job tasks delineated in the board of directors job descriptions must be meaningful and reflect the empowerment and accountability inherent in the position. All expectations of the position need clear description. There should be substantive participation from each committee chair when designing job descriptions in their distinct areas. They are the experts in their fields and will have definitive insights on the board of directors positions and responsibilities.

Figure 5.1. **Board of Directors Position and Committees Template**

Chairman of the Board of Directors
Liaison with Athletic Organization and Community, Management of Board of Directors Operations, Leadership (Delegation, Empowerment, and Accountability), Annual Board of Director Planning

Chair of Committees Volunteer
Recruitment, Selection, Job Descriptions and Duties, Training, Assignments, Evaluations, Recognition, Succession Planning

Budgetary
Monitoring Budgets of All Fundraising Events/activities/programs, Board of Directors Accounting (Expenditure and Revenue Sources), Reporting Obligations (Internal and External), Forensic Accounting/Auditing (if necessary)

Fundraising Solicitation
Lobbying, Large Donation Solicitation, Legacy Programs/Endorsements, Planned Gifts, Community Public Relations, Private/Corporate Donor Database, Research, Personal Selling Supervision

Fundraising Events and Activities
Development, Implementation, and Evaluation of All Fundraiser Program Events and Activities, Supervision of Volunteers in Specific Events and Activities

Legal Advisory
Consultations, Review of Contractual Arrangements, Supervision of all Legal Aspect of Board of Directors Operations

** While the above committee chair positions are generally accepted as a requirement of a fundraising board of directors, the dimension of each division is determined by the size of the athletic organization and future growth objectives. For example, in a large collegiate athletic organization, the legal advisory committee chair may lead a board of directors division of multiple lawyers and legal consultants.

* Special Note: Due to federal and state regulations dealing with non-profits (as well as IRS reporting regulations), an athletic organization's fundraising board of directors should have at least one lawyer and CPA as either board members or program consultants. The complexity of legal and regulatory stipulations for nonprofit management is far beyond most athletic organization administrators.

- Because of volatile economic circumstances, most board of directors positions have become, by necessity, more than ceremonial. A fundraising board member must be a functioning, integral component of the fundraising program's operations. However, for significant donors who do not have the time (or inclination) to be operational board members but want to be integrated into the athletic organization's operation, honorary board of directors titles can be a compelling tactic for their inclusion without damaging active board of directors functions.

- The formation facet of a fundraising board of directors should be centered on standing committees as well as ad hoc committees (temporary extemporized committees that are for exclusive projects and programs). Most long-term fundraising programs (2-5 years and beyond) will need standing committees which have cohesive groups and demarcated positional responsibilities. Conversely, special fundraising events and activities with terminal time frames should be structured around ad hoc committees. In other words, ad hoc committees are project-oriented groups which are formed and focused on a specific fundraiser, then disbanded upon its completion.

Fundraising Tip

When presenting a fundraising board of directors job description to a potential new fundraising board member, complete disclosure of all responsibilities should be prioritized (the good/desirable as well as the difficult/demanding). This practice will circumvent any surprises and provide a comprehensible list of duties and expectations.

Operational Elements

The subsequent points (which are in no special order) are conceptual elements that are universal to the operation of nearly all nonprofit boards of directors. These assumptions can be adapted to an athletic organization's fundraising board of directors.

- The ultimate objective of effective budgeting is to furnish the board of directors, fundraising administrators, and athletic organization executives with essential information for the allocation of limited operational resources. Budgetary responsibilities, along with fundraising program fiscal monitoring, should be through a collaborative affiliation between an in-house fundraising administrator and a designated board member (customarily the budgetary committee chair). Moreover, year-end reports which are presented to the fundraising board of directors and athletic organization administration need to be professionally constructed, precise, and agreed upon by all budgetary/accounting personnel.

- When acquiring board members to fill vacant positions, formalized interviews should be conducted with the prospective member and athletic organization executives, fundraising administrators, chairman of the board of directors, and selected board members. Even though the interview process is prearranged, due to the volunteer nature and importance of each board of directors position, interviews need to be conducted in conjunction with meals (in high quality venues) or at selected athletic organization functions. The interview should have an atmosphere of solicitation rather than selection.

- Once the position has been offered and accepted, a letter of commitment will need to be generated which itemizes the specifics of a board of directors position. "The nominating committee should write the specifics of the board committee letter for approval...The letter should be revised annually, as the needs of the non profit vary from year to year" (Weisman, 2002, p. 11).

- An operating priority should emphasize the entire board of directors' (as well as each distinct standing and ad hoc committee's) cross-functionality. Cross-functionalism is defined as a "team made up of technical specialists from different areas" (Kreitner/Kinicki, 2008, p. 325). A board of directors with complementary skills is a more competent, well-rounded, and adaptable unit. However, while board members are separate in functional responsibilities, they must be a unified team with a singular purpose of raising funds and support for the athletic organization.

- For efficacious operations, the concept of unity of strategy must be a foundational component of any board of directors. In this case, unity of strategy is when the overall athletic organization's mission and strategic goals flow down and are the basis of the fundraising's program's mission and strategic goals— from there, the fundraising program's mission and strategic goals flow down and are the basis of the board of directors' specific mission and strategic goals. Simply stated, all facets of an athletic organization are all operating on the same page and working toward the overall athletic organization's mission.

- The board of directors' obligation to athletic organizational communication (and public relations) is contingent upon each individual's commitment and personal, dynamic style of speaking. Board members must embrace and utilize their distinct individuality and charisma to communicate with the community and to enhance the fundraising program's image. Public speaking, media interviews, promotional events, and public service messages are just a few of the potential communication opportunities. It is highly advisable to have all messages that represent the athletic organization reviewed and approved by athletic organization personnel (e.g. public relations staff, sports information department).

- The idea of intrinsic rewards becomes exceptionally relevant when discussing fundraising board members. Individuals who volunteer to help an athletic organization raise funds have a zealous need for intrinsic appreciation. Fundraising administrators must recognize this need and continuously reward these individuals. Intrinsic rewards can range from acknowledgment at public events (such as banquets and competitions) to accessing organizational resources (within reason).

Board of Directors Effectiveness Factors

© MinervaStudio | Dreamstime.com

A significant factor for the effectiveness of a fundraising board of directors is the group's clear loyalty to the athletic organization and fundraising program. This allegiance is best exemplified by the statement 'walk the talk.' Plainly stated, board members must donate their time and monetary resources to the athletic organization. The amount of their support is up to their discretion and financial situation. However, 100% participation is a critical imperative. If financial resources are unavailable, in-kind donations and support (with relevant value) are just as appropriate. The benefit of and necessity for board members' contributing to the fundraising program in which they belong can encompass the following:

- It increases the level of ownership that board members feel toward the organization and permits them to ask others for money.

- It shows others that board members are good stewards.

- It helps your organization raise funds from foundations and other entities that ask "How much has the board given?" (Lysakowski, 2005, p. 25)

Fundraising Tip

Some board members have an inherent apprehension toward soliciting charitable gifts and contributions from others. The notion of asking an associate and/or family member for money could be a potent deterrent to a board member's involvement in fundraising endeavors. The best advice is to request their assistance in solicitations, not mandate it.

This manner of contribution (through personal support, financial and/or in-kind gifts and trade) makes a profound statement throughout the entire athletic organization.

If possible, to enhance and encourage board of directors diversity and to dynamically involve the entire community, the fundraising program should embrace the mirror principle when recruiting board members. The mirror principle in business (also known as occupational parity) is defined as a "situation in which the proportion of minorities and women employed in various occupations within an organization is equal to their proportion in the organization's relevant labor market" (Byars & Rue, 2008, p. 49). If a board of directors' membership can emulate the fundraising market, donations and fundraising potential will be amplified.

The concept of diversity of a fundraising board of directors also embraces the demographic characteristic of age and volunteerism. In her article "Including young people on non-profit boards of directors," Getha-Taylor (2003) discusses some compelling reasons to include young members on non-profit boards, "including: New views and experiences, succession planning and special technical knowledge...incentives for young people include improved leadership skills, recognition, social contracts and an opportunity to help make a difference in the community" (p. 4). Age should not be a precluding factor for board of directors membership. The level and extent of assistance and support should be the inclusion (or exclusion) elements.

Another relevant issue that is essential for a fundraising program's success is the resilient, cooperative environment that exists between the internal fundraising professionals and the external board of directors. No individual is of greater consequence to this affiliation and rapport than the fundraising program's director/executive administrator. The collaboration between a fundraising program's director/executive administrator and the athletic organization's board of directors can be encapsulated by the following:

> As a developmental person, you may find a big difference in your relationship with the Board in a small, medium, or large non-profit. In a small agency, you may have a close, team-like relationship with the entire Board. In a large organization, you may work only with the developmental committee, and even that relationship may have a formal flavor to it. (Mutz & Murray, 2000, p. 66)

With that being said, no matter what the size of the athletic organization, the atmosphere must be one of trust and teamwork. This is not to claim that individuals will not have interpersonal conflicts. The most vital element for fundraising program achievement is that these interpersonal divergences do not sidetrack the groups (both fundraising administrators and board of directors) from the program's mission and goals.

A core element to a fundraising board of directors' worth is the chief operating officer/chairman of the board. For a successful fundraising board of directors, this individual must have a commanding presence.

Fundraising Tip

Fundraising board members should have little or no prescribed operational governance or oversight over internal athletic organization and fundraising operations. Their primary duties are to act as liaisons with boosters and the community as well as to participate actively in fundraising events/activities/programs; however, their internal operational input should be valued and considered in all decisions.

Whether referred to as president or chair, the leader of the board is pivotal to its functioning. The best board leaders:

- Talk change
- Collaborate with staff leadership
- Have a vision of the possible
- Don't try to carry all tasks on their own shoulders. (Walsh, 2002, p. 17)

Finally, there may come a time when a board of directors and fundraising program needs to make a difficult decision regarding a board member. If a board member or members "are uninvolved or and don't come to meetings, maybe they don't have the time or interest to continue to serve. The trick is to have them leave as friends" (Weisman, 2002, p. 13). However, if it is a choice between retaining a sub-par board member, and a project or event deteriorating and even failing because that board member is not fulfilling his/her obligations, the decision to eliminate and replace that individual must be as expeditious and subtle as possible.

VOLUNTEER CORE

The essential benefit of having a passionate and dedicated volunteer core for an athletic organization's fundraising program cannot be overstated. They are frequently the primary human resource foundation of a fundraising program. They should be considered just as vital as the fundraising administration, departmental staff, and board of directors. Their enthusiasm and work ethic is unequivocally connected to the success of fundraising events/activities/programs. Their recruitment, supervision and development should be a top priority for the fundraising program.

Appreciating what motivates volunteers to take part in nonprofit activities (in this case, athletic organization fundraising events/activities/programs) is a decisive factor in their acquisition and retention.

All individuals volunteer for some combination of the following reasons:

- *Values* – to express or act on important values like humanitarianism;
- *Understanding* – to learn more about the world or exercise skills that are unused;
- *Enhancement* – to grow and develop psychologically;
- *Career* – to gain career-related experience;
- *Social* – to strengthen social relationships;
- *Protective* – to reduce negative feelings or to address personal problems. (Gazley & Dignam, 2008, p. 92)

A key to understanding volunteers from these six possible reasons is to initially acknowledge that each person has their own introspective motivation (or motivations) for contributing his/her time and energy. Comprehending each person's individuality requires time. However, the proactive effort put forth in sincerely knowing volunteers individually will help with keeping them a critical part of the athletic organization.

> **Fundraising Tip**
>
> An imperative note of warning: A fundraising board member's contribution and involvement can have no hidden agendas. Board membership must be for altruistic reasons and not for clandestine control and power over the athletic organization's operation.

> **Fundraising Tip**
>
> Individuals in a fundraising program's volunteer core can (and regularly do) become board members. There are many benefits of utilizing general volunteers to become board members: (1) They are familiar with the athletic organization and the fundraising program's operations; (2) they are a known quantity inside the fundraising program (work ethic and dedication); and (3) they have an established rapport with other fundraising stakeholders.

Volunteer Recruitment

The concepts of demand shift analysis and manpower planning for fundraising program employees, discussed in Chapter 4, apply (in most cases) to the recruitment of volunteers. For example, during the planning process for a fundraising event, activity, or program, a demand assessment (also known as a needs assessment) should be conducted to clarify the fundraiser's human resource and volunteer requirements. The fundraiser should be systematically examined from the following perspectives:

- What positions are considered necessary for the event, activity or program?
- How many volunteers will be necessary to fill those positions?
- What level of operational skill and expertise will those volunteers need?
- Does the existing volunteer pool satisfactorily fulfill the event's, activity's or program's need?

If your current volunteer pool is sufficient, then volunteer recruitment need not apply. If the fundraising program's needs assessment shows a deficiency in volunteers, either quantity or skills required, the fundraising program will need to aggressively recruit zealous, capable individuals.

© iStockphoto.com/mangostock

Sources of Volunteers

The viable sources for an athletic organization's volunteer core are only limited by the fundraising program's efforts in reaching out to various community groups. Occasionally, groups with unique demographic characteristics that 'on paper' show the least promising pool of talented volunteers transpire to be the athletic organization's most ardent and consummate supporters. Is this to say that volunteer groups should not be scrutinized as to their motives and qualifications? Absolutely not. However, it is to state that casually overlooking different groups because one thinks they will not be participative or appropriate for the fundraising program could be a costly oversight. Remember—a worst case scenario when it comes to fundraising operations is to have an event, activity or program impeded by not having enough qualified volunteers. This can only be compounded by the actuality that viable volunteer groups and individuals were overlooked.

While some believe that one of a board member's central occupations is volunteer recruitment (which it is), boards of directors are not the only group to be accountable for recruiting capable volunteers for the fundraising program. Internal stakeholders such as athletic organization executives, fundraising administrators, and program staff should all assume a committed role in recruiting volunteers. Another prominent source for recruiting future volunteers is the current group of functioning volunteers. Their recommendations of family, friends, and business associates are typically judged to be strong due to the fact that they know the volunteer positions and what it takes to be a successful volunteer.

Weaver, in her article "Staffing fundraising in small organizations," delineates three potential groups where an athletic organization fundraising program can obtain volunteers—seniors, interns and work-study programs.

> Seniors are dependable and wonderful at donor relations, making thank you calls, sending acknowledgement letters, staffing phone lines—time consuming tasks that are critical to development efforts…College and high school interns are another source of volunteer staff…they make great volunteer staff members because, of course, their final grade depends on the quality of their work and attendance…Federal work-study programs are another viable resource…these students usually have limited formal work experience, but are good data entry clerks, research assistants, typists and receptionists. (Weaver, 1998, p. 47-48)

If the fundraising program (board of directors, administration, and staff) recognize up front the limitations of these three potential volunteer groups, their productivity and service to the athletic organization can be maximized.

Another feasible recruitment strategy that a fundraising program could exploit in acquiring volunteers is through cooperative relationships with select business entities in the athletic organization's local/regional area. This mutually beneficial alliance between the business and the athletic organization's fundraising program can assist both enterprises in numerous ways. Businesses that provide volunteers can experience the benefits described in the following paragraphs.

The business' employees who volunteer to support an athletic organization's fundraising endeavor(s) can develop a sense of community within the business operation. This cooperative spirit and atmosphere developed from fundraising volunteering will amplify teamwork inside the business which, in turn, will augment employee productivity. Volunteering will also engender a new level of community awareness among a business' employees. Most of the employees will reside in the same area as the athletic organization. By volunteering to be a part of community-wide athletic organization fundraising events, activities and programs, employees can reattach themselves to their locale and have a vested interest in where they live.

The business name, often along with its products and services, will be exhibited (through fundraisers) in the community. This goodwill can go a long way toward heightening brand awareness and future sales. It should be emphasized that these passive marketing communications benefits (from positive public relations) should not be seen as the business' primary motive for having its employees volunteering in the athletic organization's fundraisers. In other words, the business' employees should not 'push' sales and the building of clientele during a fundraising event, activity or program. They are there for the athletic organization. It will immediately negate the possible goodwill/public relations benefits from volunteering. A premeditated and tactful notice of who the volunteers represent (event signage or clothing with company name and logo) will suffice.

Fundraising Tip

Even if the pool of volunteers is adequate to satisfy current fundraising program events/activities/programs, the recruitment of volunteers should nevertheless be an active component of the fundraising program operations. Just because volunteers are not needed now does not mean they will not be needed in the future.

Athletic organization supporters will recognize and appreciate the business' help.

The business can use volunteering activities as a method to nurture leadership talent in its employees.

> A major corporate volunteer effort can thrust the employee into a leadership role above and beyond the one assumed during the normal business day...The leadership opportunities are so likely, in fact, that the company should be careful to provide such an employee with consummate challenges back on the job. It would be a shame if the return to one's responsibilities in the office is considered a step-down by the volunteer fresh off the front lines of an exhilarating community project. (Carrison, 2010, p. 6)

For this purpose, a sound communication system which encourages openness between the fundraising program and business must exist. If the business wants to foster an employee's leadership, then the fundraising program should make a concerted effort to accommodate.

Employees volunteering in an athletic organization's fundraiser can learn and appreciate the concept of being in self-managed teams. For a fundraising event, activity or program, employee volunteers could be assigned tasks and projects independent of direct supervision and allowed to develop strategies and implementation plans for their completion. While the fundraising program administration will monitor and evaluate the team's work product, the volunteers will attain a strong self-concept and motivation, which is an invaluable component of modern business operations.

There is a noticeable risk in using business employees as volunteers. Korngold points out the danger when utilizing a business' employees as volunteers by stating, "A nonprofit can leverage the skills of business people only when business volunteers take the time and effort to learn about the nonprofit and its particular circumstances. Volunteers can add value when they join nonprofits with humility and a willingness to learn" (Korngold, 2005, p. 104). The employee volunteers must be totally committed to the fundraising program's mission. This allegiance can be mandated by the business' executives, but the employees' involvement is much more vigorous if they believe in the athletic organization and aspire to be part of its fundraising efforts. Only then will there be a win-win scenario between the business and athletic organization's fundraising program.

For the fundraising program, the benefit of business working events, activities and programs is apparent. The fundraising program will acquire a competent and multi-talented workforce with real-world business experience. The athletic organization, while getting a new pool of volunteers, will also get a new pool of supporters.

Additional recruiting strategies for fundraising program volunteers are described in the following paragraphs.

Fundraising Tip

Volunteers cannot have ulterior and concealed motives when participating in the fundraising program's events, activities and programs. They must genuinely believe in the mission of the athletic organization and want to assist in its expansion and advancement without any covert agendas of their own.

The athletic organization's fundraising program could institute a public relations campaign to notify the community about the fundraising program's upcoming fundraisers and volunteer needs. The negative aspect of utilizing this tactic would be with the initial quality control over the potential volunteer pool and supervising a substantially greater recruitment base.

Competition for 'blue chip' volunteers will be intense. A blue chip volunteer is one who is favorably known in the community and has a durable track record of volunteer performance. Acquiring these individuals can take additional time and energy beyond general recruiting tactics. Personal selling techniques (such as 'wining and dining,' complementary tickets to an athletic organization's sporting event, personal invitations to spotlight fundraising events and activities) will need to be applied. The pay-off for attaining blue chip volunteers can be the legitimization of the fundraising program and a new level of quality volunteers and supporters.

Similarly, the acquisition of a celebrity/public figure volunteer could stimulate a great deal of attention in the fundraising program. Community leaders, entertainment personalities, and former high-profile athletes could become ceremonial volunteers whose main function would be to help gain working volunteers. Additionally, these individuals would be the 'face' of the fundraising event, activity, or program. This, in turn, would motivate community members to participate as volunteers or to contribute financial support for the athletic organization.

Never blindly reject volunteer assistance because of its perceived limitations. For example, if a business wishes to get involved in a certain fundraising event (and that event only), appreciatively accept the generous offer, whether it be manpower, resources, or in-kind trade. Would the fundraising program like to only have long-term productive relationships? Absolutely. However, those do not happen overnight. An operational philosophy should be that minor volunteering today can turn into long-term volunteering tomorrow.

Volunteer Management and Effectiveness

The supervision and efficient utilization of fundraising volunteers can use many of the identical principles of business employee management with some subtle but consequential differences. The most precarious disparity between managing employees and managing volunteers relates to the volunteer's capacity to walk away from an athletic organization's fundraising program without any ramifications, but potentially major consequences to the fundraiser. In basic terms, if the volunteer's intrinsic incentives and feelings are not (in his/her mind) outweighing the effort, time and resources given, this disconnect will have the individual eventually leaving the fundraising program. To maintain the volunteers' active participation and excitement about the fundraising program, the fundraising administrators must exceed their intrinsic expectations. The following points can help fundraising administrators manage and amplify volunteer productivity while increasing each individual's intrinsic motivation.

An important key in maximizing the effectiveness of volunteers and strengthening their commitment to the fundraising program is to "…target their strengths. Once a volunteer's specific interests and expertise are determined, align them with the appropriate area to keep them engaged, productive and confident in the value of their involvement" (Frels, 2006, p. 15). Nothing could extinguish volunteers' excitement and dedication more than to position them in a situation in which they are not comfortable and to which they are infrequently contributing. Their strengths and weaknesses go beyond tangible expertise to include personality traits. The most influential trait to examine and comprehend is an individual's introversion or extroversion. For example, putting a gregarious, extroverted person in a behind-the-operation data entry position would be a demoralizing personnel error. Conversely, putting an introverted and withdrawn individual in a position of public contact and speaking would be disastrous. The best way to discover a volunteer's strengths and weaknesses is to openly discuss his/her participation wants and desires. From there, endeavor to match these elements with fundraiser functions available.

Fundraising volunteers need to go through their own distinct orientation to get acclimated to the program's operational environment. Selected orientation elements (from Chapter 4) that apply to fundraising program employees can be employed with volunteers to assist in their inclusion in the athletic organization and its fundraising program. The more comprehensive the orientation activities, the more comfortable the volunteer will be with participating in the fundraising program.

A distinct endeavor that could be a precursor to a formal orientation program for volunteers is to have them attend a fundraising program event or activity as a patron/supporter rather than a volunteer worker (free of charge). While the fundraiser might experience additional operating expenses associated with this orientation strategy, a volunteer will get an authentic living example of a program's fundraising and what responsibilities could be expected from him/her in the future.

The efficient supervision of volunteers is augmented by the operational philosophy that a volunteer's time is precious. With this in mind, fundraising program organization should be the main concern in assuring that all tasks, responsibilities, and time schedules are planned and structured for minimal downtime for the volunteer. One of the most dispiriting feelings a volunteer can experience is 'standing around' for hours with little or no chance to assist in a fundraiser, which is why they are there.

The fundraising program's board of directors should be the most ardent supporters of the volunteer core. There are seven things every board member should do to help support volunteer participation.

1. Regularly devote time to volunteer issues at board meetings.

2. Analyze data about volunteer involvement.

3. Participate in volunteer recruitment. Each board member can:

    •   Refer volunteer candidates.

- Distribute volunteer recruitment materials when doing public speaking.
- Arrange for the volunteer office to have access to his/her circle of contacts to share recruitment information.
- Be a visible advocate.

4. Take part in volunteer recognition events.

5. Make volunteers as visible as possible.

6. Form a board committee to offer ongoing advice to the volunteer program staff.

7. Think about it. Too many boards are thoughtless when it comes to volunteers. The best way to maximize volunteer involvement is to become thoughtful on the subject. Know why you want volunteers, provide adequate resources and successful strategies will follow. (Ellis, 2003, p. 21)

To improve the value of a volunteer, after an event, activity or program the individual needs to be evaluated for his/her productivity, development, and ultimate continuance in the fundraising program. Evaluations (discussed in Chapter 4) should be objective, timely, and based on the potential of the volunteer to play a role in future fundraising endeavors. The modifications needed in evaluating fundraising volunteers compared to fundraising employees relates to the tone of the discussion. For a fundraising staff member's evaluation, a positive but straightforward approach could be used. For a fundraising volunteer, an appreciative tone is established immediately with performance suggestions rather than mandates. One note—just because the mood of the evaluation is 'softer' with a volunteer, the message must still be clear and precise. When the volunteer leaves the evaluation meeting, he/she must understand completely all future expectations.

Aberle (2009) discusses five elements that can contribute to a volunteer's effectiveness. These volunteer effectiveness factors are:

1. Ask me to volunteer.

2. Show me the benefits for the mission and myself.

3. Help me succeed.

4. Tell me how your organization works.

5. Allow me a 'time-out' rather than a retirement. (Aberle, 2009, p. 14)

Amending these five concepts to an athletic organization's fundraising program could considerably strengthen the overall effectiveness as well as long-term retention of a strong volunteer pool.

1. *Ask me to volunteer.* A fundraising program should proactively dissect the pool of potential volunteers to assess their abilities and assertively solicit their assistance. While some privileged and well renowned athletic organizations need simply to notify the community that they are seeking volunteers, most athletic organization fundraising administrators and boards of directors will need to seek out individuals and groups to 'sell' potential volunteering with the athletic organization.

2. *Show me the benefits for the mission and myself.* The benefits for the fundraising program are apparent—volunteers are the labor pool needed to achieve profitable fundraising events, activities and programs. The benefits to the volunteers relates to what motivates them to participate in an athletic organization's fundraising program. Once again, this goes back to the concept of extrinsic (tangible) versus intrinsic (introspective) rewards. While one might assume extrinsic motivators are more powerful, they are not (especially for volunteers). The primary intrinsic motivator that must be continuously conveyed to volunteers is their importance to the athletic organization. They must be told time and again that their volunteering is the outstanding 'X' factor in the fundraising event, activity, or program's success.

3. *Help me succeed.* Nothing could be worse for a volunteer when it comes to them donating their time and effort than the management tactic of 'being thrown in the deep end.' Not only will they resign from an event, activity, or program (perhaps at the most critical juncture), they will warn other potential volunteers about their experience. A volunteer should never be put into an athletic organization fundraiser without being completely aware and trained on his/her duties, and knowing that he/she has an immediate communication system to get assistance when needed.

4. *Tell me how your organization works.* More often than not, volunteers are the 'face' of the fundraising program. For them to interact with potential patrons and supporters, they should have an intimate knowledge of the athletic organization as well as a familiarity with all of the fundraising program's specific events/activities/programs.

5. *Allow me a 'time out' rather than a retirement.* This is Aberle's (2009) most essential statement in regard to long-term retention of a volunteer. Fundraising events, activities and programs can be tremendously arduous in both time given and work completed. A fundraising administrator and board of directors should know when to balance the needs of the program with the needs of the individuals. Each volunteer is unique. For example, a retiree might want to have continuous volunteer responsibilities while a mid-life professional can commit

to one event, activity or program per year. These mid-life professionals will need some 'down time' from the fundraising program. Stay in
contact, be empathic to their needs, and let them determine when they
are ready to resume volunteering with your athletic organization.

Training for volunteers should go beyond the 'nuts and bolts' of the event, activity or program. Remember, volunteers are the athletic organization's most important
ambassadors.

> Training a volunteer is training a marketer! Volunteers come from various
> segments of the community. Even when they are not actually working in
> the agency's office or program site, they continue spreading information
> about the nonprofit by telling its story to their friends and wherever they
> interact with people. (Wendroff, 1999, p. 117)

A fundamental key to the retention of a fundraising program's volunteer core is
providing individuals with a sincere 'thank you' and celebratory recognition for their
contributions.

You can find many, many ways to recognize a special volunteer. If you are creative
and genuine in giving your thanks, your volunteers are sure to feel appreciated.

- Say it with a smile and mean it.
- Send a card with a personal note.
- Invite the volunteer to lunch.
- Have a recognition dinner for special volunteers.
- Give out certificates of recognition.
- Submit a 'thank you' note to your local paper.
- Mention the volunteer's work in your organization's newsletter.
- Ask the volunteer to speak to a group of new volunteers.
- Have a plaque of recognition made.
- Dedicate a publication or event to your volunteers. (Mutz and Murray, 2000, p. 82)

SUMMARY

The correlation between a successful fundraising program and its board of directors
and volunteer core is unmistakably apparent. A formidable board of directors and
volunteer core not only provide resources and manpower for a fundraising program,
they furnish an enthusiasm that energizes the entire athletic organization. With their
dedication and passion, an athletic organization's fundraising program can achieve
tremendous financial and public relations goals. Because of these factors, boards of
directors and volunteers must be skillfully cultivated and professionally managed. To
do otherwise would be to waste their enormous potential and expertise.

REVIEW AND DISCUSSION QUESTIONS

1. What are the distinct differences between in-house fundraising administrators/staff and board of directors/volunteers?

2. What is the mirror principle/occupational parity, and how can it apply to board of directors membership?

3. What are the six possible reasons that individuals volunteer their time and effort?

4. What are seven things every board member should do to help support volunteer participation?

5. What are some tactics to thank and recognize volunteers?

6

Marketing for Fundraising Programs

INTRODUCTION

Marketing is an organizational discipline that interfaces with almost all of the athletic organization's functions, especially fundraising. From a fundraising standpoint, marketing can control a majority of the program's operational components. The term *marketing* is probably one of the most misused and misinterpreted words in today's business and athletic world. The first impression that one associates with marketing is advertising. The function of advertising is just one facet of the total concept of marketing. Marketing also involves product selection, customer research, distribution of the product, pricing decisions, and numerous other administrative elements.

The essential importance of understanding marketing fundamentals cannot be stressed enough when discussing the role of promotion and marketing communication in fundraising programs. To jump into advertising and promotion without consciously knowing the fundamentals of marketing would be, at best, a hit or miss proposition. Understanding a fundraising program's market communication and promotion requires an appreciation of:

- market information and research;
- target market determination and segmentation;
- marketing mix components; and
- all communication mix elements in a blended approach.

Finally, the importance of public relations as a strategic element of the fundraising program's marketing plan must be discussed. While the creation of a positive image is an important goal of publicity and public relations in a fundraising program, it must be emphasized that the primary intention of public relations is to be a part of the fundraising program's all-inclusive marketing concept. Marketing communication techniques such as advertising, direct marketing, sales promotions, and personal selling are all applied harmoniously with public relations. Explicitly stated, public relations, as a fundraising tool, directly and indirectly facilitate support and donations.

IMPORTANCE OF MARKETING IN FUNDRAISING PROGRAMS

The significance of the marketing function for all business enterprises (including fundraising programs) cannot be emphasized enough. Marketing produces customer value, satisfaction, and relationship development through the model of utility.

> Utility is the satisfaction, value, and usefulness a user receives from a good or service in relation to the user's wants…marketing function creates place, time, and possession utility…Place utility is the value added to goods and services as a result of having them available where the customers want to buy them…Time utility is the value added to goods and services by having them available when the customer wants to buy them… Possession utility is the value added to goods and services that comes about as a result of the passage of legal title to the buyer through sales transactions. (Schoell & Guiltinan, 1990, p. 7)

The concept of utility is especially important for fundraising programs. This is due to the fact that a sponsor/donor/supporter's satisfaction with a fundraising event, activity, or program will have a profound effect on their current and future financial assistance. The more value added (either perceived or actual), the more they will contribute to the fundraising program and athletic organization. In addition to utility, marketing presents the fundraising program with elements such as:

- information on the external operating environment (which can facilitate long- and short-term strategic decisions);
- details on the make-up of the fundraising program's supporter base (which can concentrate and conserve operational resources);
- details on the make-up of the fundraising program's competitors (which is an indispensable component of survival); and
- a logical process to developing new fundraising products, pricing options, where to place fundraising products/services, and promotional considerations.

MARKETING INFORMATION AND RESEARCH FOR FUNDRAISING PROGRAMS

Learning how to plan, organize, implement, and analyze marketing research for fundraising programs goes far beyond a chapter in a textbook or a course in college. Marketing research is a lifetime profession that takes years of theoretical knowledge and practical application to master. However, from a fundraising program administration viewpoint, marketing research can impart vital information that can assist a program administrator's decision making. The question then becomes: How can a fundraising program administrator solve the conundrum of obtaining critical information to support decision making while knowing that marketing research is beyond their typical life experience and education? The answer relates to the delineation of primary research versus secondary research.

Basic Primary and Secondary Research

"Primary research is data gathered and assembled specifically for the research project at hand. Secondary data is data that has been previously collected for some project other than the one at hand" (Zikmund, 2000, p. 58). In other words, primary research is conducted by the fundraising team for an exclusive fundraising program need or problem. Secondary research is conducted by someone else to solve a particular need or problem.

To conduct primary research, a fundraising administrator would require substantial resources, time, and research experience. The benefit from performing primary research study is obvious; the information accumulated (if done correctly) is focused on the fundraising program's explicit needs. The decision a fundraising administrator has to make when performing a primary research study is whether the information gathered from an internal primary research investigation is worth the time and expenditures associated with this type of study. A cost-benefit analysis can answer this question.

Secondary research has noteworthy advantages and disadvantages in relation to primary research. The advantages are predominantly in expense and time savings. Secondary research just needs to be uncovered rather than conducted. In some cases the time and outlay saving is enormous. The disadvantages of secondary research include three elements:

1. *Problem to fit.* Does the secondary research fit the fundraising program's special need or problem?

2. *Outdated information.* Since the research was done in the past, how obsolete/archaic has it become?

3. *Confidence in research.* Was the research completed by credible researchers who were objective and dispassionate?

If the fundraising program administrator can answer that the secondary research fits the fundraising program's situation, it is timely, and was prepared by a trustworthy source, then secondary data is tremendously valuable.

In conducting secondary research for the fundraising program, there is one resource that is indispensable—librarians. Librarians are remarkable when it comes to resolving informational needs. They can help define research problems, direct administrators to sources that will correspond to the fundraising program's needs, and can assist in the follow-through to solve administrators' fundraising data collection obstacles.

Environmental Research

The next question becomes: What elements are important for a fundraising program to research? The answer is the external environmental elements that affect all organizations (both business and athletic). The seven external environmental factors that must be continuously monitored by a fundraising program are technology, competition, natural, social, economic, political/legal, and demographic. These seven factors will affect how the products (a fundraising program's events, activities, or ongoing programs) are perceived, accepted, and desired by the program's target market. The seven factors are discussed below.

Technology Factor

The first environmental factor that the fundraising administrator should research is technology. There is virtually no business that is not profoundly affected by the accelerating changes in technology, and fundraising programs are no exception. Computers, cell phones, advanced training systems, and the Internet are just a few of the technological advancements that need consideration. The technological investigation should focus not only on currently available technology

Table 6.1. **Basic Primary and Secondary Research Sources and Tools**

Primary	Surveys (developed in-house or purchased)
	Questionnaires (hard copy or online)
	Focus Groups and Panels
	Observations
	Interview and Telephone Research
Secondary	Library (both public and academic)
	E-Library/Commercial Sources
	Periodicals/Journals/Magazines/Newspapers
	Electronic Sources/Internet (general search engines—Google, Yahoo, Bing—or site-specific)
	United States Governmental Resources and Publications (statistical abstracts and geographic data sources)
	Directories and Trade Association Publications
	Commercial Research Groups (outsourcing primary research)
	Athletic Department Media Guides

Your Site Name

Your slogan or something else

Home | About Us | Services | Contacts

● **About Us**

Lorem ipsum dolor sit amet, consectetur adipisicing elit, sed do eiusmod tempor incididunt ut labore et dolore magna aliqua. Ut enim ad minim veniam, quis nostrud exercitation ullamco laboris nisi ut aliquip ex ea commodo consequat.

About Us | Services | Solutions | Support | Contacts

Copyright © 2010

© Suprijono Suharjoto | Dreamstime.com

but on how projected technological advancements may affect the fundraising program's operations in the future.

Nature Factor

For most fundraising programs, the natural environment might not be as consequential an environmental factor to research as the other six external factors. Obviously fundraising events/activities/programs that are outdoors need to address geographical weather patterns, pollution, and other possible natural/nature concerns that could affect their operations and marketing.

Social Factor

The factor of the social environment is defined as "the people in a society and their values, beliefs, and behaviors...Marketers describe this environment in terms of who the people are (their ages, incomes, hometowns, and so forth) and the characteristics of their culture." (Churchill & Peter, 1998, p. 38)

From this definition, the leading questions that surface for fundraising programs are:

1. How does society view our athletic organization and fundraising program?
2. What marketing opportunities for the fundraising program are possible from this perspective?
3. Are some subcultures more interested in our athletic organization and fundraising program than others?
4. Does society expect our athletic organization and fundraising program to act in a socially responsible way?

Economic Factor

The economic environment deals with a region/nation's purchasing power and its discretionary income. An economic environment that is stable or growing has stronger purchasing power. The stronger the purchasing power, the higher the discretionary spending (which is essential for fundraising). This presents numerous marketing opportunities. Conversely, the more financially deprived the economic situation in a city, region, or nation, the less the purchasing power and discretionary spending in that area. A climate of economic downturn and recession presents significant marketing concerns for fundraising programs whose 'life blood' is based on unencumbered discretionary spending.

Political/Legal Factor

The political/legal factor in environmental research is the legislation affecting a fundraising program's operation. From a sports standpoint, fundraising programs have two tiers of legislation to identify and monitor. The first is U.S. governmental legislation that all businesses have to recognize and with which they must comply. Examples of this can range from the IRS to the INS to the EEOC. The second tier is the particular sport's governing body and its regulatory legislation concerning fundraising. The concentration and intensity of regulations, bylaws, and directives is sport specific as well as level specific (e.g., high school, NCAA, NAIA).

Fundraising Tip

When environmentally researching the influential external component of technology, only review relevant technologies that will influence the fundraising program. Do not spend time on technological advancements that will have little or no impact on the fundraising program's goals.

Fundraising Tip

Economic examinations should be in line with contingency or scenario analysis. Evaluate the economic impact on the fundraising program of both ideal economic conditions as well as depreciated states of economic affairs.

Demographic Factor

Another critical external environmental element a fundraising program administrator needs to research relates to the demographic characteristics of both the overall, comprehensive market and the fundraising program's target market segment. Demographic forces are

> the characteristics of a population, such as age, gender, ethnic origin, race, sexual orientation, and social class. Like other forces in the general environment, demographic forces present managers with opportunities and threats and can have major implications for organizations. (Jones & George, 2006, p. 204)

By understanding demographic characteristics, a fundraising administrator can uncover details on the make-up of the existing market as well as predict changes in the future market. From a current perspective, demographic analysis is the foundation for constructing a fundraising profile. Fundraising profiles are instruments that definitively catalog all of the relevant demographic characteristics of a fundraising program's target market. With a profile, fundraising programs can concentrate (sometimes limited) resources directly on a specific supporter base. From a futuristic standpoint, demographic knowledge can help a fundraising program predict/strategize the best course of action for its future supporters. Supporters transform and change. By knowing the fundraising program's current supporters, a fundraising administrator can predict what they will be like in the future.

Competitive Factor

The final and often most consequential area a fundraising program needs to research is its market competition. As previously stated, there has and always will be a limited amount of money for fundraising programs. This is even truer now with drastic limitations on discretionary income sources. The competition for limited monetary resources is fierce. A fundraising program administrator must understand (through research) the competitive forces affecting his/her fundraising efforts and make sound decisions based on that understanding. An excellent tool for researching competitive forces is called the Five Forces Model.

FIVE FORCES MODEL – FORCES GOVERNING COMPETITION IN AN INDUSTRY

The Five Forces Model is a theoretical representation that delves into the five foremost external competitive components in a market. In the case of this textbook, the industry is fundraising in athletics. In order to adapt this concept, fundraising administrators must take the comprehensive categories given by Porter (1998) and research each for their particular fundraising program and marketing efforts.

- Threat of new entrants
- Bargaining power of suppliers
- Threat of substitute products or services

- Bargaining power of customers
- The industry: Jockeying for position among current competition (Porter, 1998, p. 22)

Additionally, before elaborating on each individual factor of the model, it must be stated that the stronger (or more influential) the force, the more of a threat it is to the fundraising program. Conversely, the weaker (or less influential) the force, the more of an opportunity it is to the fundraising program.

POWER OF SUPPLIERS

As the model is examined, the first external competitive segment that needs to be researched is the bargaining power of suppliers. Suppliers furnish the inputs for the fundraising program's outputs. In fundraising programs, the outputs are the program events, activities, and ongoing programs. From there, ask some of these elementary questions:

- Who provides these inputs for the fundraising programs outputs?
- Will they control the working association or does the fundraising program have influence over the situation?
- Do fundraising program administrators need to pursue them or do they approach the administrators?

In almost every sport, athletic organizations (and their subsequent fundraising efforts) are divided into strata or tiers. If the athletic organization is classified as a tier one program (which has a high profile and commanding history of achievement and exposure), the fundraising program administrator can characteristically dominate the relationship with the suppliers. The fundraising administrator will have, in most cases, the opportunity to 'pick and choose' from the elite suppliers. However, if the athletic organization is a lower tier program (not as high profile or well financed), dealing with the suppliers of the fundraising program's inputs will be a different experience. Analyze all of the inputs into the program and formulate the input strategies from there.

Returning to the above example—if the athletic program is not an upper-tiered program, what strategies can one select to obtain quality, reliable supplies/inputs at a good value? What strengths can be emphasized and weaknesses minimized to secure the inputs? The less power the organization has, the more creatively the program administrator needs to strategize.

When conducting marketing research into suppliers, adopt the best value philosophy. This position emphasizes researching which organization can provide the fundraising event, activity, or program with the highest quality input (quality being determined by factors such as functionality, durability, customer perception, appearance) for the lowest cost. Two significant points:

1. The better values acquired (quality versus cost), the more 'bottom-line' effect on revenue from the event, activity, or program.

2. Never sacrifice quality for cost. This short-term thinking can drastically affect the fundraising event, activity, or program while alienating supporters from future fundraising events, activities, or programs.

BARGAINING POWER OF BUYERS

As fundraising administrators, this exterior determinant relates to the target market's discretionary income and their willingness to donate and support the fundraising efforts. Along the same thoughts as the prior example, if the athletic organization is a tier one level program that has elite athletes and a solid track record, in most cases,

© Creostudio | Dreamstime.com

fundraising activities are a distinct opportunity. If the athletic program is a lower strata program, finding supporters could be a consequential program threat. The administrator's method of support procurement would, in most cases, need to be inventive and continuous.

Case in point, a major athletic organization with a well-documented history of success can apply more impersonal tactics to solicit support from a broad (sometimes huge) donation base. The buyer research into these instances would encompass how to segment this broad base into various targeted market groups and tailor the athletic organization's fundraising efforts toward each group. Conversely, a small athletic organization would need to focus its buyer research on finding and defining supporter groups. While large athletic organizations often have supporters seeking them out, lower tiered athletic organizations need to find and delineate which groups will be potential supporters. Potential supporter research would focus on demographics (characteristics such as age, education, income), psychographics (lifestyles and interest), geographical elements (location/region), and behaviors (patterns and frequency of support/donations).

SUBSTITUTES

The concept of substitutes relates to the convenience and accessibility of other fundraising programs that supporters can sponsor instead of the athletic organization's fundraising program. In our situation of athletics, support of the fundraising program is in direct relationship to the consumer of a business product. For example, if the athletic and fundraising program is located in a region where there are a limited number of other athletic organizations and fundraising programs, then direct substitutes would be less of a threat to the program's supporter base. On the other hand, if the athletic organization and fundraising program is located in an area with abundant substitute athletic organizations and nonprofit fundraising programs, support (as well as fundraising program publicity and interest) would be a more tenuous issue.

To distinguish all of the possible substitutes to the fundraising program, list all of the principal components of the fundraising program, prioritize those elements, and carefully examine each for the danger of substitutes. The more meaningful and significant the ingredient of the fundraising program, the more the program administrator will need specific actions to minimize the effects of any possible substitute fundraising organizations.

Substitute fundraising organizations are not considered direct competitors. However, their fundraising efforts can have a substantial indirect effect on an athletic organization's fundraising program. When conducting research on a potential indirect fundraising program, the administrator should focus on organizations that are targeting the fundraising program's primary and secondary supporters. If a substitute fundraising organization is conducting fundraising efforts outside of the administrator's primary and secondary supporters, they should be removed (but not forgotten) from the list of potential substitute threats.

RIVALRY AMONG EXISTING FUNDRAISING PROGRAMS

Besides buyer power, this classification is the most discernible and tangible of the Five Forces Model. The fundraising program's immediate competition is the one strategic element of which fundraising administrators tend to be mindful. The fundraising program's results are a direct reflection of its competitors' results. The stronger each of the fundraising program's direct competitors, the more of a threat those competitors are. The same comparable format for strategizing can be utilized in this category. List all of the fundraising program's legitimate direct competitors (athletic organizations of the same size, make-up, number of sports, etc.), prioritize them by competitive potency, and develop strategies to competitively fundraise against each. Additionally, do an internal strength/weakness appraisal of each fundraising competitor to form a more effective strategy.

When researching competing athletic organizations' fundraising programs, focus the research on the following questions:

- Who are they? What is their make-up (both of the overall athletic organization and their fundraising efforts)?

- Who is their primary supporter base? Who is their secondary supporter base? What are the demographics, psychographics, geographics, and behaviors of their targeted supporter groups?

- When do they schedule major fundraising efforts? What type of events/ activities/programs have they run in the past? What has been their success with these types of events/activities/programs?

- What does their current fundraising calendar look like?

- Where is their geographic operating area? Are they local, regional, national, or global in scope?

- What is the size and structure of their fundraising program? What is the strategic importance of the fundraising program in their athletic organization?

Through research, the answers to these and other such questions will have a direct impact on the fundraising program's marketing and overall strategies.

NEW ENTRANTS

The final broad segment in the Five Forces concept that can be adapted to fundraising programs is the examination of potential new fundraising programs (direct or indirect) entering the external environment. In other words, who has the capability to penetrate the competitive fundraising environment and what do they offer? New entrants can be start-up athletic organizations with no prior history of fundraising or they can be from established athletic organizations trying to expand into different arenas. By far, this category is the most difficult to predict. Suppliers, buyers, competitive rivalry, and substitutes are already-existing components that are tangible in nature and grounded in reality. New entrants require more guesswork and anticipation than research because of uncertainty.

In investigating this classification of the model, one needs to comprehend the concept of barriers to entry. The higher the barriers, the more difficult it would be for a new competitor to penetrate the fundraising program's competitive environment. The opposite is also true. The lower the barriers, the more of a danger new entrants can be to the fundraising program. To strategically dissect this section of the model, define all of the barriers to entry, then recognize who could fulfill these requirements, then finally determine whether they will enter the fundraising program's competitive environment.

MARKETING MIX: 4 PS OF MARKETING

After researching external marketing environmental factors, a fundraising administrator should consider the internal marketing process known as the marketing mix or 4 Ps of marketing. In the business world, the marketing mix is defined as:

> the proper blending of the basic elements of product, price, promotion and place into an integrated marketing program...the right product for the target market must be developed. Place refers to the channels of distribution. Promotion refers to any method that communicates to the target market. The right price should be set to attract customers and make a profit. (Megginson, Byrd, & Megginson, 2006, p. 187)

All four of these marketing elements play a role in fundraising programs. However, fundraising programs can often produce services that have entertainment value rather than actual tangible products. "Services have four unique characteristics that distinguish them from goods; intangibility, inseparability, heterogeneity, and perishability" (Lamb, Hair, & McDaniel, 2003, p. 267).

As stated earlier, fundraising events/activities/programs are in the entertainment market. These events, activities, programs are commodities that are typically consumed via supporter participation and involvement. They may or may not generate a tangible product. The inseparability of a service refers to the concept that the consumer (in this case fundraising program supporter) is using an event/activity/program service at the same time as he/she donates to the service. In other words, the supporter is often present during the delivery of the entertainment. The characteristic of heterogeneity refers to the fact that while fundraising products can be very similar (if not precisely alike), fundraising services are distinct and dynamic. Finally, services such as fundraising entertainment are perishable because they are time specific. Once a performance is over, a supporter can never see it again in present time. With this distinction between services and products given, we can definitively adapt the marketing mix concept to fundraising program's tangible products and intangible events/activities/programs.

Product/Service/Output/Performance

As a fundraising program administrator, the primary concern is with the product (in the case of this text, fundraising event/activity/program). Inside that theme, there should be an unconditional single-mindedness on quality and value. Quality can relate to a fundraising program's performance, presentation, facilities, operational administration, and any other aspects that directly or indirectly influence its output. Without quality, marketing and promotions break down.

Another product/service issue relates to the uniqueness of an administrator's fundraising program. Uniqueness is used to separate the fundraising program from its competition and to confirm and sustain the image (also known as branding) of the fundraising program in the mind of the supporters.

One more major marketing product/service consideration is the selection of the type of events/activities/programs the overall athletic organization and its fundraising program are currently offering and which products and services it is going to emphasize in the future. Some fundraising programs may be, at a given point in time, restricted to stressing base fundraising events/activities/programs. Lack of resources, inadequate staffing, and insufficient stakeholder cooperation are a few of the reasons to contemplate a single fundraising strategy. However, in most cases, fundraising programs have capabilities to mature beyond the base events/activities/programs. Expanding the service into instruction, merchandising, and new fundraising endeavors are just some of the ways to diversify (see Section 2 of the text).

New Fundraising Developmental Process
To develop new fundraising events, activities/programs (fundraising products), one should follow a step-by-step process that generates ideas and appraises their feasibility. The New Product Development Process (which can be easily adapted for fundraising programs) is as follows:

1. Idea Generation

2. Idea Screening

3. Business Analysis

4. Product Development

Fundraising Tip

When attempting to conceive new fundraising programs, avoid gimmicks and publicity stunts that will damage the integrity of the athletic organization and fundraising program. While these marketing techniques will direct short-term attention to the fundraising program, their long-term effects could be irreparable. Uniqueness with a high-class reputation will bring extended growth.

5. Test Marketing

6. Commercialization (Churchill & Peter, 1998, p. 260)

STEP 1: IDEA GENERATION

Idea generation is the origination of new, relevant ideas for expanding, improving, or developing new fundraising events/activities/programs. Idea generation can be through various avenues such as formal requests, informal conversations, brainstorming, etc. A key to idea generation is to get as many internal and external stakeholders involved in the process as possible.

STEP 2: IDEA SCREENING

This stage takes the aggregate list of new fundraising ideas from Step 1 and weeds out all the notions, thoughts, and conceptions that are inappropriate for the fundraising program. Idea screening, like idea generation, is typically qualitative and subjective in nature. The program administrator and the fundraising program team's expert opinions are customarily the determining factors. In a formal or informal setting, the fundraising team will talk through each new event/activity/program idea to gauge its merits and appropriateness for the athletic organization and fundraising program now, and more notably, in the future.

STEP 3: BUSINESS ANALYSIS

This phase involves a more quantitative analysis of the fundraising program's capabilities and resources. The analysis is performed in order to determine the feasibility of an idea. Resources include the fundraising program's capital and financial situation, building and facilities, and other tangible assets that it possesses and that can be utilized to help realize new fundraising idea. Capabilities include the fundraising program members' intangible skills and knowledge. These are some of the questions asked in the business analysis stage:

- Does the idea fit the overall mission of the athletic organization and fundraising program?
- Do we have the finances to pursue this new event/activity/program idea?
- In the future, will we have the finances (or potential to raise the funds) to pursue this event/activity/program idea?
- Does our current building or facility have the ability to support this new fundraising idea?
- Does the fundraising idea have the potential to generate profits?
- Will there be additional labor associated with the new fundraising idea? If so, how will that affect our current personnel structure and budget?
- Do we have the technical and logistical knowledge to pursue and realize this fundraising idea?

The list of questions is extensive. Logically, the more detailed the questions are and the more that is known about the proposed fundraising idea, the less chance of poor decisions and failure.

Fundraising Tip

In the preliminary stage for idea screening, it is always critical to keep current and potential supporters in mind. Their enthusiasm is a notable predictor of whether a new event/activity/program will work. In others words, ask if the idea will generate value and benefits for present supporters and future projected supporters.

STEP 4: PRODUCT DEVELOPMENT

After a fundraising idea has been probed, scrutinized, and is determined to be desirable and feasible, the next phase is event/activity/program development. For tangible fundraising products, this step necessitates that engineering and production experts come up with a prototype of the product. Unfortunately, with the exception of merchandising, fundraising programs characteristically deal with intangible services, so the best that a fundraising program administrator can do is to put together a comprehensive plan for the new event/activity/program. In essence, the event/activity/program plan is a complete step-by-step written description of what the new fundraising idea (fundraising event, activity, or program, instructional camp, athletic endeavor, etc.) is about. It must be reiterated that since we are unable to visualize and hold this intangible fundraising service, the fundraising plan must be as comprehensive and as carefully delineated as possible. The fundraising event/activity/program plan is at the core of the next-step—test marketing.

STEP 5: TEST MARKETING

Test marketing

> is an experimental procedure that provides an opportunity to measure sales or profit potential for a new product or to test a new marketing plan under realistic marketing conditions…the major advantage to test marketing is that no other form of research can beat the real world when it comes to testing actual purchasing behavior and consumer acceptance of a product. (Zikmund, 2003, p. 217)

From a fundraising program vantage, testing out a new event/activity/program concept has notable advantages. Test marketing allows program members to observe how the supporters react to a new idea or concept in authentic, real-world situations. Such real-world testing is critical to determine:

- whether an alteration in the fundraising event/activity/program is necessary;
- whether modifications are needed to make the new fundraising program event/activity/program more desirable for customers and fans; and
- whether a new idea should be scrapped rather than moved into full production.

Testing should be done on a cost-sensitive and timely basis. Additionally, open discussions or surveys of supporters should be employed.

STEP 6: COMMERCIALIZATION

The final section in the new product development process is commercialization. Plainly stated, this is the 'go for it' stage where the fundraising administrator has appraised and tested the fundraising idea and found it to be a sound proposition. At this point, commit the fundraising program's allotted resources to producing the new event/activity/program. Effective utilization of Steps 1-5 will decrease the possibility of concept failure. Will it remove the possibility of failure completely? No. However, implementing the stages will give the program the best opportunity of launching a new and successful fundraising event/activity/program.

Pricing

Now that there is a viable, desired fundraising event/activity/program (whether a recognized, conventional one or an innovative concept), one will need to price it for maximization of profits while still maintaining and increasing the fundraising program's supporter base.

> Price is the amount of money a seller is willing to accept in exchange for a product at a given time and under given circumstances…no matter how well a product is designed, it can not help an organization achieve its goals if it is priced incorrectly. Few people will purchase the product with too high a price, and a product with too low a price will earn little or no profit. Somewhere between too high and too low there is a "proper" effective price for each product. (Pride, Hughes, & Kapoor, 2003, p. 399)

Once again, comprehending the intricacies of pricing a product (fundraising event/activity/program) is beyond the scope of this book. However, by understanding the central concepts of pricing, a fundraising program administrator can be more conscious, in general, of pricing decisions and how they can affect the fundraising program.

Price Elasticity

Price elasticity is a concept that connects changes in price with changes in demand. Specifically, price elasticity reveals how sensitive the change in demand for a fundraising event/activity/program is when there is a change in price for the event/activity/program. If the price is considered elastic, then adjustments in price produce radical swings in the number of people who want it. For example, assume that the price being charged to attend one of the fundraising program's fundraising banquets is $100.00 per plate. Assume that at the $100.00 level, the attendance is at 1,000 attendees. The price would be considered elastic if an increase in the cost by $20.00 is associated with the banquet losing 500 attendees. In this case, a 20% increase in the price yields a 50% decrease in the attendance. This example shows high price elasticity. Using the same example, once again the plate price is increased from $100.00 to $120.00 but the decrease in attendees was from 1,000 to 950. This situation is known as inelastic demand. A 20% change in price only resulted in a 5% decrease in attendees. There is also a premise known as unitary demand. This is when a percentage change in the price furnishes an exact percentage change in the demand. This is illustrated from the above example by changing the price from $100.00 to $120.00 and the attendance decreases from 1,000 to 800 (a 20% change in price has a 20% change in demand). Whatever service offered (e.g., attendance at an event, activity, instructional camps), it is important to understand the elasticity of the item, which, in turn, will show what flexibility one has in pricing it.

Pricing Objectives and Goals

Once a fundraising administrator has a picture of the price elasticity of the event/activity/program, he/she will need to generate pricing objectives and goals. The administrator should price the fundraising program's products/services to keep them in harmony with the fundraising program's overall goals. These objectives should be straightforward and easily understandable. An objective fixed on survival is essentially an emergency approach to pricing that is designed to keep the athletic organization and fundraising program afloat. The only consideration is to situate the price at whatever level makes it possible just to keep athletic organization and fundraising program going. Pricing for a targeted/predetermined return is principally done by establishing a desired profit over and above the estimated costs and working the price of the event/activity/program to achieve the projected amount. Strengthening/enlarging the fundraising programs market share and maintaining competitive position is basing the price on not only what the competition is doing but on how one can aggressively establish and acquire more supporters.

Additional Pricing Considerations

THREE METHODS OF PRICING

To price a fundraising program's events/activities/programs, three distinctive facets must be considered—cost, competition, and value. From a cost viewpoint, prices must be established to 'cover' expenditures associated with the event/activity/program as well as additional fixed fundraising program operating costs. A fundraising administrator must formulate a break-even analysis (which is a breakdown of costs associated with projected revenue) to know when the fundraising program's outlays/expenses are covered at a certain price level. The second factor to research relates to the fundraising market and a comparison of competitors' prices. Clearly stated, how competitors price their similar fundraising events/activities/programs will directly affect the foundation of how the athletic organization's fundraising program prices out its events/activities/programs. The final component of pricing deals with the value supporters put on the athletic program's events/activities/programs. The more value (and subsequent demand) the supporter places on the program's offerings, the more price control a fundraising administrator has over the product and services.

It should be stated that each of these can be used separately to devise a fundraising program's price structure. However, blending all three methods (cost, competition, and value) will give a more precise and realistic representation of the price configuration of the fundraising program.

PRICE SKIMMING VERSUS PRICE PENETRATION

The concept of price skimming versus price penetration corresponds to the pricing philosophy of new offerings (fundraising event, activities, and programs) in a fundraising program. Price skimming is introducing a new event/activity/program into the market with a high price. The core rationale for doing this type of pricing strategy is to recapture as much initial developmental costs as possible with limited sales. Price penetration is introducing a new event/activity/program into the market at a minimal cost to gain as many new supporters as possible. The prime incentive for this type of pricing approach is to get as much of the overall fundraising market share as immediately as possible.

PSYCHOLOGICAL PRICING

Pricing a fundraising program's events/activities/programs can have a psychological influence on current and prospective supporters. An event/activity/program with a high price can convey superior quality (whether quality exists or not). This type of psychological pricing is known as prestige pricing. Conversely, an event/activity/program with a low price could communicate a lack of quality (whether quality exists or not). Another psychological pricing technique is odd-even pricing. Odd-even pricing is when a price is established that makes a supporter think that the price is lower than it really is. For example, $19.99 is essentially $20.00, while customers will often acknowledge the price as $19.00. Bundle pricing can also be a psychological pricing tactic. By combining a set of events/activities/programs together, a fundraising administrator can increase sales of multiple items, increase offerings, and utilize psychological perceptions of a better overall fundraising package price.

There are six additional considerations when instituting prices for a fundraising program's events/activities/programs:

1. What should be the balance between costs, the competition, and customer when arriving at a price?

2. Will the deal be a once-only transaction or the beginning of a relationship with potential long-term benefits?

3. Is the price to be a fixed number (or schedule) or something that will be negotiated, bargained for, and possibly changed over time?

4. Are we dealing with a single customer, guest, or buyer or with a group of people?

5. Which parties to the deal have sufficient power to influence the outcome of a negotiation and what is the source of this power?

6. Does the price in question require pricing a single, specific service or does it involve a full schedule of prices? (Lazer & Layton, 1999, p. 291)

DISCOUNTS

In addition to the six considerations when pricing a fundraising event/activity/program, discounting is utilized when a fundraising program wants to stimulate sales in a condensed timeframe. In other words, discounting an established price is a short-term solution that can only be applied for limited periods. If it is discovered that the price level established is elastic at a certain level, the possible re-evaluation of the event/activity/program's price should be examined rather than repeatedly discounting. The variety of discounts can encompass:

- *Quantity discounts* – provide supporters with discounts proportional to the amount they purchase.

- *Seasonal discounts* – used to balance out cyclical fluctuation in event/activity/program support.

- *Early-payment discounts* – used to encourage immediate donations, decrease accounts receivables to the athletic organization, and increase cash flow.

- *Special event discounts* – promote a fundraising program's special event and increase awareness.

- *Repeat business discounts* – special discounts provided to repeat supporters.

Place/Distribution of Fundraising Activities, Events, and Programs

The elementary difference between a tangible fundraising product and an intangible service (event or activity) is most evident when discussing distribution. There are two ways to dispense a fundraising event or activity: Either the supporters come to the athletic organization's location or the fundraising program's service must be taken to them. The key to making a good choice between these two is accessibility. Ask which approach has the greatest potential to get the event, activity, or program the largest number of supporters. For example, if the athletic organization is extremely visible, in a heavily populated area, and is easily accessible, the fundraising program's service distribution would undeniably be to have the supporters come to the program. However, if the athletic organization is in a remote location with inadequate exposure, creative distribution might be required. The fundraising administrator may need to take the event or activity to an auxiliary locale to maximize supporter interaction and donations.

Promotion

Promotion is the fourth and final component of the marketing mix.

> Promotion is communicating information between sellers and potential buyers to influence attitudes and behaviors…The main promotional job is to tell targeted customers that the right product is available, at the right price, at the right place…What the marketer communicates is determined by customer needs and attitudes…How the message is delivered depends on what blend of various promotional methods the marketing communicator chooses. (Perreault & McCarthy, 2006, pp. 318-319)

Promotion and advertising will be examined at length later in the chapter.

TARGET MARKETS AND MARKETING SEGMENTATION

A market is "a group of individuals, organizations, or both that have needs for products in a given category and that have the ability, willingness, and authority to purchase such products" (Pride, Hughes, & Kapoor, 2003, p. 333). A target market is merely a group of people inside a market with even more explicit attributes, in which a fundraising program converges all of its marketing effort. For example, the all-encompassing market for athletic programs is entertainment. One can then break down the broad market classification of entertainment into the more detailed (but still sizeable) category of sports entertainment. From there, dissect the sports entertainment market into the precise target market of fundraising supporters for a specific sport, in a particular geographic area, with a distinct income level, etc. The more clear-cut the fundraising program's target market, the more systematic and efficient the program's marketing efforts.

Market Segmentation

Once fundraising program administrators have an underlying insight into the marketing mix, they should concentrate on the overall fundraising market, how to divide it up and, subsequently, which 'piece of the pie' the fundraising program is going to target. In Ross' (2007) article "Segmenting sports fans using brand association: A cluster analysis," sports market segmentation's importance is delineated by the following passage:

> The practice of pinpointing groups within the current fan base is necessary for success, because a sports organization cannot gain a strong foothold within the market place if these individuals are not identified and managed appropriately. As a way of optimally meeting the needs of all fans and establishing a strong position in the sports marketplace, an organization should not only identify the distinct groups of members, but also develop marketing strategies that are tailored to these different groups. This process of identifying well-defined clusters of consumers is knows as segmentation, and a wide variety of strategies have been used to achieve organizational goals. (Ross, 2007, pp. 15-24)

Once again, from a fundraising administration perspective, an athletic organization's inclusive market falls under the broad umbrella of entertainment. From there, one can narrow down the overall entertainment market to the smaller (but still substantial) sports entertainment market. The market of sports entertainment is the one fundraising administrators need to analyze, examine for niche opportunities, and approach in a manner that capitalizes on the fundraising program's superior competitive position. Moreover, from the definition of marketing segmentation, to commit all of the fundraising program's existing resources to the correct target market segment, a fundraising program administrator must:

CHAPTER 6

1. Categorize and segment the market into clear-cut, defined segments.

2. Select the most appropriate piece (or pieces) to focus the fundraising program's marketing mix—the 4 Ps.

In identifying segments, a fundraising administrator needs to research all of the possible bases for segmentation. He/she needs to investigate how the market is broken down into precise, identifiable groups. The potential ways to break down a fundraising market into distinct segments are presented below:

Geographic features – Global location/country, financial level of geographic area, urban/rural, population concentration, geographic environmental elements (temperature, terrain, etc.)

Demographic features – Male/female, maturity level/age, earning potential, household factors (spouse, children, relatives, etc.), profession, educational degree, religious convictions, ethnic group, social caste

Psychographic features – Standard of living, activities, qualities, interests

Behavioristic features – Patterns of consumption, capacity, previous encounters, allegiance to a product/service, consumer preference

In essence, demographics are associated with population characteristics; geographic criteria relate to locations; psychographics are lifestyle choices; and behavioral features are an individual and/or group's use of the product or service.

To get all-inclusive and accurate market segmentation, each category and subcategory must be dissected for its relevance to the fundraising program. By questioning a market's demographics, geographic features, and purchasing behavior, one is developing segmentation profiles of individual and group supporters. For example, some segmentation categories might not have a significant effect on how a market is segmented. In fundraising, typically city size and density is not applicable for potential supporters that come from diverse city sizes and densities.

A fundraising administrator should go through each category with his/her particular fundraising program in mind, and develop a specific profile of the target market groups. Ask the following questions:

1. Who are they? Go through the demographic and psychographics subcategories.

2. Where are they? Go through the geographic subcategories.

3. When will they contribute/support? How will they contribute/support? Why will they contribute/support? Go through the behavioral subcategories.

A few relevant points on identifying target market segments:

*   Each fundraising program will have its own distinctive segment (or, as the definition describes, niche).

- Is it feasible to have more than one target market segment? Absolutely. One might come up with several target market segments in which the group profile is ideal for one's fundraising program.

In selecting the target market(s), a fundraising administrator should consider the following criteria:

Measurable – Can you quantify the segment?

Accessible – Do you have access to the market?

Substantial – Is the segment of sufficient size to warrant attention as a segment? Further, is the segment declining, maturing, or growing?

Profitable – Does concentrating on the segment provide sufficient profitability to make it worthwhile?

Compatible with competition – To what extent do your major competitors have an interest in the segment? Is it an active interest or of negligible concern to your competition?

Effective – Does your organization have sufficient skills and resources to serve the segment effectively?

Defendable – Does your firm have the capability to defend itself against the attack of a major competitor? (Paley, 2000, p. 163)

If the fundraising administrator can verify that the segment being evaluated is in an attractive group that presents an opportunity, that it has good profitability and growth potential, and that it is in line with the fundraising program's mission and resources, then it is a segment worth pursuing.

PROMOTIONAL TOOLS FOR FUNDRAISING PROGRAMS

The fourth P in the marketing mix is *promotion*. Promotion is, in fact, marketing communication. Marketing communication consists of five major tools:

Advertising – any paid form of non-personal communication, by paid announcements in the print, broadcast, or electronic media, designed to gain acceptance of the advertiser's message.

Direct Marketing – selling directly to customers, rather than via a mass medium. It includes methods such as direct mail and telemarketing.

Sales Promotion – selling aids, often at point-of-purchase, which reinforce other types of promotion. (Shim, 2006, pp. 11, 122, 344)

Personal Selling – a form of person-to-person communication in which a salesperson works with prospective buyers and attempts to influence their purchase needs in the direction of their company's products and services.

Public Relations – identifies, establishes, and maintains mutually beneficial relationships between sports organizations and the various publics. (Shank, 2005, pp. 316, 324)

Fundraising Tip

In selecting target markets, know the fundraising program's resource boundaries and limitations. For small fundraising programs, a niche/ focus strategy can present a strong competitive advantage. If the target market niche is successfully captured by the fundraising program first, the program will be identified with that niche and be on the ground floor of future increased support.

MARKETING COMMUNICATION GOALS FOR FUNDRAISING PROGRAMS

Prior to discussing the five promotional and communication tools, a fundraising program administrator will need to examine strategic goals pertaining to marketing communication.

1. *Create awareness.* Inform markets about products, brands, stores, or organizations.

2. *Build positive images.* Build positive evaluations in people's minds about the product, brand, store, or organization.

3. *Identify prospects.* Find out names, addresses, and possible needs of potential buyers.

4. *Build relationships.* Increase cooperation among stakeholders (internal and external).

5. *Retain customers.* Create value for customers, satisfy their wants and needs, and earn their loyalty. (Churchill & Peter, 1998, pp. 445-446)

As a fundraising program administrator, map out the program's objectives for a promotional communication campaign. Can an administrator undertake and achieve multiple goals with a single campaign? Absolutely. In other words, can a fundraising team put together a promotional communication strategy (by using advertising, direct marketing, sales promotions, public relations, and personal selling or a combination of these) that not only generates recognition for the fundraising program but also fosters positive perceptions and relationships while retaining and even increasing the fundraising program's supporter bases? Yes. It is more complicated to have multiple goals but if the administrator is imaginative and can think the campaign through, there are no limits.

After conceiving and defining the goals for the fundraising program's promotion, examine the communication tools of advertising, direct marketing, sales promotion, public relations/publicity, and personal selling. Once again, it should be noted that a close examination of each of these tools is well beyond the scope of this book. In fact, each of these areas offers opportunity for study and is a specialized career. Thus, it is not the purpose of this text to enable each reader to become an authority on these tools and their use. It is the purpose of this book to enable the reader to gain a working knowledge that will allow each of these tools to be adapted and utilized with purpose within the fundraising program.

> **Fundraising Tip**
>
> It is advisable to align certain marketing communication goals with selected marketing communication tools. For example, the goal of a fundraising program could be to create awareness for the event, activity, or program. This might be best accomplished through advertising techniques in the operational area.

ADVERTISING

The prime promotional communication tool at a fundraising administrator's disposal is advertising. Advertising is

> a non-personal sales presentation communicated through media or non-media forms to influence a large number of consumers...it is a common method for promoting products and services. Although advertising

is generally more expensive than other methods, it can reach many consumers...Brand advertising is a non-personal sales presentation about a specific brand...Comparative advertising is intended to persuade customers to purchase a specific product by demonstrating a brand's superiority by comparison with other competing brands...Reminder advertising is intended to remind consumers of a product's existence...Institutional advertising is a non-personal sales presentation about a specific institution...Industry advertising is a non-personal presentation about a specific industry. (Madura, 2007, p. 529)

From Table 6.2, the fundraising administrator can begin to uncover which advertising communication tool is desirable. In the 2003 text *Principles of Marketing*, Lamb, Hair, and McDaniel expound on the advantages and disadvantages for each type of advertising/media communication tool. The following is an extrapolation of their impressions.

Table 6.2. **Advertising Media**

Media Advertising	Newspapers Magazines Trade Journals Specialized Publications
Brochure Advertising	Media Guides Game-Day Programs Specialized Literature
Broadcast Media	Television (local, regional, national) Radio (local, regional, national)
Exhibitions	Special Events Trade Show Displays
Internet	Websites Banners
Video/Film	Promotional Videos/DVDs and Films
Outdoor	Posters Point of Purchase Displays Billboards Transit/Transportation Advertising Signage Arena and Sports Facilities Special Events Aerial Advertising Mobile Billboards Movie Theatre Advertising

Newspapers:

- *Advantages* – Geographic selectivity and flexibility, short-term advertiser commitments, year-round readership, high individual market coverage, short lead time.

- *Disadvantages* – Little demographic sensitivity, limited color capabilities, low pass-along rate, may be expensive.

Magazines:

- *Advantages* – Good reproduction, color, demographic selectivity, regional selectivity, local market selectivity, relatively long advertising life.

- *Disadvantages* – Long-term commitments, slow audience buildup, lack of urgency, long lead time.

Radio:

- *Advantages* – Low cost, immediacy of message, can be scheduled on short notice, highly portable, short-term commitments, entertainment carryover.

- *Disadvantages* – No visual treatment, short advertising life, high frequency required to generate comprehension, background sound.

Television:

- *Advantages* – Ability to reach a wide, diverse audience, low cost per thousand, creative opportunities, immediacy of message, entertainment carryover.

- *Disadvantages* – Short life of message, skepticism about claims, high campaign costs, long-term advertiser commitments, long lead times required for production.

Outdoor Media:

- *Advantages* – Repetition, moderate cost, flexibility, geographic sensitivity.

- *Disadvantages* – Short message, lack of demographic selectivity, high "noise" level distracting audience.

Internet:

- *Advantages* – Fastest growing medium, reach narrow target audience, short lead time required for creating web-based advertising, moderate cost.

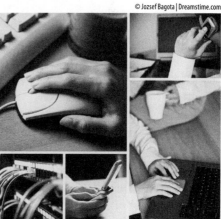

© Jozsef Bagota | Dreamstime.com

- *Disadvantages* – Difficult to measure ad effectiveness and return on investment, ad exposure relies on "click through" from banner ads, not all consumers have access to the Internet. (Lamb, Hair, & McDaniel, 2003, p. 449)

After researching each type of advertising communication tool for its germane advantages and disadvantages, the ultimate criteria for selecting an advertising mix (which is a package of tools to promote the fundraising program's events/activities, programs) is financial. The advertising goal from a financial standpoint is simple and uncomplicated. Which advertising tool (or tools) should the fundraising program employ to amplify its target market exposure and get the most from its limited advertising dollars? This is where the previously discussed subject of fundraising program marketing comes into play and affects advertising communication. Knowing the customers (prospective supporters) is the most important key. Through market segmentation and subsequent target market selection, a fundraising program administrator can get a well-defined profile of current and potential supporters. This segment profile will furnish answers to questions such as the following:

- Who are they?
- Where are they?
- What type of people are they?
- What are their demographics? Psychographics? Geographics? Lifestyles?

The vital key to any paid advertising campaign is reaching and then having an effect on the target market. Within budget constraints, ask which advertising tools will have the most influence on the projected audience and will most efficiently provide the fundraising program with the most powerful message.

- When is the best time to communicate with them?
- How often do they need promotional communication?

With these supporter profile questions answered (through marketing planning), the question of how to contact and persuade the supporter becomes easier. In the simplest terms, the fundraising administrator must know the current and potential fundraising program supporters before he/she can promote and communicate with them. After determining who the supporters are, the administrator must match the financial resources up with the most effective advertising tools the program can afford and hope that the program's financial budget will support those tools.

Once connected with the fundraising program's potential supporters, the concept of creativity comes into play. Marketing communication for fundraising events/activities/programs should follow the AIDA concept. The acronym is explained below.

Attention: The advertising tools utilized must first secure the supporters' attention. In a majority of all advertising, one has a precious few seconds to achieve this. Since people are saturated with a continued bombardment of advertising, if one does not 'catch and grab' the prospective supporter's attention, he/she will move on.

Interest: After successfully getting the supporters' attention, the advertising communication must seize their interest. In other words, once they are grabbed they must be held until the message is delivered.

Desire: Subsequent to getting the prospective supporters' attention and interest, one must get them to desire the program's product (or in the case of this text, fundraising event, activity, or program). If the advertising is imaginative and directed toward the fundraising program's target market, developing the desire for the service is the next progressive step in the AIDA progression.

Action: This is the final stage. If A, I, and D are fulfilled, getting the individual to support the fundraising program should fall in line.

In today's world, the concept of creativity in advertising is crucial. If one wants to achieve AIDA, the creative advertising work must be focused on what the customers (in our case supporters) are interested in. Actual inspiration and generation of ideas typically comes from non-structured techniques such as brainstorming and free association methods.

DIRECT MARKETING

Direct marketing is

the use of consumer-directed (CD) channels to reach and deliver goods and services to customers without using marketing middlemen. These channels include direct mail, catalogs, telemarketing, interactive TV, kiosks, websites, and mobile devises. Direct marketing is one of the fastest growing avenues for service customers. Direct marketers seek measurable response, typically customer order. This is sometimes called direct-order marketing. Today, many direct marketers use direct marketing to build long-term relationships with the customer (customer relationship marketing). (Kotler, 2003, p. 620)

The key to contacting large volumes of individual prospects though direct marketing techniques comes from advances in technology and is known in business as mass customization. Mass customization enables mass-produced products (or in this case, advertising and promotion) to be customized for each individual.

Another important aspect of direct marketing is the development of a substantial database of qualified target market supporters. The operative word in the last sentence is qualified. While a phone book may be a viable database of potential supporters, it probably would not be a qualified database for fundraising programs. How does one find a suitable database to use for direct marketing purposes? Such a database should come from the market segmentation process.

To review:

1. Identify the fundraising program's overall operational market.

2. Break down the market into segments of people with similar needs, wants, characteristics, and purchasing behavior.

3. Select the most appropriate segment on which to focus organizational efforts.

4. Profile the selected segment to find the most efficient way to contact prospects through one of the aforementioned direct marketing techniques.

As mentioned, direct marketing techniques are managed through databases. There are two ways to gain access to a database. The first and more difficult way is to construct one's own. To do so, find potential supporters, design the system of data retrieval and use, and then catalog and computerize the list. The second option is to utilize a database that already exists. The sources of databases that already exist are plentiful and, through the ever-growing power of computers, the number of relevant lists available is continuously increasing. Whether it is a geographic, demographic, psychographic, or behavioral database, never forget that the fundraising program's segment profile will determine which one (or ones) to utilize.

As with all forms of communication, direct marketing involves extensive planning and research as well as creativity tactics, cohesion of concepts, target market appeal, AIDA, and production and distribution systems. Whatever direct marketing techniques are selected to reach the fundraising program's target market segment(s), the program administrator must know the marketing concepts behind each technique.

It would serve a fundraising program administrator well to do a cost-benefit analysis to evaluate if direct marketing is warranted and financially feasible. The

Fundraising Tip

A conspicuous danger in direct mailing is saturation. Temper and monitor the amount of direct contact the fundraising program has with its supporters. If the fundraising program exceeds tolerable direct contacts with its supporter groups, not only will the message be disregarded, but it might instill a negative perception of the athletic organization and fundraising program in the eyes of the supporters.

investment of time and money in putting together a direct marketing plan is extensive. Once again, the ultimate determinant of whether to utilize any promotional tools is the supporter (or potential supporter). Through analysis, if direct marketing is proven to be effective and the financial resources of the fundraising program can support a direct marketing campaign, then it is a powerful and focused promotional instrument.

SALES PROMOTIONS

Sales promotions are defined as

> non-personal marketing activities other than advertising, personal selling, and public relations that stimulate consumer purchasing and dealer effectiveness…sales promotion has emerged as an integral part of the promotional mix. Promotion now accounts for close to half as many marketing dollars as are spent on advertising and promotional spending is rising faster than ad spending. Sales promotion consists of forms of promotion such as coupons, product samples, and rebates that support advertising and personal selling. (Boone & Kurtz, 2006, p. 463)

These nonrecurring techniques are used to create awareness and to stimulate support. Some of the possible sales promotion techniques include rebates, coupons, samples, etc. From a fundraising administrative perspective, the creativity that goes into sales promotion techniques can be rich and rewarding.

Sales Promotional Techniques

The following list details sales promotional techniques along with their relative cost and time considerations:

> *Free samples* are especially useful in generating interest in a fundraising program's event/activity/program. They can be distributed in the mail, passed out at other events or high traffic areas, or made available upon request from a potential supporter.
>
> *Price oriented programs* seek to reduce the supporter's real cost per unit in some way, e.g. cents-off coupons, mail–in refunds or rebates.
>
> *Premiums* – another item is given away or offered at an attractive price if a certain number of units are purchased.
>
> *Tie-Ins* – similar to premiums, but involves joint promotion of two items… Typically, the two parties share the cost of the promotion.
>
> *Continuity Program* – a reward is given in recognition of continuing relationships.
>
> *Contest/Sweepstakes* – used to generate excitement about product. (Lal, Quelch, & Rangan, 2005, p. 267)

Once again, it must be emphasized that while relative cost and time are important considerations in choosing a sales promotion, the most critical choice factor is the fundraising program's target market and that market's receptivity to a certain sales promotion technique. No matter how time- and cost-effective a sales promotional method could be, if it does not stimulate support, it is inappropriate and will squander limited fundraising program resources.

PERSONAL SELLING

Personal selling is one-on-one, face-to-face interaction between a fundraising program administrator (or fundraising team member) and a prospective supporter. The benefits of a successful sales call can be immeasurable. Not only can a personal sales call 'close' an immediate donation, it also establishes a personal rapport for future encounters. This, in turn, can lead to 'positive word of mouth' networking that creates more support. Virtually every marketing and advertising text goes through a step-by-step procedure to make a sales presentation (or to close a personal sale). While there are slight variations in the stages, content, and sequencing, in order to be successful, each salesperson (in our case fundraiser) must have certain general traits.

> While no ideal set of characteristics has been found to guarantee success, a number of factors are strongly related to performance: hard work, working smart, the ability to set goals, maturity, a good appearance, communicative ability, dependability, honesty, and integrity. In some cases, the individual may possess these traits instinctively, but in all cases, these characteristics can be developed through thought and careful practice. (Marks, 1997, p.55)

The following is one of the many step-by-step procedures that can be used in making a sales presentation and closing a sale.

Step 1: *Prospecting for new customers*

Step 2: *Set effort priorities*

Step 3: *Select target customer* – Identify who influences purchase decisions and/or who is involved in buyer-seller relationship

Step 4: *Preplan sales call and presentation* – Prepare presentation

Step 5: *Make sales presentation* – Create interest, overcome problems/objectives, arouse desire

Step 6: *Close sale* – Get action

Step 7: *Follow up after the sales call* to establish relationship and follow up after the purchase to maintain and enhance relationship. (Perreault & McCarthy, 2006, p. 360)

Personal selling goes beyond a generic communication tool. Personal selling has been referred to as a business skill or science that takes hard work and extensive experience to master. It is composed of:

- building relationships both short-term and long-term;
- providing adept demonstrations;
- interpersonal recommendations;
- showmanship and presentation dynamics;
- tactical negotiation;
- networking and campaigning; and
- role playing and performing for effect.

For a fundraising administrator or team member to exploit this methodology in fundraising program promotion and communication, he/she must set aside the time to appreciate and understand the process as well as rehearse and practice its use.

STRATEGIC ALLIANCES IN MARKETING COMMUNICATION

A potential solution to fundraising program marketing communication deals with the concept of strategic alliances. Many strategic alliances take the form of marketing alliances. The fundraising program could piggyback on a marketing communication plan of another organization. The significance of this type of alliance is that the two organizations have a mutually beneficial relationship. Simply put, by working together on cooperative marketing/promotional activities, the fundraising program and outside organization are both profiting from the joint promotion. Shared promotions devices can encompass alliances in advertising, sales promotions, special events, sponsorships, and public relations.

The second form of strategic alliance deals with having an external marketing agency supply all of (or a portion of) the fundraising program's marketing communication and promotional activities for something of value that the fundraising program could provide in return. The key to this strategic alliance is the value-for-value trade-off between the fundraising program and the external marketing agency.

MARKETING COMMUNICATION BUDGETING

Budgeting is the control function that assists a fundraising administrator in establishing and maintaining guidelines for spending. When constructed accurately, these benchmarking tools help forecast needs and describe circumstances through quantitative parameters. However, budgeting money for marketing communications/promotion in a fundraising program is as much a philosophical issue as it is financial. In other words, an athletic organization's way of thinking about designating money to the function of marketing communication for fundraising will often influence the extent to which that 'line item' is financed. Some athletic organization directors possess the attitude that marketing communication for fundraising is a luxury and whatever is available at the end of the financing/budgeting process is what will be apportioned to the fundraising program's marketing communication. More progressive athletic organization directors realize the indispensable worth of marketing communication in fundraising and prioritize its budgeting/financing.

Specific techniques associated with the 'nuts and bolts' of marketing communication budgeting for fundraising can include the following methods:

Arbitrary Allocation – The simplest, yet most unsystematic, approach to determining promotional budgeting is called arbitrary allocation. Using this method, sports marketers set the budget in isolation of other critical factors…promotional budgets are established after the organization's other costs are considered.

Competitive Parity – Setting promotional budgets based on what competitors are spending (competitive parity) is often used for certain product categories in sports marketing.

Percentage of Sales – The percentage-of-sales method of promotional budget allocation is based on determining some standard percentage of promotional spending and applying this proportion to either past of forecasted sales to arrive at the amount to be spent…it has a number of shortcomings…With sales declining, it may be more appropriate to increase (rather than decrease) promotional spending. A second major shortcoming of using this method is the notion that budgeting is very loosely, if at all, tied to the promotional objective.

Objective and Task Method – Objective and task method could be characterized as the most logical and systematic. The objective and task method identifies the promotional objectives, defines the communication tools and tasks needed to meet those objectives, and then adds up the cost of the planned activities. (Shank, 2005, pp. 290-291)

One final point on marketing communication budgeting for fundraising programs: There are clear dangers in under-funding a fundraising program's marketing communication and promotional activities. Under-funding restricts the effectiveness of communication tactics and limits a fundraising program's projected exposure. Conversely, over-funding marketing communication strategies can be just as detrimental to a fundraising program. Precious resources (time and money) will be wasted, and other strategies the fundraising program might want to pursue will be missed due to the lack of funds. The key to a good marketing communication budget is knowing the resources needed to accomplish communication goals and dispersing the capital and resources to achieve those objectives.

PUBLIC RELATIONS AND PUBLICITY

From an academic standpoint, the concepts of public relations and publicity have numerous definitions that vary in substance and structure. For the purpose of this book, the following description encompasses the fundamental nature of publicity and public relations for fundraising programs:

Publicity – Promotional tool in which information about a company or product is transmitted by general mass media…publicity is free. Marketers usually have little control over publicity, but because it is presented in a news format, consumers often regard it as objective.

Public Relations – Company-influenced publicity directed at building goodwill with the public or dealing with unfavorable events…A firm will try to establish goodwill with customers (and potential customers) by performing and publicizing its public-service activities. (Griffin & Ebert, 2004, p. 379)

A core consideration that these definitions underscore is the need to develop and preserve a highly regarded public image. This corporate identity (in this case, athletic organization and fundraising program identity) is the context not only for the way people think of the fundraising program now, but also for the way they imagine the fundraising program in the future. If the athletic organization and fundraising program's image is one that elicits upbeat, positive feelings, the fundraising program's public relations foundation is formidable and can support the operation. If the current athletic organization and fundraising program image has little or no response (neither positive nor negative) associated with it, one can look at this situation from a 'clean slate' viewpoint—the fundraising program's public relations outlook is an opportunity for growth. Finally, if the athletic organization and fundraising program's image provokes negative connotations, the fundraising administrator will need to 'stem the tide' of disapproving opinion and start the lengthy process of building an optimistic picture for the fundraising program.

As with most business applications, public relations and publicity need formal proactive planning. For fundraising programs, public relations have two distinct elements. The first is known as campaign public relations and the second is perpetual public relations. The difference between the two is captured by the factors of frequency and duration. Public relations campaigns are one-time projects with a fixed, terminal timeframe. Perpetual public relations is a continual process set up (through a public relations system) to operate as long as the fundraising program is functioning. Campaigns are associated with intensive development efforts and attempts to reach identified fundraising goals, while perpetual public relations systems are characterized by long-term maintenance and consistency.

Public Relations Campaigns for Fundraising Programs

The listing below identifies the stages in a public relations campaign.

- Situational analysis
- Problem statement
- Goal statement
- Targeted publics

- Tentative strategies
- Statement of limitations
- Management liaison (generated from Kendall, 1996, text concept)

Situational Analysis

The initiating phase in a fundraising program's public relations campaign, situational analysis, is known as a 'where are we now' perspective. A situational analysis

> is the unabridged collection of all that is known about the situation, its history, forces operating on it, and those involved or affected internally and externally. A situation analysis contains all the background information needed to expand upon and to illustrate in detail the meaning of a problem statement…a situation analysis begins with a thorough and searching review of perceptions and actions of key actors in the organization, structures and processes of organizational units relevant to the problem and the history of the organization's involvement...The internal situation analysis also includes a "communication audit"—a systematic documentation of an organization's communication for the purpose of understanding how it communicates with its public…an analysis focuses on the external factors, both positive and negative. The starting point may be a systematic review of the history of the problem situation outside the organization. (Cutlip, Center, & Broom, 2000, pp. 347-348)

Additionally, during this current-time analysis, the program administrator should conduct a preliminary public relations S.W.O.T. investigation into both the athletic organization and its fundraising program. A S.W.O.T. analysis involves a thorough evaluation of the fundraising program's internal strengths and weaknesses along with its external opportunities and threats. A S.W.O.T. study is appropriate for all business functions within a fundraising program, especially public relations.

Problem Statement

A problem statement summarizes the overall condition of the organization's public relations. While the phrase *problem statement* has a pessimistic connotation, it does not have to be negative in context. With the help of a S.W.O.T. analysis, the fundraising administrator may have discovered encouraging opportunities and notable strengths. The problem statement should be as clear-cut and concise as possible. Clarity is essential since the fundraising program's public relations campaign, whatever it is designed to achieve, will emanate from this declaration.

Fundraising Tip

As with all introspective program investigations, the public relations situational analysis must be as unemotional and as dispassionate as possible. A truthful assessment is the key to a thriving public relations campaign.

Fundraising Tip

Dig deep to expose the fundraising program's true public relations problem, not just its symptoms. Even though the symptoms might initially seem like they are bona-fide predicaments, they are more than likely superficial signs of something more profound.

Goal Statement

A goal statement

Fundraising Tip

Since public relations campaigns for fundraising programs have precise time frames, their goals should be very time specific while focusing directly on the validated public relations problem. In other words, can the campaign's goals be accomplished within its operational deadlines?

should be evaluated by asking (1) does it really address the situation? (2) is it realistic and achievable? and (3) can success be measured in meaningful terms? Public relations basically have two kinds of goals: informational and motivational. Informational objectives are goals designed primarily to expose audiences to information and create awareness... the difficulty with an informational objective is in measuring how well the objective has been achieved...motivational objectives try to change attitudes and influence behavior...because they are bottom-line oriented, they are based on measurable results that can be clearly quantified. (Wilcox, Ault, Agee, & Cameron, 1998, p. 148)

From a fundraising program viewpoint, an informational public relations goal could be to provide a website for fans and supporters to access data about the athletic organization's players and staff as well as fundraising events/activities/programs. A motivational public relations objective could be to inform and energize the fundraising target market (through various media) about upcoming events. The quantifiable measurement to see if this goal is accomplished could simply be by the amount of tickets sold and/or donations given. Once again, it is essential to understand that whatever type of objective the program administrator chooses, the objective should be aligned with the athletic organization's and fundraising program's public relations problem statement, which is directly aligned with the marketing mission statement, which, in turn, closely reflects the fundraising program's mission statement.

Targeted Public Relations

Fundraising Tip

When considering the statement of limitations, inventory the internal weaknesses (in order of priority) that might impair the fundraising program's public relations campaign, and then set achievable solutions to combat those weaknesses. Evaluate the prospective outcomes from a resources viewpoint— time, money, and manpower being the primary considerations.

The idea of targeted public relations segments corresponds with the marketing concept of target markets. In other words, fundraising administrators should find the targeted public relations groups the same way that they established (and exploited) the target market group(s). Look at the public as a whole, segment it into groups with similar wants, needs, characteristics, and perceptions, and then select the target groups on which the fundraising program will concentrate its available resources. Will the public relations target group be the same as the marketing target group? Possibly, perhaps even likely, but not always. It depends on the goals, the situation, and what the program administrator is attempting to achieve. From a bottom line approach, motivational goals will produce very comparable public relations and marketing targets. Inspirational goals might be broader in nature because they are trying to create awareness of fundraising efforts in a larger population.

Tentative Strategies

Tentative strategies in the planning process are exactly that: preliminary strategies to achieve the fundraising program's public relations goals. From targeting, the fundraising administrator knows whom he/she is going to attempt to reach. This stage answers questions like the following:

- How am I going to reach them?
- What type of media would best get their attention?
- What message do I develop? What story do I want to tell?
- What type of creativity should I employ?
- How frequently do the targeted groups need to be exposed to the message?
- When should I reach them?
- Is my P.R. message ethical? Legal? Factual?
- If they get our message, when should we see results?
- Ultimately, will the PR strategy work?

As one goes through the inventory of strategic questions, each specific tactic will have its own distinct set of issues. The more thoroughly these types of questions are asked, the higher the likelihood that the chosen tactic will work and the fundraising program's public relations goal will be realized.

Statement of Limitation

The statement of limitation is principally the 'W' (weaknesses internally in the program) of the S.W.O.T. investigation. In other words, what internal deficiencies (lack of skills and/or resources) does the fundraising program have that might affect its projected public relations strategies and goals? Skills can relate to managerial abilities, knowledge base, and technical know-how, among others. Resources directly relate to personnel, time resources, and, ultimately, financial constraints.

Management Liaison

The concluding step in the public relations campaign process, management liaison, might not pertain to all fundraising programs. If the fundraising program is considered autonomous and thus functions without peripheral, external influences, the managerial liaison phase is not applicable. However, if the fundraising program operates as one unit within a larger department or if it has a controlling board or committee, then the fundraising program administrator must act as the managerial liaison. The managing group will need to (in some cases) authorize the fundraising program's public relations plan, sanction it through funding, provide its input and insight, etc. Each situation and program will have different reporting criteria.

Perpetual Public Relations

Perpetual public relations are how, on a permanent and continuous basis, a fundraising program administrator enlightens, informs, and communicates with the media and the public. Public relations deal with business concepts of operating systems, policies, and procedures. The public relations system in which the fundraising program communicates externally is the way staff members interact with the community.

Fundraising Tip

In the capacity of managerial liaison, keeping everyone continually informed throughout all stages of the fundraising program's public relations campaign is an essential point. Conversely, one needs to balance the amount of information given so as to not inundate people with trivial information.

Fundraising Tip

Perpetual public relations systems require time to cultivate key media relationships and feedback. As the fundraising program's visible leader, spend time developing positive relations with key media personnel. Goodwill and trust must be earned, so be patient and persistent.

Public relations policies and procedures within established systems are more specific rules and step-by-step 'how-to's.

Before developing and implementing a perpetual public relations system for a fundraising program, it is crucial that the program administrator both define what a system is and delineate its components. While the system concept in the 2003 text *Management: A Practical Introduction* is geared toward administrative/managerial applications in organizations, the authors do provide the structural definition and essential ingredients to describe any system. The following is an abridged explanation of the system concept and its functions:

> A system is a set of interrelated parts that operate together to achieve a common purpose…the systems viewpoint regards the organization as a system of interrelated parts. By adopting this point of view, you can look at your organization both as a collection of subsystems—parts making up the whole system—and a part of the larger environment. The four parts of a system are:
>
> 1. *Inputs* are the people, money, information, equipment, and materials required to produce an organization's goods and services.
>
> 2. *Outputs* are the products, services, profits, losses, employee satisfaction or discontent, and the like that are produced by the organization.
>
> 3. *Transformation* processes are the organization's capabilities in management and technology that are applied to converting inputs into outputs.
>
> 4. *Feedback* is information about the reaction of the environment to the outputs that affects the inputs. (Kinicki & Williams, 2003, pp. 48-49)

From this description of systems, a fundraising administrator can develop a fundraising program's public relations system and procedures. Ask the following supporting questions to systematize the fundraising program's public relations. These questions are nonspecific and in no particular order. The athletic organization's fundraising program operating environment will dictate the precise questions.

Inputs/Resources

- What type of equipment will the fundraising program need to have for a professional, proficient public relations communication system?
- What type of human resource needs will the fundraising program's public relations system demand?
- What individual qualifications and expertise will be needed on the program's public relations staff?
- What type of printing service is available? Postal services? Email and database availability?

Fundraising Tip

The concept of systems in business operations is a prominent feature of fundraising program operations. Systems provide flow and lessen haphazard work and outputs. Think analytically when blueprinting systems. Continually monitor and streamline systems for fundraising program enhancement.

- What access does the fundraising program have to internal organizational staff that could be utilized for speaking engagements and interviews?
- What type of statistical tracking software is considered necessary?

Processing: Converting Inputs to Outputs

- Who is accountable for:
  - press releases;
  - compiling statistics;
  - assembling press kits;
  - securing interviews;
  - speaking engagements; and
  - public relations events?
- What are the step-by-step actions for constructing the above fundraising public relations items?
- Who is responsible for scheduling, organizing, and operating public relations functions?
- Are the fundraising program's conversion processing activities computerized? If so, are these procedures the most up-to-date for efficiency?

Outputs/Final Product

- Is the final public relations product for the fundraising program professional?
- Is it factual and accurate?
- Is it relevant to the reader/listener?
- Does it 'tell the story' that one would like?
- Is it reaching the media in an opportune, timely manner?
- Is the produced output targeted toward appropriate fundraising sources?

Fundraising Tip

When putting together a fundraising program's public relations system, remember that it will not happen overnight. Public relations systems take far-reaching thought and planning.

Two other components that are of great consequence to a high-quality public relations system are feedback and control. Questions that will refine the fundraising program's public relations system that deal with these two components are as follows:

Feedback/Reverse Communication

- What was the external reaction and opinion to the public relations communication?
- Is the fundraising program getting the public relations exposure expected?
- Is the public relations output the same as the public relations media coverage given?

Control/Adjustments to the System

- Is the fundraising program attaining its public relations goals?
- If not, how can the fundraising administrator modify the program's inputs, processes, and outputs to improve results?

Table 6.3. **PR Media and Communication Avenues**	
Electronic/Technological	Internet Blogs
	Newsletters
	Industry-Wide Electronic Publications
	Direct Electronic Communication
	Athletic Program Websites
	Chat Rooms/Discussion Boards
	Search Engines
	Video Teleconferencing
	E-Conferencing
	Social Networks
Traditional Methods	Public Relations Community Events/Sponsorships
	Public Appearances (top internal personnel)
	Press Releases and Press Kits
	Correspondence Inserts/Billing Inserts
	Traditional Advertising Media (TV, radio, periodicals, direct mailing, etc.)
	News Stories
	Interviews
	TV and Press Conferences
	Brochures and Internal Fliers
	Paraphernalia (cups, hats, t-shirts, pens, etc.)

To reiterate, the key to putting together a well-designed public relations system is to establish successful procedures and to monitor the overall process.

Types of Media Avenues of Public Relations Communication

Table 6.3 is a listing of possible media and communication avenues for fundraising program public relations communication.

It should be noted that the ultimate goal of selecting the right media and communication techniques is to generate positive word of mouth for the athletic organization and the fundraising program.

SUMMARY

Marketing is the business function that facilitates exchanges in a corporate enterprise (in the case of this text, fundraising programs). Externally, it helps fundraising program administrators:

- delineate outside environmental factors that influence a fundraising program;
- analyze supporter behavior and the decision-making process; and
- evaluate the overall market of fundraising and the segmentation of that market. In addition, segmentation will identify niche opportunities that give a fundraising program a defined target market in which to exert its efforts.

Internally, fundraising program marketing:

- examines product selection and development (events/activities/programs);
- provides foundations for pricing a fundraising program's endeavors;
- elucidates the choices of distribution of fundraising program endeavors; and
- communicates the benefits to potential supporters of the fundraising program.

The practical application of marketing by a fundraising administrator will intensify the program's exposure as well as increase revenue/support. It creates desires and a call to action in fundraising program supporters and, if utilized correctly, it can transport a fundraising program to a higher operational level and competitive position.

From a marketing communication perspective, promotional tactics that can be used by a fundraising program encompass five primary elements: advertising, direct marketing, sales promotion, personal selling, and public relations. The promotional mix of these devices is through a planned process that takes into account fundraising goals, budgets, and, ultimately, the fundraising program's target market. The combination of these tools can maximize a fundraising program's exposure, image, and support. However, it should be reiterated that marketing communication is a part of the whole concept of marketing. By itself and without the proper background concepts of the marketing mix, it will inescapably fail to achieve its intentions.

The potential for the use of public relations campaigns for fundraising programs is considerable. The most important point to remember is that the expenditures associated with public relations are, in comparison to other promotional and marketing communication techniques, minimal. For fundraising programs with few resources, public relations can be a compelling, cost-effective tool. Another significant aspect of public relations is the perception by the public that it is more reliable and convincing in comparison with paid promotional approaches. Other promotional techniques, such as advertising, are seen as manipulative while public relations articles and editorials are taken as more accurate and sincere.

REVIEW AND DISCUSSION QUESTIONS

1. List the seven external environmental elements that a fundraising program administrator must always research and monitor.
2. What are the components of the five forces model?
3. Describe the four components of a marketing mix.
4. What are the five tools of marketing communication? Briefly describe each.
5. What are some of the major advertising media avenues a fundraising administrator can pursue?

7

Fundraising Control and Evaluation

BUDGETING CONCEPTS FOR FUNDRAISING PROGRAMS

Before a discussion of budgeting for fundraising programs can commence, it must be stated that the process of budgeting (in most athletic organizations) is fairly simple to understand. So why does the mere mention of the term evoke extreme mental distress for most fundraising program administrators? Three prominent reasons stand out. The first is that budgets are predictions, and predictions deal with uncertainty and ambiguity. The second is that to do them accurately, budgets take time, thought, and effort. If a fundraising administrator is not detail oriented, budgeting can be an arduous process. The third is that budgets customarily deal with a very critical and carefully scrutinized organizational resource—money. Money is the one fundraising program resource that elicits immediate attention from all organization stakeholders. This third reason is even more prevalent in fundraising program budgeting. Due to the fact that the fundraising program's primary goal is to put money into the athletic organization, budgeting what will go out (money and other resources) is extremely important and visible.

While budgeting is primarily focused on financial resources/money, almost all internal fundraising resources can (and should be) budgeted. Resources such as personnel and work time, materials and supplies, and facility and equipment usage are just a few of the athletic organization and fundraising program items that can be budgeted. For our intentions, we will concentrate our dialogue on the internal resource of capital/money.

Budgeting Defined

The most comprehensive use of the term budgeting is exemplified by the following definition:

> A budget is simply a forecast of future events…budgets perform three basic functions for a firm. First, they indicate the amount and timing of the firm's needs for future financing. Second, they provide the basis for taking corrective action in the event budgeted figures do not match actual or realized figures. Third, budgets provide the basis for performance benchmarks that management can use to evaluate the performance of those responsible for carrying out those plans and, in turn, to control their actions. Thus, budgets are valuable aids in both the planning and controlling aspects of the firm's financial management. (Keown, Martin, Petty, & Scott, 2001, p. 151)

Budgets are typically for a specific time period (ordinarily a fiscal year). For fundraising programs, they can also be for an annual period for the entire fundraising program or they can be constructed for each specific event, activity, and program. The best use of budgeting for fundraising programs would be to construct budgets for all of the projected events/activities/programs and to use those individual budgets as the foundation for the fundraising program's overall annual budget. In other words, develop parts to make up the whole.

BUDGET

Sales	1,000,000.00
Cost Goods Sold	300,000.00
Gross M. in	700,000.00
Expenses:	
Sales Expenses	150,000.00
Marketing Expenses	000.00
G&A Expenses	
Total Expenses	
Operating Income	100,000
Other Expenses	15,000.00
Net Income Before Tax	**85,000.00**
Taxes	21,250.00
Net Income	**63,750.00**

© Dave Frederick | Dreamstime.com

While budgets are utilized for projecting future resource allocation, they are grounded in historical data. What is spent in previous budgetary periods will be the foundation for the projections into succeeding budgetary periods. Once again, this concept can be broken down into events/activities/programs. What was spent on an individual event, activity, or program in the past should be the underlying basis for future budget projections.

Budgeting promotes planning and coordination; it enhances performance measurements and corrective actions.

Planning – The budget formalizes and documents managerial plans, clearly communicating objectives to both superiors and subordinates.

Coordination – The budgetary process forces coordination among departments to promote decisions in the best interest of the company as a whole.

Performance measurement – Budgets are specific, quantitative representations of management's objectives. Comparing actual results to budgeted expectations provides a way to evaluate performance.

> *Corrective action* – Budgeting provides advanced notice of potential shortages, or other weaknesses in operating plans…Budgeting advises managers of potential problems in time for them to carefully devise effective solutions. (Edmonds, Tsay, & Olds, 2008, p. 295)

Situational Budgeting

In fundraising administration, budgeting can take two different forms. The first and most difficult is that the fundraising program administrator is also the owner of the athletic organization. In this case, one must budget extensively and apply detailed accounting procedures to all athletic organization and fundraising program operations. This circumstance is similar to entrepreneurial and corporate accounting. In this type of athletic organization and fundraising operation, it is advisable (unless the fundraising administrator has a formal accounting and business background) to employ and directly work with an accounting consultant. The consultant will help set up all of the athletic organization's and fundraising program's financial statements, projected budgets, and year-end fiscal reports. Documents such as cash flow statements, balance sheets, and income statements (both actual and projected) are typically beyond general fundraising administrative knowledge.

The second form of budgeting is the one that is relevant for the majority of fundraising administrators—operating/expense budgeting. This is a system where the fundraising program is a part (or unit) within an institutional athletic organization. In this case, the process of financial statement generation is completed outside the fundraising program. The fundraising administrator is provided with specific parameters within which the fundraising program must operate. In other words, the fundraising program's athletic administration (in a high school, junior college, or senior college) stipulates a specific dollar amount for the fundraising program to operate. The projected amount can be divided into predetermined line items (which are delineated by pre-established expense categories) or it can be an aggregate total (which is the 'bottom line' amount the fundraising program has to operate). In the latter case, the fundraising administrator determines the allocation for each individual line item from the total amount given.

Traditional Expense Budgeting

Traditional expense budgeting is focuses on the disbursement/expense side of the income statement. The first step is to identify all of the fundraising program's costs. This concept is not as simple as it seems. A good place to start is with the identification of historical data. The expense categories that the fundraising program has had in the past and present are the foundations for the future projected categories. However, this is not the end of the process. The fundraising program, through planning and goal definition, has a futuristic viewpoint that is possibly very different from its current and historical position. In this instance, discover what new possible expenditures (based on the fundraising program's mission, goals, and direction) need to be defined. The fundraising

Fundraising Tip

While consultants' (such as lawyers, accountants, etc.) up-front costs could be considered exorbitant, skillful consultants over the long term can pay for their services many times over. If the fundraising program cannot finance consultants on a permanent basis, hire them to set up operational systems that are self-sustaining.

administrator needs to think this step through from every possible angle, looking at the fiscal year completely as well as each specific event, activity, and program.

Once the fundraising program's expense categories have been determined, enter the dollar amounts that are believed to be accurate. As with budget category definitions, historical data is a good starting point in determining the dollar amount for each line item expense. From that starting point, each expense must be looked at individually to determine fundraising operating variables from past years to present. Check to see if fundraising operations remain essentially the same. If so, then the utilization of historical expense information is relevant, applicable, and defensible. If a fundraising administrator has evaluated and subsequently changed any aspect of the operation, then an increase or decrease in a line item might be warranted.

Zero-Based Budgeting

As previously discussed, budgeting is the administrative responsibility that projects and calculates future fundraising program resource allocations. Budgets provide a tangible framework within which the different components of the athletic program can operate.

> In the traditional approach to budgeting, the manager starts with last year's budget and adds to it (or subtracts from it) according to anticipated needs… Under a zero-based budget, managers are required to justify all budgeted expenditures, not just changes in the budget from the previous year. The baseline is zero rather than last year's budget. (Garrison & Noreen, 2003, p. 380)

From a fundraising program outlook, zero-based budgeting is considerably more challenging to develop because of the fact that each expense line item is considered a new expense, and its projected amounts are derived from original data. While traditional budgets are considered 'rollovers,' zero-based budgets primarily stem from new budgeting research. If done accurately, zero-based budgets give a truer picture of the fundraising program's financial situation and budgetary projections. A fundraising administrator needs to determine if the additional accuracy of the zero-based budget's primary research warrants the additional time needed to construct. A possible option is to assemble zero-based budgets every other fiscal period to maintain accuracy of the traditional numbers as well as to keep the program using up-to-date primary figures.

Budgets as Fundraising Administrative Controls

Budgets, as a fundraising control tool, have

> four principle purposes: (1) to fine-tune the strategic plan; (2) to help coordinate the activities of the several parts of the organization; (3) to assign responsibility to managers, to authorize the amounts that they are permitted to spend, and to inform them of the performance that is

expected of them; and (4) to obtain a commitment that is a basis for evaluating a manager's actual performance. (Anthony & Govindarajan, 2007, p. 382)

Since budgets deal with the most critical and limited resource in a fundraising program (money), all internal stakeholders need to have a guide for operating and spending. For this reason, budgets need to be continuously monitored by the fundraising program administrator and fundraising team. A good practice is to keep an expense ledger (usually by computer) that shows a fundraising program's individual line items. The line items can be broken down into fiscal budget, actual expenditures, and operational variances. Another ledger technique could be similar to a personal checkbook where dates and running balances show the remaining funds as well as when expenditures were incurred. Furthermore, if one can accurately maintain encumbrances against running totals, it will give a clear picture of the account/line item. Finally, any major deviations from projected to actual spending should be narratively recorded and explained for budget review clarification at the end of the fiscal year.

Budgeting and Fundraising Goals

Because the ultimate ambition of a fundraising team is goal realization, budgeting and the budgeting process must always have the objectives of the athletic organization and fundraising program in mind. The budgets established should be a productive tool in the achievement of the fundraising program's goals. The worst-case scenario in dealing with budgets is that they are a hindrance and a deterrent to achieving goals. "Problems can arise if (1) the budget goal is unachievable (too high); (2) the budget goal is very easy to achieve (too loose); or (3) the budget goals of the business conflict with the objectives of employees (goal conflict)" (Warren, Reeve, & Fess, 2002, p. 820). A fundraising program's budget must be challenging but achievable to maximize the athletic organization's financial resources.

Miscellaneous Concepts on Budgeting for Fundraising Programs

- When constructing expense items, use actual quotes whenever possible. Get all quotes in writing.
- If estimating budget line-items, overestimate all calculations and costs. Make sure all expenses are inclusive of all fees. Hidden fees can drastically change budgets.
- Shop around for the best costs and the best possible values.
- Stay consistent with the fundraising program's budget format and calculations.
- Any anomalies outside of the budgeted expenses need a narrative explanation.
- Verify the accuracy of all aspects of the budget. Triple check all calculations.

- Standardize the fundraising program's budgetary process by designing and utilizing budget spreadsheets.
- For each event/activity/program budget, work in a miscellaneous line item account for unforeseen expense.
- Use the fundraising program's budgets as communication tools. All critical stakeholders involved in the fundraising program should have an intimate knowledge of the contents of the fundraising program's operating budget.
- If the fundraising program is the primary source of revenue for the athletic organization, the use of a budgeting committee might be the most advantageous tactic.

  A standing budget committee will usually be responsible for overall policy matters relating to the budgeting program and for coordinating the preparation of the budget itself…in addition, the budget committee approves the final budget and receives periodic reports on the progress of the company in attaining budgeted goals. (Garrison & Noreen, 2003, p. 380)
- If a fundraising program (or event/activity/program) budget is limited, and most are, allocation of resources in the budget must be in 'pecking order' of importance. Think through the tough decisions prior to the construction of the budget.

Summary of Budgeting Concepts for Fundraising Programs

Before a fundraising program administrator embarks on the process of budgeting, he/she needs to have a comprehensive understanding of the operational environment in which the athletic organization and fundraising program functions. Additionally, the concepts of situational budgeting, traditional budgeting, and zero-based budgeting all need clarification. An understanding of these three components, in turn, supplies the fundraising administrator with a true financial picture of the fundraising program.

FUNDRAISING CONTROLS

Control Defined

The word control has a unique meaning to each of us. For the most part, the business world has given the functional duty of control a standardized definition. The applicable, strategic definition is as follows:

  Strategic managers choose the organizational strategies and structure they hope will allow the organization to use its resources most effectively to pursue its business model and create value and profit. Then they create strategic control systems, tools that allow them to monitor and evaluate whether, in fact, their strategies and structure are working as intended, how they could be improved, and how they should change if they are not working. (Hill & Jones, 2004, p. 411)

From this definition, the importance of the planning process in giving a fundraising program focus is accentuated. Without delineated goals and structure, there would be nothing to control. This leads to the question "Why practice managerial controls in fundraising programs?"

Why Practice Managerial Controls?

Managerial controls are designed to give fundraising administrators information regarding progress. The fundraising administrator can use this information to do the following:

1. *Prevent crisis* – If a manager does not know what is going on, it is easy for small, readily solved problems to turn into crisis.

2. *Standardize outputs* – Problems and services can be standardized in terms of quality and quantity through the use of good controls.

3. *Appraise employee's performances* – Proper controls can provide the manager with objective information about employee performance.

4. *Update plans* – Even the best plans must be updated as environmental and internal changes occur. Controls allow the manager to compare what is happening with what was planned.

5. *Protect an organization's assets* – Controls can protect assets from inefficiency, waste, and pilferage. (Rue & Byars, 2009, pp. 363-364)

© Sergey Gavrilichev | Dreamstime.com

Fundraising Tip

Control is the ultimate step in the management of fundraising programs that leads right back into the first step, planning. Management is a circular progression with no beginning or end.

These five major reasons to practice managerial controls can be related to fundraising program administration.

Through proactive planning and control, all fundraising administrators should try to avoid crisis management. The possible crisis situations in a fundraising program are unlimited. However, with strong control systems in place, fundraising administrators can minimize the possibility of a small problem turning into a major crisis.

Standardizing outputs emphasizes quality control and maximization of resources. As discussed in previous chapters, quality should be a primary goal in all aspects of the fundraising program. If the control system and philosophy stress standardized quality, then the fundraising program will consistently produce superior fundraising events/activities/programs.

In appraising fundraising team members, control revolves around maximizing all members' skills and capabilities. By their very nature, performance evaluations are direct tools that keep the fundraising program's personnel focused, not only on their personal goals but also on the fundraising program's goals. The maintenance of this type of control system has a direct effect on productivity and performance.

A fundraising program plan must be considered a flexible document that can be adapted and revised. In most cases, the only way to determine if an element of the fundraising program plan needs adjusting is to examine that element over time. Through good monitoring and controls, one can determine what fundraising goals and objectives are still relevant and which goals and objectives need to be adjusted (expanded, augmented, minimized, eliminated).

Finally, all fundraising programs (no matter how large) have limited resources. Control systems can quickly determine which functions are effectively using fundraising program resources (time, money, manpower) and which are not. For example, the fundraising program might be utilizing a certain training technique to develop a particular skill or strength in its team members. Without proper controls and monitoring, how could one know if this technique is a productive training method or if the fundraising program team member could use his/her time, resources, and efforts more effectively elsewhere?

Types of Controls

In the text *Essentials of Contemporary Management,* Jones and George illuminate three types of control systems that can be utilized by a fundraising program. The three concepts are broken down as follows:

Feed forward controls – Control that allows managers to anticipate problem before they arise.

Concurrent controls – Control that gives managers immediate feedback on how efficiently inputs are being transformed into outputs so that managers can correct problems as they arise.

Feedback controls – Control that gives managers information about customers' reactions to goods and services so that corrective action can be taken if necessary. (Jones & George, 2004, pp. 245-246)

These three types of control systems can be easily adapted to fundraising program administration.

1. Feed forward controls are proactive controls that a fundraising administrator can establish prior to any type of fundraising event, activity, or program. The important consideration in establishing these types of controls is based on the final expected fundraising endeavor.

2. Concurrent controls are used to adjust actions while the fundraising program's operations are in progress. This control method keeps the fundraising program endeavors on track and avoids tangents. A small change early in a process can avoid a large change and restructuring later. Major types of concurrent controls are Yes/No controls. Yes/No controls are essentially go/no-go decisions at selected checkpoints in the program's operations. The key to this type of control process is

discovering the points at which to make go/no-go decisions. Typically, these are called the 'points of no return' or critical decision junctions. Once again, the control decision is based on the fundraising program's goals and mission.

3. Feedback controls are the comparison of projected results and actual results after a specific time period has elapsed. This is a major premise behind the control process.

Two other distinctions need to be made when talking about types of fundraising program controls. They are bureaucratic controls and commitment (or clan) controls. They are defined by the following:

> *Bureaucratic control* – an approach to tactical control that stresses adherence to rules and regulations and is imposed by others.
>
> *Commitment (clan) control* – an approach to tactical control that emphasizes consensus and shared responsibility for meeting goals. (Black & Porter, 2000, p. 494)

In other words, bureaucratic controls can be described as rigidly enforced controls that are established and outlined in a fundraising program's policies and procedure manuals. Clan controls are cooperative and empowered shared visions that provide fundraising team members an opportunity to voice their personal concerns in quality control. In deciding which one a fundraising program should emphasize, a sound mixture of both techniques is often recommended.

The collaborative/clan approach to fundraising program control can be enhanced by the concept of Management by Walking Around. Management by Walking Around (MBWA) is exactly that. Managers (i.e., fundraising program administrators) observe operations by simply walking around and having open discussions with fundraising team members. There are some distinct advantages to doing this:

1. MBWA brings fundraising control issues to the surface much easier than through bureaucratic channels.

2. MBWA provides immediate awareness to fundraising control issues through empirical observation.

3. MBWA has an enormous side benefit of being motivational to fundraising team members.

4. MBWA establishes an open culture.

5. MBWA gains fundraising information not derived by formal reports and control documents.

6. MBWA breaks down resistance and barriers to fundraising control standards.

7. MBWA is a great idea generator and a managerial learning tool.

8. MBWA penetrates the immensely persuasive informal communication channel (known as the grapevine).

The Control Process for Fundraising Programs

© Wrangler | Dreamstime.com

The steps in the control process follow the logic of planning: "(1) performance standards are set, (2) performance is measured, (3) performance is compared to standards, and (4) corrective action is taken if needed" (DuBrin, 2003, p. 413).

Before an elaboration of each step is given, it must be emphasized that the control process is not a separate, stand-alone element of the management concept but an integrated feature of management. Furthermore, while the process of control is essentially sequential, the actual variety of applications of the control process inside the fundraising program is unlimited. For the process to be effective, it must be an ongoing activity rather than an intermittent and occasional event.

The areas on which a fundraising program administrator can focus his/her control efforts parallels corporate/business dimensions. Corporate control dimensions are evaluated along the following:

- Quality of product and service
- Quality of management
- Innovativeness
- Long-term investment value
- Financial soundness
- Community and environmental responsibilities
- Use of corporate assets
- Ability to attract, develop, and keep talented people. (Wright, Knoll, & Parnell, 1996, p. 250)

Once again, these corporate operational control essentials can be customized to fit a fundraising program's administration/control:

- From the perspective of the quality of product, fundraising administrators' quantitative control criteria are based on the superiority of their fundraising program's output (event, activity, program, etc.).

- With their pre-established human resource systems, fundraising programs can develop control elements for the performance of fundraising team members (e.g. policy and procedures, performance evaluation systems, operational manuals).

- Innovativeness control aspects relate to how well the fundraising program keeps up with external, contemporary best practices as well as cultivating original internal administrative techniques.

- Long-term investment controls examine how well current dollars are being used for future fundraising program benefit. For example, a current investment in new equipment needs to be continuously inspected as to its potential fundraising program payoff in the future.

- Financial controls are essential for all fundraising programs. Budgets are established and fundraising administrators need to have control systems in place to make sure that the budgets are monitored and maintained.

- Because of the visibility of most fundraising programs, control systems should be established with the athletic organization's community and stakeholders/supporters in mind.

- Controlling the use of athletic organization assets in fundraising can relate to a facility, transportation, or the use and replacement of equipment, office machinery, etc.

- Another human resource control system that needs monitoring/controlling relates to the fundraising program's staffing system. Questions such as "How well is the fundraising program recruiting fundraising team members?" and "What is the quality of significant personnel additions?" need to be answered and evaluated.

Establish Performance Standards

The first factor in the control process for fundraising programs is establishing performance standards.

> Performance standards tell employees—in advance—what level of performance is expected of them. They also measure how well employees meet expectations… There are many ways of developing these standards, such as intuition, past performance, careful measurement of activities, and comparison with other standards or averages. Once standards of performance are set, they should be communicated by means of written policies, rules, procedures, and/or statements of standards to the people responsible for performance. Standards are valuable for stimulating good performance, as well as in locating sources of inefficiencies. (Megginson, Byrd, & Megginson, 2006, pp. 364-365)

The planning aspect of the fundraising process stresses that the program determine specific, tangible, and measurable goals. It should be noted that fundraising goals and performance standards have to be based on reality. The mission of a fundraising program administrator and leader should be to establish goals and standards that are challenging but achievable rather than discouraging or unrealistic.

Fundraising Tip

When establishing performance standards, use historical data as the starting point, but do not finish there. Study what other similar and successful fundraising programs have instituted as their performance standards. By merging the competition's standards along with historical foundations, a fundraising administrator can develop specific controls that are rational as well as realistic.

Measure Performance

There are two ways to measure performance in a fundraising program: One is through quantitative valuation; the other is qualitative, subjective observation. Many business organizations adhere strictly to the philosophy of judging performance according to the 'bottom line results.' They look meticulously at sales margins and profits. To rely solely on numbers for measuring fundraising program performance is a monumental mistake for a fundraising administrator. Motivational administrators will augment quantitative measurements with qualitative ones such as desire, intensity, and a concentrated effort to improve and fulfill fundraising goals.

Compare Actual Results with Projected Standards

This step in the control process is the easiest to comprehend. The underlying question is "How does the actual measured performance compare to the projected performance?" The most effective tool for this comparison would be to design a performance evaluation table/chart.

Corrective Action

The control process is completed by evaluating the variance between projected fundraising goals and actual fundraising achievements. The evaluation's outcome can necessitate one of three possible actions:

1. *Do nothing* – If meeting an acceptable range of variances, then do not adjust control system.

2. *Correct deviation* – If the variable falls outside acceptable limits, corrective action will be necessary. Positive deviations should be examined for new insights into such successes while negative deviations should be the foundations of learning.

3. *Revise standard* – After learning that there are certain variances, the revision of performance standards might be necessary. This, in turn, will re-track performance into achievable goals. (Bedeian, 1993, pp. 563-564)

If the individual fundraising event/activity/program exceeds standards and goals, readjust the standards to an elevated level yet still make them achievable. If the fundraising event/activity/program is not achieving standards:

1. Ask "why?"

2. Decide if the problem can be fixed.

3. Either maintain standards or readjust them to a more realistic range.

Feedback

The primary advantage of using an organized, participative control system in a fundraising program (whether for an individual or a fundraising team) is that it provides a basis for feedback. All material variances should be discussed whether they are positive or negative. How one handles those variances is a part of one's makeup as a

Fundraising Tip

The first scenario in the appraisal of a fundraising program's performance," do nothing," is associated with a potentially perilous long-term ramification—complacency. If there is ever an option in a managerial control situation, take the challenging choice over the complacency choice, especially in significant operating areas.

fundraising program administrator and leader. In the article "Giving good feedback," McLaughlin (2007) discusses seven methods to giving good feedback controls:

1. *Ask permission to give feedback* – You will not believe the difference in the level of conversation when you ask permission. Asking permission to give feedback sets a positive framework on a situation that could be perceived as negative.

2. *Set a tone of energy and optimism* – Consciously assume an attitude that embraces both candor and sensitivity.

3. *Focus on specifics* – When sharing feedback, focus on specific situations and behavior, rather than delving into psychoanalysis.

4. *Show appreciation and say thank you* – Let them know you value their time as well as their willingness to listen to your feedback.

5. *Confront non-performance* – Don't wait for the yearly review to tackle this issue.

6. *Remember it's a dialogue* – Not a monologue. Ask questions and listen attentively to answers. Offer suggestions and support. Jointly consider options.

7. *Encourage and energize* – Get excited about the changes your direct report can make. Give them examples of how they can improve and show that you're supportive of them making these changes. (McLaughlin, 2007, p. 7)

Conversely, Lindenberger (2007), in her article "Feedback without fear," describes some feedback fouls regarding control:

- Doing nothing. Ignoring the problem in hopes it will go away is probably the most common mistake.
- Giving only negative feedback. It is only human to focus on the things that bother you.
- Giving negative feedback months after the fact.
- Criticizing things your staffers don't know how to do better.
- Blaming the need for negative feedback on someone else. Take responsibility for feedback.
- Delivering drive-by feedback.
- Criticizing in public. Besides being humiliating, a public dressing-down hardly encourages the kind of two-way dialogue that leads to improvement.
- Criticizing via voicemail, email, or little notes. (Lindenberger, 2007, pp. 34-38)

Fundraising Tip

Throughout all aspects of the management process, the program administrator should aggressively scrutinize other comparable fundraising programs and, if they are doing better than his/her program, emulate them and even improve on their concepts and operations.

A fundraising administrator must communicate to his/her fundraising team that even though they are ultimately accountable for their own performance results, they are part of a team and the top priority is to help them achieve. If the fundraising administrator can instill this feeling into them and the overall fundraising program, the fundraising team will look forward to the challenges of higher performance standards rather than dreading them.

Summary of Fundraising Controls

The managerial aspect of control is vital in helping with the smooth flow of fundraising program operations as well as the ultimate realization of fundraising goals. Proper control systems isolate and solve problems, ensure quality benchmarks, monitor fundraising team performance, and prevent an athletic organization and its fundraising program from squandering limited resources. Through the proactive application of the control process, a fundraising administrator can standardize and measure fundraising team performance while conveying essential feedback to each member for improving and maximizing potential.

TECHNOLOGY FOR FUNDRAISING ADMINISTRATION AND CONTROL

The importance of technology as an internal component of fundraising administration and control cannot be overemphasized. Technology, through what is known as Management Information Systems (MIS), is the tool for accumulating, sorting, and reporting data that is essential for fundraising program control and decision making. The factors in the construction and implementation of an MIS in a fundraising program encompass the following three elements:

1. First and foremost, the goals (both short-term and long-term) of the fundraising program...will directly affect the depth and complexity of the MIS.

2. The financial resources available for hardware and software requirements for the fundraising program.

3. The information control need of the fundraising program users as well as their computer sophistication...a general rule is the more user friendly (with accomplishing all of the needs of the MIS), the better. For small athletic organizations and fundraising programs, the learning curve should be minimal.

In his 2001 text, Dove elaborates on

two fundamental aspects to establishing a system that is efficient and effective: selecting the right system for your environment and selecting the right people to install and support that system. The 80/20 rule is an important consideration in selecting the right computer system. This rule

Figure 7.1. **Fundraising Areas to Establish MIS Controls**

- **Construction, Access, and Monitoring Fundraising Plan and Strategies (both overall plan and event, activity, and program plans)**
- **D-Base of Current Supporters**
  - By Donation Level
  - Demographic Information
  - Geographic Information
  - Activity Level
  - Complete, Updated Contact Information
- **D-Base of Prospective Supporters**
  - Donation Potential
  - Demographic Information
  - Geographic Information
  - Complete, Updated contact Information
- **Fundraising Team Member Information**
  - Applications, Vitae, Resumes
  - IRS Information
  - EEOC Information
  - Other Personnel Information
- **Communication Systems**
  - Internal – to Fundraising Team Members, Board of Directors, Athletic Organization Administrators
  - External – Current and Prospective Supporters
- **Phone Logs and Contact Records**
- **Financial Systems**
  - Internal Budgeting Documents
  - Legally Require Non-Profit Accounting Statements and Reports
- **Marketing Information**
  - Marketing Research Data
  - Marketing Competitive Analysis Data
  - Marketing Communication Effectiveness Data
- **Fundraising Program Meeting Notes – Archive for Review**
- **Operational Data**
  - Team and Hierarchical Structures
  - Fundraising Schedules
  - Project Timelines
  - Post Event and Activity Reports
  - Job Descriptions
  - Online Policy and Procedure Manual
  - Training Systems
  - Contracts and Vendor Agreements
  - Risk Management – Incident Reports
- **Fundraising Program Asset Utilization**
- **Planned Gift Administration**
- **Publications**
  - Annual Reports
  - Fundraising Literature

states that 80 percent of users just want access to data (and want it now); they need to be able to see the data and produce, quickly and easily, reports that support their business. Only 20 percent will actually use the detailed functionality of any system. Remembering the 80/20 rule is fundamental in choosing the right system. Failure to do so will have two consequences. First, the system will contain only features that support its most sophisticated users (the 20 percent). Second, your organization's information system staff will then have the expensive task of building in the features that will support the remaining 80 percent of the users. (Dove, 2001, p. 311)

Some final points on technology as a control element in fundraising programs:

- Technology costs money up front but saves money in the long term.

- A fundraising MIS is only as good as its functionality.

- It is easy to get captivated by the 'bells and whistles' associated with newer hardware and software.

- If a fundraising program's resources are limited, prioritize necessities and acquire high priority items first. As funding increases, secondary MIS items can be acquired.

- No two fundraising MIS are alike; tailor-make the fundraising program's system to its specific operation.

- Due to the confidential information contained in a fundraising program's MIS, security must be a paramount consideration.

Summary of Technology for Fundraising Administration and Control

Developing an MIS for a fundraising program has tremendous operational advantages. An MIS can sustain internal efficiencies as well as cultivate external support, and the amount of systemic uses for a comprehensive MIS in a fundraising program is enormous. The selection and utilization of each component is up to the fundraising administrator and the needs of the fundraising program.

REVIEW AND DISCUSSION QUESTIONS

1. Define the term budgeting.
2. Why are budgets considered good managerial control tools?
3. Define MBWA. What are its advantages?
4. What is the four-step control process?
5. Define MIS. What are the three factors in the construction and implementation of a fundraising program's MIS?

FUNDRAISING EVENTS, ACTIVITIES, AND PROGRAMS

8

Fundraising Events and Activities

INTRODUCTION

Once the administrative fundamentals of fundraising discussed in Chapters 1-7 have been developed and implemented, fundraising can be focused on identifiable events and activities. The depth and application of each fundraising event and activity will depend on its overall complexity, the internal competencies of the athletic organization and its fundraising team, the revenue capabilities and upfront costs, and its popularity with the target market.

In this chapter, specific fundraising events and activities will be isolated and comprehensively described. In addition to a synopsis of each event, sections within each fundraiser will provide details about operating expenses, financial resources, planning requirements, estimates for revenue potential, event operating procedures, personnel needs, marketing and promotions principles, and miscellaneous planning and operational strategies.

GOLF TOURNAMENTS

Because of their attractiveness and allure, golf tournaments (either celebrity or general) are a central feature when considering fundraising events. Golf tournaments can furnish existing and prospective athletic organization supporters with a gratifying activity while producing significant revenue for the fundraising program. Additionally, a professional, well-organized golfing event can have an enormous impact on the goodwill of an athletic organization and its subsequent fundraising endeavors. While one takes considerable planning, a superior golf tournament (along with other revenue sources) can develop into a notable, if not extraordinary, resource generator. Tournament golfing can be in conjunction with an assortment of interconnected fundraising activities such as banquets, auctions, or other entertainment. The setting of the event (golf course/country club), as well as its promotion, is a critical component to its success.

The following points epitomize an all-purpose template for a golf tournament fundraiser:

- Teams are characteristically groups of four (foursomes). If celebrities are involved, teams of three with a celebrity designate for each group is a possibility.

- The maximum number of groups would (as a general rule) be 27 for an 18-hole tournament. This is determined by 18 starting groups—one per hole—with nine groups waiting to start every other hole.

- The time frame for a golf tournament's actual on-course golfing should be between five and six hours.

- To expedite groups moving through the tournament, a best ball/scramble format could be utilized. A best ball/scramble format is when after each stroke of all four players only the location of the group's best ball/shot will be applied for the next stroke by all four players. With this system of operation, scores will be reduced and the number of strokes minimized.

- Start times and schedules should be strictly adhered to. If not, group 'bottlenecking' and subsequent frustration can ensue.

- The fee structure should be consistent. Fees can be charged per person, per group, or per organization.

Other key points to emphasize when constructing a golf tournament fundraiser include:

- location and golf club/course duties and responsibilities;

- timing of the event and its importance in the community calendar;

- format/mechanics of the event to maximize proceeds;

- marketing and sales plans for both participants and sponsors;

- contingency options in case of inclement weather;

- celebrity acquisition and deployment; and

- supplementary revenue sources such as sack lunches for a nominal fee, skills contests such as hole-in-one or closest to hole competition, photographers who will take group, individual and action shots, refreshment stations throughout course, raffle tickets for donated prizes, and selling mulligans (3 for $10.00 as standard rate—mulligans are categorized as 'do-overs').

Table 8.1. Golf Tournaments

Capital or Annual Fundraising	Typically an annual fundraiser, apart from exceptional circumstances, in large athletic organizations where capital funds can be raised.
Financial Resources Commitment	In the early years of operation, the upfront financial obligations could be classified as moderate.
Planning Requirements	Because of the high visibility and participative nature of golf tournament fundraisers, the planning requirements are considerable.
Human Resource Requirements	High commitment of staff and volunteers; see Figure 8.1 for a detailed breakdown.
Fundraising Potential	Typically moderate to high, depending on the size of the event and supplementary revenue sources associated with the tournament.

Operating Procedures

Operating procedures for a golf tournament fundraiser depend essentially on two factors:

1. The complexity of the entire program (actual golf tournament and supplementary activities).

2. The contractual arrangement/obligations of the country club where the event is taking place.

Strictly speaking, the actual logistics for running a golf tournament fundraiser are comparatively straightforward.

Pre-Event Preparation

The pre-event set-up of the golf tournament fundraiser (in most cases) will be the responsibility of the golf course/country club. Items such as course maintenance, parking, golf carts, and clubhouse amenities will be taken care of in advance. Golf fundraiser event specific set-up can range from positioning course signage, facilitating registration and start times, establishing refreshment stations, and preparing auxiliary activities for operation.

Event Operations

The leading operating goal of a golf tournament fundraiser should be focused on the smooth operation of the event. In simplest terms, a well-run golf tournament has a systematic process in place that keeps participant teams moving along while avoiding bottlenecks. A sound tactic in facilitating tournament flow is to assign individual supervisors for each of the 18 holes. Along with hole supervisors, front nine and back nine coordinators should be used to help communicate between holes and to alleviate congestion.

Fundraising Tip

The community calendar for golf tournaments must be clear of similar events. Operating golf tournament fundraisers on the same weekend (or even consecutive weekends) could negatively influence attendance at one or both events. Additionally, due to the possibility of inclement weather, contingency dates must be secured under the same assertion.

Fundraising Tip

If feasible, complete as much pre-event set-up as is practical the day prior to the golf tournament (with the club's permission and no interference with regular course operations). Because golf tournaments have early start times/tee times, it is important to get as much pre-operational set-up done in the day (or days) preceding the fundraiser.

Figure 8.1. **Golf Tournament Positions and Responsibilities**

Tournament Coordinator

This position will oversee all facets of the fundraising event. Due to the magnitude of the position's responsibilities, it is recommended that a permanent, full-time athletic organization fundraising administrator or key board of directors member be employed.

Front Nine/Back Nine Coordinators

These on-course managers will facilitate the professional, well-organized operation of their designated course areas. They will report directly to the Tournament Coordinator.

Hole Supervisors (18)

Hole supervisors' responsibility is to expedite groups through their designated holes. Each hole supervisor will need to stay in communication with each preceding and subsequent hole supervisor as well as with front/back nine coordinators.

Registration Personnel

The registration team will be accountable for items such as fee collection (if not on a pre-paid basis), distribution of course tags, course maps, promotional packets, start times and locations, tournament rules, etc.

Refreshment Station Volunteers

These individuals will dispense an assortment of refreshments to tournament teams throughout the day. It is recommended that at least two stations be operated during the fundraiser (one on the front nine and one on the back nine).

Contest Staff

If the golf tournament fundraiser is to have a hole-in-one or closest-to-the-cup skill challenge, two volunteers will be needed per contest site - one volunteer will supervise the collection of fees and teeing off shot and a second volunteer will be used at the green to measure and record attempts. Communication between the two contest facilitators will be critical.

Other Potential Positions

Parking and Valet, Caddies (through country club or by fundraising volunteers), Announcers, Float Staff

Post-Event Operations

The physical breakdown of the course facilities will normally be completed by the management and staff of the country club. The golf tournament fundraiser team will need to:

- accumulate/tabulate the final scorecards;
- distribute team awards, gifts, and prizes;
- recognize sponsors;
- coordinate post gathering event/social/banquet (if applicable);
- account for event's operations (tabulation of funds received and expenses dispersed);
- facilitate participant departures;
- develop "thank-you" correspondence for all supporters and participants; and
- assemble the golf tournament fundraiser team to gauge the success of the event.

Fundraising Tip

An effective communication system should be utilized during the fundraising event. Coordinators at each hole should be in contact with one another as well as front nine/back nine coordinators. A side benefit of a strong communication system throughout the course is the continuous updating of the master scoreboard back at the clubhouse (if applicable).

Marketing and Promotion

As with all fundraising events, a principal ambition of marketing and promotional communication is to amplify the exposure for the event while curtailing costs. With this premise in mind, the following marketing components can be summarized.

Marketing Mix Components

PRODUCT

Golf is a sport where the majority of targeted consumers (in our case targeted athletic organization supporters) have an abundant amount of knowledge. In other words, due to the familiarity and 'golf intelligence' level of participants, product quality expectations are characteristically very high. Not all golf clubs and courses are the same. The course attributes and playing echelon can span from undesirable to PGA level. The fundraising program's selection of a course is a considerable determination of the current and future success of the event. Another aspect of the product is the professionalism of the volunteers' and athletic organization's overall operation of the event. A skillfully run tournament radiates class and sophistication. Unfortunately, a badly run golf tournament exudes ineptitude and a lack of propriety.

PRICE

The pricing model for a golf tournament fundraiser must appraise costs, market value, and customer perceptions. The initial aspect of pricing—costs—is essentially examining all expenditures associated with the event, adding on a projected profit margin, and calculating a definitive price. Market value pricing involves researching other analogous events and basing the price charge on competitors' prices (also called benchmarking). The third pricing concept, customer perception, is directly impacted by the quality expectations of the product in the consumer/supporter's mind. For example, if a golf tournament fundraiser is at a PGA-quality course with numerous amenities and a tournament banquet, the fundraiser supporter's perception of the worth of the event might warrant an above-cost and above-market fee. No matter what pricing structure (by individual, group, corporate) is chosen, it is vital to merge the three pricing methods together to come up with the best possible price for both supporters and the athletic organization.

PLACE

As was previously discussed, the location of the golf tournament event is a significant strategic component of the event product's quality. Another consideration is the locality's geographical position in relation to the targeted supporters. The more central the event's location, the more enhanced the supporters' experience. With that being said, a golf tournament fundraiser at a consummate course could be outside the general geographic region and nevertheless have maximum attendance.

PROMOTION

To reduce the cost of marketing communication while increasing the event's exposure (and ultimately attendance), there are several low-cost strategies that could work well with a golf tournament fundraiser:

- *Piggybacking on the sponsor's current marketing communication tools* – When acquiring sponsors for the golf tournament fundraiser, discuss with the sponsor's management team a viable and mutually beneficial marketing communications program for the event. The selling point to sponsors for this cooperative promotional communication tactic is the positive public relations and goodwill the event will bring to their organization.

- *Personal selling* – To acquire participants and group/corporate sponsors, personal selling by all fundraising team members as well as influential Board of Director members will be crucial.

Fundraising Tip

Other low-cost promotional tactics include adding the event to the athletic organization's website, having the hosting golf club post event flyers/posters throughout their facility, and distributing leaflets, brochures, and registration forms at sport- and golf-only retail outlets.

- *Word-of-mouth promotion* – An enormously valuable promotional tactic is to enlist not only everyone involved with the golf tournament fundraiser, but everyone in the athletic organization to create a positive word-of-mouth 'buzz' about the impending event. An essential element of this strategy is to educate each person involved in promoting the event so that no misinformation is given.

BANQUET FUNDRAISERS

Banquets are influential fundraising events geared toward philanthropic recognition and appreciation as well as future charitable contributions. Additionally, other luncheon/dinner events (while smaller in scope) can be vital sources of annual funds to augment operational budgets.

The central fundraising factors for luncheons/dinners/banquets are listed below:

- For a first-time event, the honoring of a cherished individual, program, or holiday which can invigorate community enthusiasm and collaboration is imperative. Someone who is an affluent, steadfast supporter of the athletic organization could be a recipient of an annual award (or have an annual award given in his/her name).

- It is essential to single out an event date to avoid conflict with other related events.

- A per-plate price should be established. The price determination is based on the occasion and importance to the community. Benchmarking comparable events by other familiar athletic organizations is a sound starting point.

- The banquet, which may be a yearly event or one-time exclusive activity, could be a black-tie affair involving prominent community and nationally renowned speakers.

- Determinations will be needed for the banquet's food quality and service level, beverage distribution (alcohol and non-alcohol), stage management, and floor design and set-up.

- Possible banquet themes can encompass (1) a 'get-to-know' luncheon/dinner that introduces and familiarizes alumni and athletic organization stakeholders with a new coach or athletic administrator, (2) a named banquet for an annual award, (3) an athletic organization's signature team's annual kickoff banquet and/or year-end banquet, (4) an 'All Sports Luncheon/Dinner/Banquet' (for fall sports, spring sports, or the entire athletic year), or (5) a Hall of Fame induction banquet.

- Other considerations include the printing of agendas and invitations; attendees' arrivals and departures along with parking arrangements; VIPs arrivals and departures along with preferred parking arrangements; entertainment (music, speakers, etc.); inclement weather contingencies; and accounting and contractual arrangements.

Fundraising Tip

There are dangerous financial scenarios associated with banquet fundraisers. The initial expenditures absorbed (upfront costs such as facility rental, music, food costs, and personnel) can be costly. Secondly, as with all special event fundraisers, the banquet must be timed/scheduled for maximum community/stakeholder involvement.

Prior to implementing a banquet fundraising plan, the fundraising team needs to construct a proactive break-even point analysis of the event. The break-even point for a banquet is the level at which attendance at the event will cover all of the event costs. If projections of turnout are below break-even attendance, the fundraising team could still have time to cancel or modify the event to minimize losses.

Table 8.2. **Banquets**

Capital or Annual Fundraising	**Banquets can be either a distinct capital fundraiser or an ongoing annual fundraising event.**
Financial Resources Commitment	**In the majority of cases, the financial resources necessary to operate a banquet fundraiser are considerable.**
Planning Requirements	**Because banquets entail an all-encompassing (and often community-wide) significance, their planning is considerable.**
Human Resource Requirements	**High commitment of staff and volunteers is needed for banquets; see Figure 8.2 for detailed positional breakdowns.**
Fundraising Potential	**Typically moderate to high, depending on the magnitude of the event and the banquet's importance to the community.**

Operating Procedures

Pre-Event Preparation

In most cases, if the banquet plan is adeptly constructed, pre-event set-up and preparation should be reasonably straightforward. Staff and volunteer timetables and responsibilities, meticulous and exhaustive floor schematics, food and beverage policies and procedures, and other banquet elements will be formulated and communicated with the entire fundraising team well in advance of the banquet date. While fundraising team members have explicit game-day tasks, each should be equipped and trained to assist with 'at-need' issues that can surface.

The best pre-event scenario is when the physical facility set-up takes place a day prior to the actual banquet. This time frame will allow for a heightened attention to detail as well as an opportunity for a comprehensive run-through of activities and testing of technology. If pre-event preparation/set-up is on the day of the event, the plan execution could be more problematic. Add to that the possibility of the event being outsourced to independent caterers and facilities, and the pre-event day could be exceptionally demanding and stressful. The solution to a smooth and stress free event set-up in these situations is developing and encouraging clear lines of communication between fundraising team members and the independent contractors.

Fundraising Tip

Prior to implementing a banquet fundraising plan, the fundraising team needs to construct a proactive break-even point analysis of the event. The break-even point for a banquet is the level at which attendance at the event will cover all of the event costs. If projections of turnout are below break-even attendance, the fundraising team could still have time to cancel or modify the event to minimize losses.

Fundraising Tip

The use of strategic alliances and one or more signature sponsors to underwrite both upfront costs and event expenses could be a viable way to develop a new fundraising banquet program. The signature sponsors need to be appropriate for the event, and all parties should experience a mutual benefit from the event.

Fundraising Tip

Do not assume
that independent
contractors know
what you mean or
what you want.
These assumptions
can lead to major
event mishaps. State
in clear terms (in
writing and verbally)
all stipulations,
conditions, and event
elements.

Fundraising Tip

A sense of urgency
is substantially
different to a sense
of panic. One
encourages energy
and efficiency—the
other is debilitating
and often destructive.
It is important, as
the fundraiser's
administrator, to
distinguish between
the two attitudes.

Event/Program Operations

Because banquets can be (and often are) spotlight events of an athletic organization's fundraising year, their undertaking must have certain foundational operational philosophies. The following is an inventory of these philosophies for a successful event:

- *A 'whatever it takes' attitude.* All fundraising team members, staff, and volunteers must have this mind-set instilled in them from the beginning of the banquet's planning process to the actual event. A 'whatever it takes' outlook is one that parallels the old maxim - failure is not an option. The magnitude of the event must be frequently communicated to all individuals involved in the banquet's operation and a communal sense of urgency must be developed.

- *A 'no one is above a job' approach.* Situations transpire at banquets that need immediate attention. If fundraising team members, staff, and volunteers selectively choose which items they can or cannot perform, the event will most certainly have major issues. A 'no one above a job' way of thinking means that if a banquet area needs cleaning, tables need bussing, or tables need moving, all available team members (including the banquet director/coordinator) will 'roll up their sleeves' and get the job done with little or no impact on the attendees. An unsurpassed technique for banquet administrators to get this atmosphere incorporated into the banquet is to lead by example.

- *An 'attendees are everything' way of behaving.* The collective experience of all attendees must be exceptional. For the future expansion and value of the event, all attendees' pre-conceived expectations must be met, if not exceeded. Within reason, each unique request and individual attendee's needs must be prioritized. It should be noted that the bigger and more complex the event, the more difficult individualized attention becomes. However, this should not be a disqualifying factor for fulfilling special requests.

- *A 'keep on schedule' operational approach.* Nothing can impair an attendee's experience more than having a two-hour programmed banquet turn into a four-hour marathon banquet. Adhering to a timetable/agenda is paramount to meeting attendees' expectations. Attendees can be directed toward the next component of the banquet by the use of general scheduled announcements as well as banquet itineraries.

A standard nighttime banquet program could encompass the following:

7:00 – 7:30 p.m.	Arrival and check in
7:30 – 8:00 p.m.	Open reception (meet and greet)
8:00 – 9:30 p.m.	Dinner and event activities (awards, speakers, etc.)
9:30 – 10:00 p.m.	Open reception (post-event socializing)
10:00 – 10:30 p.m.	Departure

**Reception schedule flexibility allows attendees to have options regarding arrival and departure times.

There are other strategic policy elements that can enhance a banquet's value and enjoyment:

- Analyzing traffic flow in all aspects of the event. Traffic flow includes:
  - arrival traffic and car parking;
  - spacing in reception area;
  - spacing and seating in banquet area; and
  - departures and road traffic.

- Premeditated and tactical positioning of all fundraising team members, staff, and volunteers. The more banquet area covered by fundraising team personnel, the more improved the experience for attendees. Each team member working the banquet should have a name tag which designates them as a part of the fundraiser. Figure 8.2 elucidates a comprehensive hierarchical structure for a banquet fundraiser.

Figure 8.2. **Banquet Hierarchical Chart**

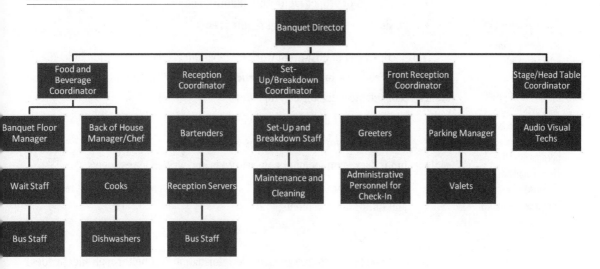

- Planned seating, festival seating, or a combination of both. Each seating scheme has its own challenges. Planned seating's foremost concern is with the assignment and placement of individuals and groups. Festival seating is logistically easier but has the confusion factor. A combination of designated and open seating can create an 'us-versus-them' feel to the event.

- In an attempt to keep the banquet stimulating, giving out door prizes, table prizes, or seat prizes can be beneficial.

- If utilizing an MC (Master of Ceremony), make certain that the personality is dynamic as well as committed to providing a quality experience for the attendees. Additionally, if guest speakers are used, confirm their appropriateness for the audience (are they speaking on a subject that has an appeal to all in attendance). Each presenter should know his/her time limits on their speech.

- Develop an event brochure and itinerary agenda. These pamphlets can contribute greatly in facilitating a smooth operating banquet.

Post-Event

The two principal factors for a banquet's post-event are facility breakdown and acquiring comprehensive feedback. From a breakdown perspective, if the banquet has been outsourced to a separate facility and/or catering enterprise, event breakdown is simplified appreciably. All the fundraising team needs to do is accumulate any exclusive athletic organization assets used for the banquet, settle accounts, and walk away. If the banquet is an in-house affair, a breakdown protocol will need to be established well in advance. The breakdown procedure could encompass:

- established checklist for each functional area;
- food and beverage storage protocol;
- inventory control on all athletic organization assets;
- inventory control on all rented/leased equipment;
- sequences of proper facility breakdown; and
- waste disposal and cleaning requirements.

The second facet of post-event work for a banquet is the compilation of feedback information. Feedback information is crucial to learning and improvement of future events. Feedback mechanisms can include:

- surveys of attendees (paper or electronic);
- formal and informal discussions with attendees;
- fundraiser team members observations and written assessments;
- fundraiser team member open forum discussions relating to event re-cap and future improvements; and
- any combination of the above tools.

Another competent source of valuable information can be through independent paid observers (in the retail industry known as secret shoppers, in the hospitality industry know as spotters). These individuals will attend the banquet just like any other athletic organization supporter. Their job during the banquet is to observe, record, and report their experience during all phases of the event. The key is to have them unknown to the fundraising team and to have them educated on the specifics that need to be evaluated.

Marketing and Promotion

Marketing Research

The two ingredients of a banquet fundraiser that need extensive research are:

1. *Community calendar* – There needs to be a collective group review of all coinciding community banquet type events for overlapping and spacing issues.

Fundraising Tip

The learning curve effect is an inherent issue with new banquet fundraisers. Banquets (and banquet type events) take experience to become effective. They should be classified as a continuous learning fundraiser.

2. *Targeted segment* – An exhaustive database must be constructed (from research) on past and future prospective athletic organization supporters as well as an all-inclusive alumni database.

An initial/inaugural banquet will have a tremendous time outlay for database formation and research. As the banquet becomes an annual event, research will build on previous years' efforts. Consequently, the time commitment for research and its expenditures will decrease.

Marketing Mix

The marketing mix components (product, price, place, promotion) must all be of superior quality, meet expectations, and have the necessary capability to generate the targeted funds of the banquet.

PRODUCT

The centerpiece of the event is focused around the quality of the food and beverages served during the banquet as well as the entertainment value of the speakers and activities. The theme of the banquet is another factor that directly affects the quality of the product (banquet). The banquet theme has to be in line with the banquet products being offered. For example, for an outdoor event with a 'picnic theme,' the food could be BBQ and the entertainment could be activity-based. Conversely, if the banquet theme is a black tie affair, the food could be steak and lobster and the entertainment could be VIP speaker-based. The key to selecting a banquet theme is that it must be one that is important to the projected audience and capable of being profitable.

PRICE

The three major pricing considerations (cost, competition, and value) are all factors that should be examined when contemplating what price to charge for attendance at a banquet event. From a cost perspective, the primary question is: At what price level can we cover all of our banquet expenses and still reach our projected revenue goals? Competitive pricing relates to benchmarking of similar banquets by rivals (athletic organizations or other not-for-profit entities). Finally, customer value is the balance between accomplishing fundraising goals and pricing according to the perceived value of the banquet in the minds of the targeted attendees. All three considerations need to be collectively examined to determine the feasibility of the event as well as its profit potential.

Unfortunately, the pricing breakdown and rationale can have a drastic impact on a banquet. One situation could be that the fundraising team, after scrutinizing the cost factors at a maximum attendance level, realizes that even with the highest possible price charged to the attendees, the fundraiser will not be able to cover all of its projected expenses. Another scenario could be that after completing a competitive analysis, the price charged to cover costs and fundraising goals is so significantly above a comparable community event that attendance will be beneath original projections. A final pricing possibility could be that the maximum value which can be provided does not meet the attendees' price expectations. All three circumstances can be devastating

Fundraising Tip

The quality of the event is a direct reflection on the athletic organization. The ultimate goal is for the attendees to leave the banquet with all of their expectations met and a sense of excitement for the next athletic organization banquet.

to a banquet fundraiser. For this reason, pricing considerations should be prioritized at the beginning of the banquet planning process.

From a logistical pricing vantage (after the above factors have been dissected), pricing structures can be based on individual seats, group rates, or table pricing. Group and table rates could be priced with built-in quantity discounts.

PLACE

Another necessary marketing mix element that can have a vast influence on the banquet event is the location of the banquet facility. In basic terms, the banquet's location has to be as convenient and accessible as possible to the highest number of attendees. The banquet's setting/ambience must be of the utmost quality and in accordance with the banquet's theme. However, having balance between a superlative facility and the cost for that locale is an underlying consideration for the event.

PROMOTION

In many cases, banquet fundraising will not use conventional promotional mix tactics (e.g. advertising, sales, promotions, direct mail). Because most banquets are by invitation, attendees (both general program supporters and VIPs) should be individually segmented and targeted. For this reason, the two primary promotional tools exploited for a banquet fundraiser will be personal selling and public relations. Personal selling will be concentrated on fundraising team members' (and B.O.D. members') exclusive communications with VIPs, alumni, and past supporters. Public relations will pursue community wide media outlets to initiate a 'buzz' about the event. Promotional material should consist of a superior quality invitation with RSVP responses incorporated.

CELEBRITY SIGNINGS

Because of the continually increasing popularity of autographed sports objects (uniforms, bats, balls, hats, etc.) and autographed paraphernalia (posters, magazines, books, pictures, etc.), an outstanding fundraising event for any size or category of athletic organization is a celebrity and/or team autograph day. A couple of noteworthy points to reflect upon when considering this type of event:

- The celebrity/team must be a 'known quantity' in the community in which the event is taking place.
- The media should be invited (and courted) to cover the event. The more the local/regional media covers the event, the more enhanced the current and future attendance for the fundraiser.
- If an athletic organization's team is the enticement for the autographing fundraiser, the occasion should be programmed as close as practicable to the start of the team's season. The primary justification for this tactic is for the promotion of ticket sales (indirect financial support), the advancement of athletic organization goodwill, and the influx of financial resources at a critical junction of the particular athletic team's season. It should be noted that the team signing date should in no way obstruct the team's (and individual athlete's) preparation and training.

Fundraising Tip

For a banquet event's continuous improvement, fundraising team members should benchmark and model components of other successful banquets. It should be noted that benchmarking should not only be used for major event elements, but small factors as well (attention to details).

- The autograph date could be a stand-alone event or could be incorporated into other fundraising activities. If integrated into other fundraising activities and events, it should not be 'buried' or obscured but be a major contributor to the combined fundraising endeavor. In fact, if the celebrity's popularity is considerable, the signing could possibly be the 'crowd-pleaser' and highlighted feature for other fundraising activities.

Table 8.3. Celebrity Signings

Capital or Annual Fundraising	Annual fundraiser except for rare instances when the participating celebrity's autograph is highly prized and could contribute to a major capital project.
Financial Resources Commitment	Modest upfront commitment, primarily for celebrity's appearance fee and pre-event marketing materials.
Planning Requirements	Relatively easy compared to other fundraising events, but planning should remain formal and event goals should still be set.
Human Resource Requirements	Low commitment of staff and volunteers; event could be completed with relative ease by 4-6 people; see Figure 8.3.
Fundraising Potential	Typically moderate to high, depending on status of celebrity, especially since upfront costs are low.

Generally speaking, a celebrity signing is a relatively easy fundraising event to conduct due to its lack of complexities regarding planning and personnel requirements. Because of the simplicity of the actual event, formal event-day volunteer training could be as little as a solitary meeting and an event-day walkthrough. Depending on the popularity of the celebrity, financial resources are generally low and there is an opportunity to generate moderate to high levels of revenue.

Fundraising Tip

It is strongly recommended that a formal contractual arrangement be made with any and all external celebrities participating in the event. As with all contracts/letters of agreement/ arrangements, legal counsel should be proactively involved.

Figure 8.3. Human Resource Positions for a Celebrity Signing Fundraiser

Celebrity Signing Coordinator
Oversees all functions of the event: marketing, celebrity liaison, contracts, ordering, and operations

Marketing Director
Accountable for all marketing and public relations communications as well as actual event-day promotions

Event-Day Volunteers

Inventory Manager
Control and distribution of tangible products

Celebrity Assistant
Needs and transportation of celebrity

Event Operations
Maintaining signing system and fan control

Operating Procedures

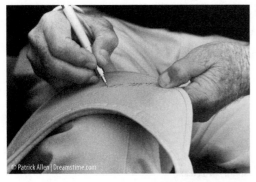

© Patrick Allen | Dreamstime.com

Pre-Event Preparation

The selection of a date and time is the first pre-planning item that must be addressed. The date and time determination for the fundraiser could be based on the availability of a celebrity or team, the fundraising program's competition and their scheduled events, the community calendar, and the target market's availability.

Once a suitable date and time are established, the next (and most vital) aspect of pre-event planning/preparation is the choice and procurement of an appealing, broad based, and well recognized celebrity. Because the most admired and fashionable celebrities have multifaceted and limited time schedules, their participation must be secured at least six months in advance (if not earlier).

Special Note: When securing a celebrity, analytically examine each prospective celebrity's net profit potential. Due to often enormous salary requirements (upfront guarantees, travel, per unit profit cuts, etc.), not all celebrities are suitable for every athletic organization fundraising program. Do not get 'swept away' in the fame and status of a celebrity without investigating whether he/she will cost more than the signing could ever generate. A break-even analysis is a judicious and sensible course of action for any celebrity signing.

Pre-planning the location of the fundraising event should encompass selecting a location that is well known, central to the community and targeted fan base, suitable for a celebrity signing, can facilitate the projected number of attendees, and exudes the image that the celebrity and athletic organization want.

Finally, sports items and paraphernalia for signing must be highly prized by the targeted market, appropriate for and approved by the celebrity, and cost effective. If possible, acquire memorabilia on consignment to limit the event's liabilities and increase the net profit potential of the fundraiser. Often, celebrities and their representatives have suggestions for this component of the event.

Event-Day Operations

The actual event day must be meticulously scheduled to maximize the limited time most celebrities can commit for this type of fundraiser. A signing system must be utilized to ensure the flow of items being signed and to supervise the interaction of fans with the celebrity. Celebrity signings are more than the tangible signatures. They include an interfaced communication between the celebrity and each individual fan/customer. A system must be planned in advance to balance celebrity and fan interaction with the expeditious use of the limited time inherent in all celebrity signings.

An inventory of memorabilia to be signed must be monitored continuously during the event. If the fundraiser has multiple lines of items to be autographed, different prices could be charged for each item. For example, if the celebrity signing has a

Fundraising Tip

Fundraising products acquired by consignment (which is the transfer of goods from one party to another without the actual transfer of ownership of those goods) is by far the best possible scenario for any type of fundraiser. At the completion of the fundraiser, a pre-established percentage of profits from sold products will be presented back to the consignment company (original owner). All unsold (and undamaged) products are handed/transported back to the consignment company without any financial burden to the athletic organization.

baseball athlete, items to sign could include photos/posters, balls and bats, helmets, and uniforms. High priced items (uniforms and exclusive collector items) could be available on a pre-ordered, pre-paid basis.

Post-Event Evaluation and Feedback

Post-event appraisals and feedback can be obtained through quantitative measures as well as subjective judgments. Quantitatively, the number of fans/attendees and the aggregate sum of revenue generated will be the fundamental determinates of the event's success. If possible, customer surveys, which can be a way to quantify the attendees' opinions, could be conducted to supplement 'hard data.' Subjectively, a frank discussion with all fundraising team members could provide opinions and insights into improving future events.

Marketing and Promotions

Marketing Research

The marketing research prior to the initiation of a celebrity signing program should converge on three primary areas:

1. The community/fan perception of the prospective celebrity.

2. The community calendar for conflicting events.

3. Cost and value expectations of the targeted community/fan base for the event.

Both quantitative (i.e., tabulated surveys) and qualitative research (i.e., personal interviews) should be used to gather relevant data.

Marketing Mix Components

PRODUCT

As previously stated, the selection of the celebrity, individual or team is the strategic key to the achievement of the fundraiser. Secondary elements of the product such as the venue and sports items to be autographed are also critical components of the overall product. Since the event is a visual component of the athletic organization and its fundraising program, it should radiate refinement and class.

PRICE

The estimated costs (both upfront and operations), the market value of products to be autographed, and the projected number of fans/customers are all fundamental considerations when constructing a pricing structure for the event. Research diligence and an overall consensus must be established when forecasting these three factors. Guesswork should never be an option. The more hard data is utilized, the more accurate the pricing decisions. Researching other similar celebrity signings is the first (but not last) step in the pricing of the fundraiser. The fundraising administrator and team must clarify all of the costs and value of the event to prospective attendees in their pricing structure decisions.

The distribution of the product (celebrity autograph) needs to be conducive to maximum participation. The primary determinants in the selection of a venue for the fundraiser should be its location (centrally situated), its level of class, and how well it represents the athletic organization and celebrity. A less important, but still noteworthy, consideration is the cost of the facility rental (if applicable).

PROMOTION

If the product, pricing structure, and location of event are well designed, then the predominant goal of the marketing communication component will be to create a community-wide consciousness and enthusiasm for the celebrity event. Some promotional tactics could include:

- attaching the celebrity signing date and time to all possible community calendars;

- piggybacking the fundraising event on related websites;

- personal selling of the event to media outlets and local news organizations (public relations tactics for a celebrity signing could be the catalyst in rallying the community and fan base);

- selection of advertising avenues (within resource limits) to maximize exposure of the event; and

- sending direct mailers to alumni and fan support groups.

Miscellaneous Information

If the initial cost of sports items is prohibitive, then the celebrity signing fundraiser could have a 'bring your own item' format. No matter what items are being signed, a standard per autograph fee or admission price could be charged. This type of format would need to be discussed and approved by the celebrity participating in the event with acceptable and non-acceptable items agreed upon in advance. Benchmarking should be employed to observe the 'nuts and bolts' of a celebrity signing. If a celebrity sports signing cannot be found, an empirical observation of a book signing could assist in establishing the right format.

DREAM AUCTIONS

Dream auctions are fundraising events that can be administered as one-time capital projects or annual events. Because of the amount of preparation required, dream auctions are not suitable as a perpetual fundraising program. The endeavor's basic structure is as follows.

The fundraising team and volunteers solicit charitable gifts and services from local, regional, and national individuals/entrepreneurs/businesses. The assortment and variety of items is contingent upon what the auction's targeted market will appreciate and be inclined to bid on. Acquisition of popular auction items for the fundraiser could include (but is not limited to) restaurant certificates, vacation packages, health

Fundraising Tip

It is important that the celebrity participating in the event receive first class treatment. Not only will this help ensure his/her future participation, it could also encourage other celebrities to participate.

club memberships, spa services, and personal training sessions, golf and tennis club memberships, sports items, and paraphernalia, entertainment tickets, professional training seminars, books and collector items, clothing and athletic wear, and miscellaneous vehicles. The observable benefits for businesses that donate products and services are (1) the generation of awareness of the business and its products/services and (2) the establishing and building of a positive public image. Additionally, all contributions are at cost and tax deductible. It should be noted that businesses are more prone to donate products/services than hard cash because products/services are valued at market prices but have cash costs at substantially reduced amounts.

The fundraising team during the product/service acquisition process should inaugurate an intense promotional campaign to publicize the event. All 'blue chip' donations of products and services should be tied into the promotional campaign to increase interest and attendance at the event.

There should be a prearranged, structured 'game plan' for the solicitation of products/services for the event. A plan of action can be constructed based on geographic factors, business delineation, or specific products/services targeted for the event. Composition of the plan should include who will be accountable for specific business contacts, timeframes for solicitations, and targeted team and individual solicitation goals. The plan should be monitored continuously by the fundraising program's administrator for progress on products/services acquired and 'gaps' in the auction's solicitations.

Fundraising Tip

All documentation and tax forms for individuals and businesses donating products and services should be prepared in advance of the solicitation program. The preparation of documentation should follow both legal (IRS and state tax regulations) and AICPA guidelines. All forms and documentation should be examined by legal counsel and tax consultants.

Table 8.4. **Dream Auctions**

Capital or Annual Fundraising	Dream auctions could be one-time capital endeavors or conducted as annual events to augment operational revenues.
Financial Resources Commitment	Depending upon the theme, locality, dimension and complexity of the auction fundraiser, the upfront costs associated with this form of fundraising event could be moderate to exceptionally high.
Planning Requirements	Due to the magnitude and intricacy of dream auctions, most will be a central component of the athletic organization's annual fundraising plan.
Human Resource Requirements	The human resource requirements for dream auctions would be considered substantial. The actual event's human resource requirements will once again depend on the magnitude and sophistication of the fundraiser; see Figure 8.4.
Fundraising Potential	If initial pre-event costs and operating expenses can be controlled, the fundraising potential from a dream auction is significant.

Fundraising Tip

To augment the actual auction event, some organizations are utilizing pre-auctioning through online bidding. This system can be established for a terminal time period or could be used as continuous fundraisers.

The affair, through a public auction format, barters and sells donated items for auctioned values. For sizeable auctions, it would be advisable to enlist the aid of a professional auctioneer to facilitate bidding. Another viable alternative is the concept of silent (both open and blind) auctions where products/services are displayed for people to bid on them in a direct format. Each item will have a starting bid displayed, and participants tender offers from that price point.

Actual Operation and Event-Day Activities

Planning for the actual event day will relate directly to the type of auction, target market, goals, and premise being utilized. No matter which type of auction is planned, there are some customary event elements which will need to be planned for.

Displays – The separate displays for each of the fundraiser's products and services must be not only positioned in an appropriate location but must be designed for their individual allure and ease of examination.

Flow of items – The pre-auction displays must be collectively 'laid out' in the most conducive system to facilitate traffic flow. Exhibits can be in straight lines and angles, circular, or pre-determined designs. The key is spacing and walking room. Additionally, items could be displayed in groups by their value, product, or service type. A floor plan of displays (or schematic) is a good option to consider when contemplating traffic flow for a dream auction. 'Blue chip' products and services should have positions of prominence in the floor plan.

Establishing an opening bid price – The formation of an opening bid price for products/services can be through a subjective determination of the worth of an item to the targeted attendees or though a standardized formula. One workable technique is the straight-line percentage rule. For example, if donated tickets to a sporting event have a face value of $100.00 and the fundraising team establishes a 75% rule on all items, then under that 75% rule the opening bid for the tickets would be $75.

Event-day program/brochure – A fundamental and indispensable component of a dream auction is the event-day program/brochure (which includes a schedule of activities as well as a directory of items up for auction and their locations). The program's structure, graphics, and narrative descriptions of items to be auctioned should be completed as early as possible. Conversely, the actual program/brochure should be printed as close to the event date as possible to include any last-minute donations. A general rule that goes with auction programs/brochures: The more detailed, while being user friendly, the better.

Food and beverages – If the auction is a major fundraiser with food, beverages, and entertainment, the complexity of pre-planning for the event will be extensive. If food and beverages are outsourced to the hosting facility, which may be a stipulation of contracting the facility, then the construction of menus, time schedules, and service type will need to be planned and agreed upon. If food and beverages are an in-house function of the fundraising program, additional planning, ordering, storage, and preparation will be added to the event.

Operating Procedures

Pre-Event Operations

The pre-event set-up will be a fundamental success factor of the dream auction. If an athletic organization's facility is being utilized, set-up should commence well in advance of the actual occasion. If an external rented facility is being contracted, set-up time may be regulated and limited. A prearranged display diagram should be utilized to expedite the configuration and construction of the event, and a pre-event conference should be conducted to reiterate the distribution of staff and volunteers as well as the redefining of event responsibilities. A centrally situated cash processing area should be assembled for the efficient handling of food and beverage purchases, miscellaneous donations, and auction settlements.

If an external facility is engaged for the event, a facility liaison should be accessible throughout the entire affair (especially during set-up/pre-event operations). It is strongly recommended that either in-house or outsourced security be employed for protecting all donated items, overseeing cash drops, and overall event safety patrol. High-value auction items should be continuously monitored by the security staff. A communication system (whether through conventional cell phones, pagers, two-way radios, etc.) should be developed so all team members can communicate with each other. It should be emphasized that this system is intended for event operations only, rather than miscellaneous, extraneous conversations.

If applicable, food and beverage storage and set-up should be controlled and well organized. Additionally, waste handling should be systematized and strategically placed in various areas of the facility. As with all major fundraisers, if food and beverages are being made available, their quality and distribution must be superb. A few planning decisions

Figure 8.4. Dream Auction Human Resource Positions

Auction Director
This position will oversee all facets of the fundraising event from pre-planning and solicitations to event management and evaluation

Solicitation Coordinator
- Pre-planning and human resource sales training
- Tracking donations
- Staff and volunteer solicitations and accountability
- Coordination of donation placement at auction
- All post-event thank-you communications

Event-Day Coordinator
- Liaison with external facility and staff
- Coordination of all food and beverage activities (inventory, distribution, etc.)
- Event entertainment and actual auction (traditional or silent)
- All purchases and cash handling/accounting
- Auction set-up and breakdown
- Supervision and coordination of all staff and volunteers
- Supervision of specialized staff (i.e. bartenders, professional auctioneers, etc.)

Auction Volunteers
The placement and individual responsibilities of the fundraising volunteers will be determined by the sophistication of the fundraiser, amount of compensated outsourced staff, and pre-planned requirements.
- Food and beverage preparations and services
- Parking valet and attendants
- Coat and hat check staff
- Set-up and breakdown crews
- Auction facilitation
- Information and patron services
- Float staff

that will affect the pre-event set-up are:

- alcohol vs. non-alcoholic event;
- cash vs. open bar;
- self-service vs. waiters; and
- buffet vs. sit-down.

Event Operations

A primary point in event operations will be adhering to the pre-established (and published) time schedules. However, there must be equilibrium between keeping schedules and rushing patrons/attendees through the event. Time schedules should have a pre-planned flexibility through 'tweener' breaks in sessions/activities. For example, a 15-minute tweener break should be worked into the transition between reception and open auction period.

During the programmed reception time prior to the actual auction, it is important for the public image of the athletic organization that both athletic and fundraising administrations socialize with the alumni and business leader guests. The athletic organization's Director/CEO should greet and welcome all incoming guests. If an open auction format is employed, a central, skillfully organized seating area should be used. If a silent auction format is utilized, winning bids should be announced in the facility's main hall. This locality should be large enough for all participants to comfortably gather inside.

The fundraiser will need to have definitive job responsibilities, timetables/schedules, and break periods for all staff and volunteers involved in the event. Each individual should have detailed knowledge of his/her exact duties throughout the entire duration of the fundraiser. In addition, a high-quality sound system should be used to communicate all event announcements. It should be tested (and re-tested) to ensure that it can be heard throughout the entire facility, both inside and outside.

There should be an organized and accurate system for the procurement of funds from auctioned items and the distribution of merchandise and service certificates. A pre-established and well-marked area of the facility should be employed. A pre-determination will need to be made on the method of payments (e.g. credit cards, on-account/billed, checks).

Post-Event Breakdown and Evaluation

The breakdown of the fundraiser should be methodical and safe. From beginning to end, dream auctions can be time-consuming events to construct and administer. The more organized the fundraiser's breakdown, the less chance of mishaps and accidents.

As with all fundraisers, thank-you notes, letters, calls, and other appreciation communications should be well organized and completely comprehensive. No one who contributed or worked the event should be omitted. From the major players, alumni, and businesses to the set-up and breakdown crews, everyone should be recognized and thanked.

If the event is outsourced to an external facility or catering operation, formulate and utilize an inventory listing of all internal athletic organization property/assets used in the event. In many cases, if an inventory system is not used, athletic organization items will be (by no fault of the external facility or catering operation) gathered and integrated into the external enterprise's supplies. The subsequent recovery of those internal program items could be time consuming and arduous.

If products and services donated are not auctioned during the event, a standard post-event policy should be to contact the donating individual/business and request to use the item(s) for other possible fundraisers and promotions. This courtesy call/contact should have a tone of continuous gratitude while conveying a new public relations and promotional opportunity for the donating individual or business.

All cash transactions (and, if applicable, credit transactions) should be tabulated and balanced during and/or immediately following the event. With the power and mobility of computers, transaction processing and recording systems should be straightforward and professional. All event reporting should be within athletic organization and governmental regulations.

The post-event evaluation should be a compilation of opinions from all concerned parties/stakeholders as well as a quantitative analysis of results (profitability of event). Opinions, which should target continuous improvement of the fundraiser, can be submitted through an open dialogue or by anonymous survey instruments.

Marketing and Promotions

Marketing Research
Some of the tactical areas on which to concentrate marketing research efforts prior to the development and execution of a dream auction encompass:

- researching community calendars and regional schedules to circumvent any possible conflicting programs;

- researching the demographic makeup of the targeted audience for the auction. A critical demographic element would relate to the income level/discretionary income of the targeted group(s); and

- researching public and business perception of the athletic organization. This community interest could also include athletic organization alumni and booster groups.

Marketing Mix

PRODUCT
As with all major fundraisers, the superiority of the product (in this case auction) is a direct reflection on the quality of the athletic organization. While the leading goal of the event is to produce substantial funds for the athletic organization, a derivative objective would be to enhance the image of the athletic organization. The key to the overall superiority of the event will be the precision and organization of the fund-

Fundraising Tip

Because of the significance and value of the fundraising event, research for a dream auction should incorporate primary research to supplement secondary sources. This blended approach of primary and secondary research should provide an authentic, true picture of the current and future fundraising capabilities of a dream auction.

raiser. An organized and 'smooth' operating event will emanate class; a chaotic event will jeopardize not only future auctions but other potential fundraisers.

PRICE

The bidding price process will be impacted by the number and nature of the participants and the desirability of the items being auctioned. As previously stated, a standardized formula could be instituted for initiating opening bid prices. Other pricing decisions involved in dream auctions could relate to:

- door admission prices;
- open vs. cash bar prices;
- per plate charges (if applicable); and
- auxiliary fundraising activities included in auction program (e.g. raffles, ticket sales).

Pricing decisions for dream auctions should incorporate all three pricing methods: cost/break-even, benchmarking similar auction prices, and the projected values of the products and services being auctioned.

PLACE

The location of the auction is very important to the fundraiser's success. The facility, grounds, parking, and overall venue all set the tone for the entire fundraiser. Place/location considerations should encompass:

- centralization in relation to the target audience;
- parking and access to the auction;
- relation to the auction theme;
- capacity and projected attendance;
- food and beverage distribution; and
- overall appropriateness of the facility for an auction fundraiser.

PROMOTION

With the product, price, and location of the event solidified, the marketing communication plan can be developed. The first component in marketing communication/promotion should be to determine the major promotional campaign goals for the event. The goals for the dream auction should entail:

- informing the community of the event and creating a collective awareness and expectancy;
- persuading the targeted audience to attend the event (by means of the AIDA technique discussed in Chapter 6);
- educating and informing the community about the fundraiser (especially if the dream auction is a new community wide event); and

Fundraising Tip

While it is very possible to be profitable the first time operating a dream auction, there is also the likelihood that the fundraiser will need multiple operations to yield the expected results. However, once the fundraiser has been 'fine-tuned' and is anticipated by the community and athletic organization alumni, its potential as a substantial source of funds is tremendous.

- 'jogging the memory' of the target audience for the fundraiser (if the dream auction is an annual fundraiser event).

With the auction's marketing communication goals identified, a wide variety of promotional techniques can be exploited. Advertising and publicity tactics, sales promotions, direct mail, and personal selling should all be incorporated into a coherent communication plan.

Miscellaneous Information

The decision on auction format is a salient one. If a silent format is chosen, a subsequent decision will need to be made about whether the silent bids will be in an open format or a blind format. An open format will typically have the auctioned products and services displayed with a bidding clipboard. Individuals bidding on the item will write their bids on the clipboard's auction sheet. Obviously, bidders will know what the highest bid is on the auction sheet. A blind format will have the item on display (and its beginning bid price) with a secured container/box for bids. Bidders will write out an individual auction slip with their personal information and bid price, and place it into the secured container/box. All bids will be evaluated at the end of submission time and the person with the highest bid gets the item. If an item's winning bid has two equal bids/bidders, a bid-off could be conducted or the item could be put back on a limited scheduled open bidding.

Fundraising Tip

When planning an entertainment fundraiser, the acquisition of the venue and entertainment should be simultaneous. Simply put, one will profoundly influence the other.

Table 8.5. Entertainment Fundraiser

Capital or Annual Fundraising	Contingent on the entertainment choice and organization's commitment to the fundraising event, entertainment fundraisers would, for the most part, be categorized as annual fundraising events.
Financial Resources Commitment	The upfront financial resource commitment for entertainment programs can range from minimal to astronomical depending on the venue, entertainment, and operational expenses.
Planning Requirements	The dimension and impact of the entertainment event will determine if it will be a primary or secondary component of the overall athletic organization's fundraising plan.
Human Resource Requirements	Each entertainment fundraiser will have its own unique human resource needs. Figure 8.5 examines different entertainment categories' staffing needs.
Fundraising Potential	The potential for an entertainment fundraiser often hinges on the definitive pre-arrangements to the actual event. A 'signature' entertainment event that employs fashionable entertainment (athletic or non-athletic) has tremendous gross profit potential. The net profit realized by the fundraiser will depend heavily on pre-determined contractual obligations.

ENTERTAINMENT FUNDRAISING EVENTS

Entertainment programs and events as fundraisers can provide an influential and diverse range of applications and benefits to an athletic organization. Because athletics and sport are by definition entertainment, athletic organization and fundraising program administrators can concentrate their attention on activities they can comprehend and appreciate. From an athletic organization standpoint, sponsoring sport-specific guest speakers, indoor and outdoor contests and tournaments, and professional and Olympic exhibitions are just a handful of athletic-exclusive events that can be used as fundraisers. Non-athletic entertainment can encompass musical groups or singers, comedians, satirists, and popular lecturers.

Operating Procedures

Pre-Event Preparation

If the event is outsourced to an independent facility, then most of the pre-event preparation and set-up will be coordinated by a fundraising team member/liaison and a representative for the venue. In these cases, a clear picture of all event prerequisites and obligations needs to be underscored in the contractual arrangement. If the entertainment event is in an athletic organization's private facility, pre-event planning and set-up is more problematic. For uncomplicated events (e.g., comedians), pre-event set-up could be as straightforward as cleaning the facility, testing and turning on the sound system, and constructing a backstage backdrop. Complex events could necessitate:

- extensive preparation (field, court, auditorium, etc.);
- coordination of a sizeable collection of volunteers;
- event purchasing and inventory; and
- food and vendor set-up.

Event Operations

As with pre-event planning and set-up, the sophistication of the entertainment along with which event mechanisms are outsourced will determine the depth and intricacy of the operation. No matter which category of event, a universal operational consideration will be maintaining a publicized time schedule (including start, breaks/intermissions, and conclusion). Observance of a pre-established schedule will not only benefit attendees but facilities managers and entertainers as well. If the admissions, entrance fees, or tickets for the event are sold in advance, event-day accounting is a minimal or even a non-issue. However, if admission, entry fees, or tickets are sold at the door, then accounting systems will need to be in position before and throughout the operation. If an entertainment event is in an auditorium (or seated facility), a major event decision will relate to whether an assigned seat format or festival seating method (first come first serve) will be used. It should be noted that for extremely popular entertainers, festival seating would not be appropriate due to the hazards involved with crowd control.

Figure 8.5. Entertainment Programs Human Resource Chart

Musical + Comedians **Event Coordinator** **Marketing and Sales Manager** **Entertainment Coordinator/Liaison** **Ticket Manager** **Stage Manager** *Seating Coordinator *Ushers *Parking Attendants **Set-Up and Break Down Coordinator** *Set-Up and Break Down Staff **Food and Beverage Manager** (if applicable)	**Speakers** **Event Coordinator** **Marketing and Sales Manager** **Ticket Manager** *Seating Coordinator *Ushers *Parking Attendants
Tournaments and Competitions **Tournament Director** **Referee Coordination** **Scoring Manager** *Court/Field/ Location Managers *Operation Staff – Referees, Scorers, Runners **Food and Beverage Manager** (if applicable)	**Exhibition Competition** **Event Manger** **Marketing and Sales Managers** **Ticket Managers** **Teams Coordination/Liaison** *Ushers *Parking Lot Supervisor and Attendants **Set-Up and Break Down Coordinator** *Set-Up and Break Down Staff **Food and Beverage Manager** (if applicable)

Bold - *Positions that should be occupied by permanent/employed fundraising administrators and/or staff.*

***Asterisks** - Positions that should be filled by event-day volunteers.*

Post-Event Procedures

Post-event procedures, evaluations, and feedback could include the following:

- breakdown and clean-up of facilities (either outsourced or by an in-house group of volunteers);

- accounting reconciliation with advanced sales, at door sales, and actual attendees; and

- post attendance surveys for both attendees and volunteers which focus on continuous improvement of the event.

Marketing and Promotion

Marketing Research

Marketing research for this type of fundraiser extends beyond the examination of the community calendar to include a comprehensive assessment of whether the proposed entertainment is appropriate for a targeted audience. This entertainment feasibility study can utilize research instruments such as surveys, focus groups, interviews, and benchmarking analysis.

Fundraising Tip

The entertainment must match the targeted audience. If the entertainment is adult in nature (which includes many contemporary comedians, satirists, musical groups, and speakers), proper safeguards must be put in place to ensure that the audience is mature.

Marketing Mix

PRODUCT

Over and above the primary product (i.e. the entertainment), a fundraising team needs to examine the possibilities of supplementary products that will (1) complement the entertainment and (2) generate substantial funds for athletic programs. Items to consider can consist of, but are not limited to, the following:

- in-house athletic department merchandise sales (e.g. apparel, paraphernalia);
- a percentage of profit for selling the entertainer's merchandise;
- food and beverage sales;
- other opening acts;
- parking and valet services;
- backstage passes, VIP seating, and post-event social gatherings; and
- CDs and recording sales of the entertainer's performance.

If these and other products are developed and utilized to supplement the entertainment fundraiser, they should be properly positioned, visible, and designed to attract sales.

PRICE

The price charged for the entertainment fundraiser will directly impact the turnout for the event and most of the subsequent variable costs associated with the program. While pricing decisions concerning the entertainment should include a scrutinizing of costs and competition, the uppermost price method should be the market value (or what the market/customer can and is willing to pay) for the entertainment. Knowing aspects of the target market (such as how much appreciation and significance the customer places on the entertainment) is a necessary preliminary consideration pertaining to whether the fundraiser will be able to cover all of the event's fixed and variable costs, as well as reach all of the projected fundraising earnings goals. To determine the market price of the entertainment, some foundational factors will include:

- comparing pricing structures of other similar entertainment fundraisers, not only generally but for the specific athletic organization's geographic region;
- goodwill the athletic program has with the targeted supporters/attendees and how that will affect market price flexibility (for example, a high profile athletic program that has strong community goodwill can add to the perceived value of an entertainment event because of what a customer is willing to pay to support that program);
- current economic conditions and how they impinge on the target market's discretionary income;
- demographic characteristics (especially earning levels) of the event's target market; and

- the prestige of the entertainment and how that can sway the price the target market is willing to pay.

A final notation on pricing: from all the above components (and other event-specific elements), the demand for the entertainment fundraiser is the key. The more state-of-the-art and popular the entertainment, the greater the price the customer is willing to pay for it.

PLACE

As discussed throughout this fundraising component, the selection of a venue is a principal consideration for an entertainment fundraiser. Cost, capacity, location, adaptability, availability, perception, and all-inclusive suitability are primary considerations in the selection of an appropriate venue.

PROMOTION

The promotional communication element in the marketing mix for an entertainment fundraiser should be a profoundly accentuated aspect of the entertainment fundraiser. The achievement of the fundraiser will unquestionably depend on it. The primary marketing communication goals should be two-fold. First, the fundraising team should generate a community-wide awareness for the fundraiser. Secondly, the fundraising team should solicit direct sales from the marketing communication tactics employed.

All five marketing communication tools should be used to maximize interest and attendance. Advertising (mass paid communication), sales promotions and discounts, personal selling, public relations, and direct marketing should be blended into a cohesive and aggressive plan that will accomplish the primary goal (getting people to attend and maximum contributions). Creativity and capitalizing on dollars spent has to be a philosophical foundation of the marketing communication plan.

Fundraising Tip

The pre-game, in-game, and post-game events should in no way impinge on coaches or athletes. They need to focus their cognitive and physical preparations on their competition. The fundraising activities should be known and endorsed by all parties associated with the main competition.

Table 8.6. Game-Day Events

Capital or Annual Fundraising	These types of fundraising activities will be considered indirect annual fundraisers due to the fact that the revenue generated from their operation will be from increased athletic competition attendance and ticket sales.
Financial Resources Commitment	Depending on the game-day activity selected by the fundraising team, the upfront costs can be exceptionally low to comparatively high.
Planning Requirements	The extent of game-day event planning as a component of the aggregate athletic organization's overall fundraising plan depends on the type of activities being considered. However, no matter how complex the game-day fundraiser, an individual event plan should be developed for each activity.
Human Resource Requirements	The scope of human resource requirements for game-day events is vast. Straightforward game-day fundraisers can have minimal human resource requirements while sizeable game-day events may have substantial human resource obligations.
Fundraising Potential	A succession of well-publicized and energetic game-day events should see steady revenue growth throughout an entire athletic season.

GAME-DAY EVENTS

A popular fundraising activity that can be adopted by a wide variety of athletic organizations is game-day events. Some of the game-day event fundraising activities in which current and potential supporters of the athletic program can participate include pre- and post-game meals, youth contests, preliminary and post-game competitions (in conjunction with the main event), and pre- and post-game entertainment. Not only will these endeavors raise money (through increased ticket sales and donations), they will also develop community awareness and long-term athletic organization patronage and goodwill.

Operating Procedures

Once again, due to the eclectic mixture of feasible game-day activities, there can be no standardized operating procedures. Nevertheless, there are some basic operating policies that should be followed.

Pre-Event Preparation

As previously discussed, the game-day activity should not obstruct or interfere with the competitors' coaches, support staff, and athletes. Additionally, the game-day event should in no way encumber/interfere with the customer's experience and enjoyment of the athletic competition. Pre-event procedures should be carefully organized and all volunteers should be aware of their participation roles.

Program/Event Operation

With superior preparation, a critical operational focus (especially with a limited time in-game fundraising activity) should be on facilitating a controlled and skillfully structured event. The event should have a formidable leadership authority that instills a sense of timely urgency in concert with a smooth operating activity. For example, an in-game activity such as a half-time youth contest should include (through strong pre-planning of set-up and breakdown measures) ample time for the participants to finish the activity while vacating the facility prior to the beginning of main athletic competition's second half.

Post-Event Procedures

As previously discussed, if game-day events are successful, the quantitative determination of that success will be a spike in ticket sales and attendance at the athletic organization's competitions. However, that should not be the only post-event measure of success. Feedback from participants and fans/supporters (by using such instruments as survey/questionnaires, interviews, and focus group discussions) should be solicited.

Marketing and Promotions

Marketing Research

From a marketing research perspective, a principal focus should be on the proposed game-day event(s) and the receptiveness of the target market groups (current and potential supporters) to those events. Research questions such as the following need to be resolved:

- What is the market potential (in support and attendance) for the game-day event?

- Does the game-day event match and appeal to the current fan base in attendance? In other words, will it be an activity that fan want to see, participate in, and support?

- Is the game-day event/activity reasonable given the athletic organization's competition? Is there an opportunity for piggybacking?

- What is the potential goodwill generated in the community by the game-day event? Could and will this goodwill lead to increased financial assistance for future athletic organization fundraising endeavors?

Answering these and equivalent questions will help clarify what type of events would do well, their cost structure, how the events will be run, and the basic foundations of how to promote the events.

Marketing Communication

The marketing communication strategy for game-day events can include two separate but interrelated components. The first marketing communication strategy can be to attach and incorporate the game-day events promotion with the athletic organization's already established competition promotion. Consider blending promotional items such as scheduled cards, TV and radio advertisements, game-day brochures, interviews and public relation announcements, and athletic department media guides into the competitive marketing tactics for the game-day fundraisers.

The second marketing communication strategy is to create an independent game-day event promotional campaign which is separate but in concert with the athletic organization's competitive/game/team promotions. Depending on the marketing budget for game-day events fundraisers, a unified approach that includes advertising, public relations, personal selling, sales promotions, and direct marketing should be designed and implemented. If game-day promotional dollars are limited (which they most likely will be), linking game-day event promotions to existing competitive promotions might be the only option available.

Miscellaneous Information

Because game-day events are visible to (hopefully) sizeable audiences, their quality must be exceptionally high. In fact, in the long run, having no game-day fundraising activity is better than having one that is shoddily administered. Once again, the keys to quality for game-day events relate to planning and organization as well as having an excellent game-day event team. Quality will also be determined by efficiency and strong program leadership.

Fundraising Tip

Contingency planning is of great consequence for game-day event fundraisers. The optimal strategy is to anticipate all feasible operational scenarios and attempt to have a back-up plan in case modification is necessary. All team members and outsourced employees must be made conscious of all contingent possibilities and subsequent plans.

MISCELLANEOUS FUNDRAISING EVENTS

The ensuing fundraising activities, while inconsistent and limited as major revenue producers, are popular and comparably straightforward to organize and conduct. There are conceptual, structural, and operational points that are universal to each endeavor:

- The most decisive component for the success of each fundraising activity is the acquisition of a sizeable and zealous volunteer pool. The volunteers, who will frequently act as sales representatives as well as the activity's operational personnel, must be trained in both the fundamentals of the activity as well as the athletic organization's mission and history.

- Due to each activity's somewhat low to moderate profit potential, a significant, if not the entire, contingency of community support will be essential for net revenue generation.

- Each fundraising activity is categorized as an annual fundraiser owing to its restricted income potential in relation to high-cost capital projects. However, due to their relative ease of development and execution, each fundraiser could be administered several times during a fiscal year to augment a substantial portion of athletic organization's operating expenses.

- An overriding appeal of game-day activities is their nominal financial obligations and risk. While not entirely risk-free, each has a minimal chance of squandering substantial athletic organization assets and cash.

Product and Holiday Sales

Product and holiday sales are worthwhile fundraising activities for annual operations, but are ordinarily impractical for capital programs because of their constrained financial potential. Underlying principles of product and holiday sale fundraisers are listed below:

1. The fundraising director will engage and enter a contractual relationship with a consignment sales/fundraising enterprise.

2. Because the sales are on consignment, the athletic organization and fundraising program undertakes no liability for unsold products.

3. The sales force can be composed of both designated (or mandated) internal stakeholders and selected external stakeholder volunteers. Targeted goals should be specified for every individual involved in the sales program. Sale incentives and awards can be employed to intensify participation and targeted goal achievement.

The potential list of products and services can encompass, but is not limited to, the following:

- *Candy* – Brand name candy as well as favorably known local merchants' candy

Fundraising Tip

The principal disadvantages to consignment product sales are that they are fairly limited as fundraising activities because (1) most items being sold have a low retail value, (2) the sales force is not trained in professional selling techniques, and (3) the commitment factor necessary for success is extensive. However, product sales are an admirable, rapid source of funds for the athletic organization's operations while harvesting middle to lower socio-economic community members.

Table 8.7. Product and Holiday Sales

Capital or Annual Fundraising	Due to their limitations, product and holiday sales are annual fundraisers.
Financial Resources Commitment	If the fundraising program contractually arranges to set up product and holiday sales on consignment, the activity has little or no financial commitment.
Planning Requirements	Product and holiday sales fundraisers are secondary components of an athletic organization's overall fundraising plan. Nonetheless, basic planning for them is vital for their success.
Human Resource Requirements	The human resource ingredient of a product and holiday sales fundraiser is critical. The larger the pool of volunteers, the more potential the activity has.
Fundraising Potential	The extent and commitment of the volunteer and human resource pool will be the primary determinant in the net income potential for the fundraising activity. Typically, these activities are classified as very restricted fundraisers.

- *Food* – Advance sales of pizza, subs, donuts, etc.
- *Discount/promotional cards* – Punch cards for discounts and free products and services (brand name as well as local participating businesses)
- *Holiday gifts* – Specialty items geared toward a specific holiday (Christmas, Valentine's Day, etc.)
- *Athletic apparel* – Products and merchandise from the athletic organization (T-shirts, hats, etc.)

The variety and choice of products and services is almost limitless and directly related to the community/region where the fundraising activity is located. Knowing the community and its desires for identifiable product and services will focus the activity and maximize results.

Pre-Activity Procedures

The pre-activity procedures for a product and holiday sale fundraiser should center on the logistical facilitation of the endeavor. Pre-activity operating procedures include the following elements:

1. *The administration of the fundraiser.* The administrative positions for the fundraiser include the following:
   - Fundraising director – This program manager will be responsible for product selection, volunteer recruitment, cooperation with the consignment organization, periodic monitoring of sales and revenue, and overall administration of the fundraiser.

Fundraising Tip

Human resource training for sales volunteers depends upon the goals of the fundraiser and the experience of the collective sales force. With aggressive sales goals, basic sales presentation skills become extremely important. The sales presentation step-by-step process is found in Chapter 6.

- Inventory manager – This detailed-oriented person will be accountable for distribution and collection of products, ordering and re-ordering, storage and safety of products, quality control, and recording and accounting.
- Bookkeeper – The primary duties of this administrative employee/volunteer include revenue collection, reconciliation, bank deposits, and fundraiser sales spreadsheet.

2. *The acquisition and distribution of products and services.* The products and/or services obtained for the fundraiser must be, with the cooperation and contractual arrangement of the consignment company, delivered and received on a pre-determined date. This date and time needs to be conducive for the expeditious distribution of the products to the sales staff and volunteers. If products and/or services are sold to supporters without being physically present during the sale, after-sales distribution to the purchaser needs to occur within an acceptable and guaranteed time frame.

3. *A fundamental pre-activity sales seminar.* The seminar should be programmed as soon as all internal stakeholders and volunteers working the fundraiser are solidified. The sales force for product and holiday sales fundraisers is not composed of professional retailers/sales specialists. However, a generalized sales presentation which emphasizes key selling points (as well as program policies and procedures) could be instrumental in helping volunteers 'move' the products and services.

4. *The development of an operational schematic.* The fundraising team should map out geographic sales territories. The geographic plotting should focus on capitalizing sales and community coverage.

5. *Goal setting and accountability.* Through cooperative agreements, all participants should have sales objectives for the fundraiser. The sales objectives should be challenging but achievable. The fundraising administrator should have systematically scheduled accountability meetings with each volunteer to review their current sales levels and any possible factors that could assist in increasing sales.

6. *Developing a listing of gifts and prizes for volunteers who surpass sales goals.* These motivational items should be prized by the sales staff as well as cost effective for the fundraising program.

Fundraising Operations

If the pre-activity facets of the product and holiday sales fundraiser are designed and executed competently, the focal point of the actual operation will be to monitor the pre-established procedures in place. Two operational areas to scrutinize on a continuous basis are (1) sales levels and (2) inventory and product protection.

Fundraising Tip

If product and holiday sales are on consignment, while ownership rests with consignment business, responsibility and liability lies with the fundraising program. Inventory control and product protection/safety should be decisively accentuated in a product and holiday sales fundraiser. Damaged goods are considered bought goods by the consignment company.

By monitoring sales levels, quick adjustments can be made to facilitate additional sales. A case in point could be if volunteers have surpassed sales goals and require extra products to continue. Through active monitoring and controls, products can be rapidly dispersed from the fundraising program's inventory of supplies or reallocated and distributed from low sales volunteers.

A vital issue for the monitoring and control of a product and holiday sale fundraiser is the maintaining of accurate and sufficient inventory levels. The worst situation that can occur in a product sales fundraiser is to have transactions outgrow existing inventory levels, which, in turn, could jeopardize program income and athletic organization goodwill.

Post-Activity Processes and Evaluations

There are two conventional features that are universal to all fundraising programs when concluding a product and holiday sales fundraiser:

1. *Secured/safe return of unsold products to the consignment company.* This is accomplished through pre-planned and organized reverse distribution channels (collection system) from sales volunteers to a central location. During the gathering of unsold (and hopefully undamaged) products, a general examination of the products must be done. These inspections should isolate any missing or damaged items while reconciling product distribution with revenue collection and returned items. A pre-established course of action (describing product return responsibilities and policies on damaged or missing merchandise) should be communicated to every internal stakeholder and sales volunteer prior to the commencement of the fundraiser.

2. *Overall accounting of the fundraiser.* Once all returns and revenues are collected from each individual sales volunteer, the fundraising team should construct a comprehensive sales spreadsheet which isolates each volunteer's sales and revenue. The aggregate total of all volunteers' sales units and revenue should equate to the actual cash on hand for the fundraising activity. Additionally, the report can be used to quantitatively highlight top sellers, delineate the exact type of products sold, illustrate geographic areas with the highest sales volumes, and identify individuals and groups who did not attain promised and agreed-upon objectives. If product and holiday sales are going to be an ongoing fundraising program activity in the future, the spreadsheet statistics will be indispensable in fine-tuning upcoming endeavors.

Marketing and Promotions

Marketing Research

The marketing research associated with this form of fundraiser is fundamentally (1) identifying which fundraising products will be coveted by the community/target market and (2) checking if any other non-profit organizations are engaging in competing product and holiday sale fundraisers. Product selection for the fundraiser can be conducted through empirical observation, fundraising team brainstorming and qualitative assessments, and /or historical sales from previous product and holiday sales programs.

Marketing Mix

The marketing mix elements for the product and holiday sale fundraiser are as follows:

PRODUCT

While matching the fundraising products with what the community will purchase is an overriding fundraising concern, meeting the quality expectations of the customers is just as significant. A well-known brand name product has a pre-conceived quality perception and image in the potential target market's mind. If the prospective consumer has a positive impression of the product, the selling process for the product will be unproblematic. Conversely, a novel, unknown product will add a sales challenge due to the purchaser's possible skepticism about the product and its quality.

PRICE

The pricing element of the fundraiser necessitates the balancing of revenue goals (raising substantial funds for the athletic organization) with the value given to the customer/supporter. Typically, the pricing for product and holiday sales items can be slightly above market value because the not-for-profit athletic organization is benefiting from the sale. In most cases, the price for products on consignment is established in advance by the consignment company. With pre-established consignment pricing, the fundraising team should decide if the price fits the target market's expectations prior to committing to the product. If the products are unique and/or developed by the athletic organization, pricing research will entail examining costs as well as market value for items being sold.

PLACE

The distribution system for product sales (regular and holiday) must be planned, organized, and staffed proficiently. As previously stated, distribution systems for product and holiday sales are comprised of:

- taking delivery of products from the manufacturer or consignment company;
- inventory management and security;
- allocation of products to sales force;
- receiving unsold products back into inventory (reverse distribution); and
- transporting unsold inventory back to consignment company (if applicable).

Fundraising Tip

Direct distribution from the manufacturer to the final consumer could be utilized to simplify operations and eliminate inventory and storage responsibilities.

Protecting the product (from forward distribution, and receipt through reverse distribution and return of unsold products) should be a paramount concern for the fundraising team. If the product is perishable, the securing of an external storage area (possibly refrigerated) may be compulsory.

PROMOTION

Because of the unpredictable profit potential of the fundraising activity, paid marketing communication/advertising should be kept to a minimum. Overall community awareness through public relation tactics could generate community-wide positive word of mouth. The principal marketing communication strategy will be through personal selling by the sales staff or volunteers.

Car Washes

© iStockphoto.com/RobMattingley

Car washes are popular, but often limited, fundraising program activities. Their attractiveness stems from the fact they are straightforward in their construction and uncomplicated in their execution. This is not to say that they are easy fundraisers to implement, but that their conceptual understanding is undemanding. Unfortunately, their fundraising revenue potential is restricted because of time constraints and volume limitations associated with their operation. The fundamental elements of a car wash fundraiser encompass the following:

- *Acquiring a high-volume motor vehicle traffic location that allows for the facilitation of the fundraiser with maximum visibility.* This site should be through a mutually beneficial strategic alliance. The business (retail

Table 8.8. Car Washes

Capital or Annual Fundraising	Funds raised from this type of venture supplement annual operating expenses and special projects.
Financial Resources Commitment	The financial resource commitment for car wash fundraisers is exceptionally low, with negligible upfront costs.
Planning Requirements	Depending upon the dimension and complexity of the car wash fundraiser, planning could be low to moderate in comparison to other potential fundraising events and activities. Car wash fundraisers would be a secondary component of the athletic organization's overall fundraising plan.
Human Resource Requirements	Car wash fundraisers are human resource driven events. The service imparted is the work furnished by the volunteers.
Fundraising Potential	The aggregate fundraising potential for car wash fundraisers (in most instances) would be regarded as low.

outlet, gas station, restaurant, etc.) will get amplified publicity while the fundraising program has a cost-free location out of which to operate.

- *Securing fundraising volunteers to perform the activity.* The volunteers could be athletic organization team members, selected administrators and coaches, or general athletic program stakeholders. Because of the hands-on nature of the fundraiser, the personnel working the fundraiser should be in good physical condition.

- *Purchasing supplies for the fundraiser.* The equipment and operational materials purchased for the activity could include car washing soap, car polish/wax, tire cleaning liquids, detailing sprays, and vacuuming devices. Getting donations of supplies could be a viable alternative for controlling expenses and boosting net income.

Pre-Event Preparation

The following points are pre-activity requirements for a car wash fundraiser:

1. *Planning* – Planning items for a car wash fundraiser include
   - date and operating times;
   - acquisition of volunteers based on projected volume;
   - supplies purchased based on projected volume;
   - marketing communication and community awareness;
   - signage at the event;
   - logistical facilitation of customers;
   - safety concerns;
   - quality control on services given; and
   - contingency plans in case of inclement weather.

2. *Car wash facilitator* – An indispensable position for a car wash fundraiser is the event coordinator/facilitator. This individual is in complete command of the fundraiser and is responsible for:
   - directing staff and personnel;
   - overseeing operations and expediting the flow of service;
   - quality control;
   - managing revenue intakes and expenditures;
   - overseeing supplies inventory; and
   - public relations with customers.

3. *Venue* – The acquisition of a suitable location at which to have the fundraiser is the first and most notable element for the activity. Keep in mind that the business/venue's proprietor must be enthusiastic about having the fundraiser at his/her locality. Some concerns that must be prioritized are:
   - measurement (length and width) of the car washing area;
   - multiple water sources;

Fundraising Tip

Event coordinators should consider themselves conductors of the event. They will focus on delegating tasks and controlling the operations. While at peak times they could 'roll up their sleeves' and give assistance in working the event, they should not have a permanent line job during the operations.

- visibility to traffic;
- minimal congestion and disruption of the venue's normal operations;
- water drainage; and
- a seating area for customers.

4. *Inventory of supplies* – From the anticipated capacity and volume of the fundraiser, an inventory of operational materials and equipment will need to be prepared. The following are likely car wash necessities that will need to be requisitioned and inventoried:
   - Hoses
   - Sponges, brushes, and towels
   - Soap and wax
- Tire cleaners
- Bug/tar remover

5. *Advance ticket sales* – In an effort to enhance sales and capitalize on capacity, advance car wash tickets could be sold prior to the event. The tickets, which are sold by fundraising team members, will function as pre-paid vouchers for the customer to present on the day of the car wash. The tickets should be numbered and catalogued for regulation and control.

6. *Staff* – Once again, owing to the physical prerequisites of the fundraiser, the targeted volunteers for the activity must be physically capable of meeting all work requirements. However, no volunteer should be turned away. There are low-impact activities (such as facilitating food and drinks, customer assistance, public relations) that can be delegated to non-car washing volunteers.

Event/Activity Operations

The conceptual operation of a car wash fundraiser is comparatively simple in relationship to other fundraising activities. Nevertheless, there are critical event-day elements that must be highlighted for the smooth operation of the fundraiser:

- *Safety* – It is imperative that the safety and wellbeing of volunteers and customers be the number one event-day priority for a car wash fundraiser. A safety walkthrough by all fundraiser team members should be a compulsory component of the operation.

- *Job responsibilities* – As a feature of quality control, each volunteer should be given definitive job duties for the endeavor. If a job rotation system of operation is employed, all quality expectations need to be communicated for every responsibility.

- *Collection procedures* – All incoming proceeds from the fundraiser must be accumulated and accounted for. Since the fundraiser is an exposed outdoor activity, security over revenue collected should be a core consideration.

Fundraising Tip

If utilizing advance sales vouchers, provide each fundraising team member with ticket booklets that are sequentially numbered and have all pertinent information for customers. Triple confirm that the total booklets (tickets) do not surpass maximum capacity of the fundraiser.

- *Volunteer management* – Due to the physical nature of the fundraiser, volunteers will need to be given breaks throughout the event. It is strongly recommended that food, snacks, and drinks be available to all who participate in the fundraiser.

- *Logistical operation* – There are two workable methods for the careful direction and cleaning of cars/vehicles. The first is an assembly-line operation where cars are 'pushed through' a series of stations, each with a separate function. Station set-up could be handled as follows:
  - Payment and voucher collection
  - Wash and rinse
  - Dry
  - Windows and tires
  - Vacuum and interior wipe-down
  - Customer exit

The logistical issue with the stations layout is bottlenecking. In other words, some stations could take longer than others triggering a backup in the system. Reshuffling personnel could alleviate this possibility. The second method is by all-inclusive areas/compartments/stalls. Each stall will be its own autonomous car washing area. An intrinsic issue with this format is monitoring each unit's productivity, inventory, quality control, and traffic flow. No matter which method is adopted, safe traffic flow is critical. To help with traffic flow, a single facilitator and clear directions should be established. The use of cones and signage is strongly recommended.

Post-Event Procedures

When the car wash fundraiser is concluded, there are four primary duties that must be fulfilled.

1. *Clean-up* – The fundraising team should leave the facility precisely as (or better than) it was before the car wash fundraiser began. After the event's clean-up, there should be no residual signs of the activity.

2. *Inventory* – An ending inventory of fundraising equipment and supplies should be made at the conclusion of the fundraiser. This closing inventory will be the beginning inventory for future car wash fundraisers.

3. *Accounting* – All revenue sources and expenditures should be accounted for, reconciled, and paid at the conclusion of the fundraiser.

4. *Thank-you notes* – All volunteers should receive thank-you notes for their involvement in the event. Furthermore, a special thank-you to the facility's owner/managers should be provided.

Special Note: If the facility used for the car wash fundraiser is sizeable, the event coordinator should employ a speaker or 'bull horn' to assist in facilitating the activity.

Marketing and Promotions

Marketing Research Requirements

The marketing research for a car wash fundraiser would be categorized as negligible in comparison to other fundraising events/activities. Some basic topics to research can include:

- investigating at which times the proposed facility/location has the most traffic flow;
- conducting a community survey to see if there are any similar, overlapping events;
- targeting advanced ticket sales toward certain demographic groups/ households; and
- researching pricing structures at professional car washes (to be discussed).

Generally speaking, the target market for a car wash fundraiser is anyone with a vehicle in the vicinity of the event, so researching activities for the event will be minimal.

Marketing Mix

PRODUCT

While the car wash fundraiser is not a professional service, the product/service aspiration should be to provide as close to a professional car wash quality as possible to each customer. All cars/vehicles should be inspected by the owner and a designated volunteer before leaving the site. This 'personal touch' will generate positive word of mouth for the remainder of the event as well as for future car wash events. Another product concern relates to the supplies employed for the event. Quality supplies should be used, while keeping things as economical as possible.

PRICE

Important considerations for pricing include customer expectations and competition. The price structure must be within an acceptable range for the services provided. This range can be discovered through competitive pricing (benchmarking) of local car wash businesses or from historical pricing of past events.

If multiple services are offered by the fundraiser, various pricing levels (from competitive research) could be instituted on the following ascending services:

Level 1 – Basic wash and dry

Level 2 – Previous level plus vacuum and interior cleaning

Level 3 – Previous levels plus tire treatment and windows

Level 4 – Previous levels plus waxing

Level 5 – Previous levels plus a complete vehicle detailing

Once again, the geographic region and the competition will provide what fees are to be charged at what levels of service.

PLACE

As discussed throughout this fundraising segment, the determination of a location for a car wash fundraiser is a crucial strategic factor in the success of the fundraiser. To assist a fundraising team in deciding on a location, a pre-established listing of basic factors could be used to survey locations. The form should be in a descending prioritized design.

PROMOTION

Due to the financial limitations of the fundraiser, there should be little or no paid advertising. However, there are a number of elemental marketing communication tactics that could be applied to support the event's success. The following are some of the possible tactics:

- web-based and email announcements to stakeholders and alumni;
- positive word-of-mouth promotion through the collective effort of the entire athletic organization;
- signage on the day of the event;
- piggybacking on other athletic organization promotional campaigns;
- pre-event ticket sales through personal selling;
- pre-event sales promos and discounts; and
- announcement at athletic organization competitions.

OTHER POSSIBLE FUNDRAISING ACTIVITIES/EVENTS

Bowl/Walk/Swim-A-Thon

These types of fundraising activities are based on pledged dollar amounts to volunteers for their fulfillment/attainment of targeted goals. Some broad-spectrum points associated with this classification of fundraiser are as follows:

1. Dollar amounts pledged are specifically connected to the endeavor. Each activity must have a maximum and minimum donation level for the benefit of donors.

2. A designated time period needs to be instituted for pledge solicitation. The pledge period should be well ahead of the actual event to capitalize on donations without being so prolonged that patrons forget about (and possibly disregard) their pledge commitments.

3. The event day should be fun and filled with stimulating activities for the participating volunteers. Awards and gifts should encourage peak involvement and the growth of future events.

4. Financial resource commitments, while considered nominal for these types of fundraisers, still need serious consideration. The possible expenditures (both upfront and post-event) could encompass:

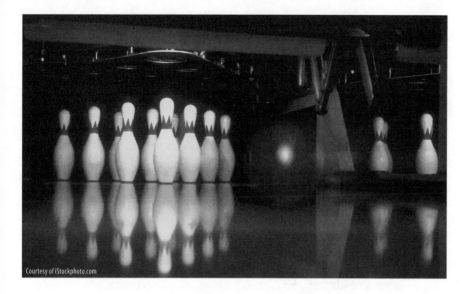

Courtesy of iStockphoto.com

- facility rental/usage (bowl- and swim-a-thons);
- event-day operating costs such as food, activities, T-shirts, prizes;
- event security and medical staff; and
- general administrative costs.

5. Each volunteer should have challenging but achievable donation goals, with top performers receiving recognition for their work.

6. Pre-event planning for a pledged fundraiser can include the following administrative duties:

- *Construction of pledge sheets* – These statements/records should itemize names, addresses, phone numbers, emails and pledged amounts from all donors. It should also be noted that direct donations to the athletic organization (without the activity) should also be documented and accepted. For walk-a-thons, contingency pledges could be used in case the event is cancelled due to inclement weather. Carbon copy sheets are advisable.

- *Securing of a facility/course* – If conducting a walk-a-thon, a closed course is the safest and most controllable alternative. Bowling and swimming fundraisers should have a set minimum number of lanes at the facility devoted to accommodate participating volunteers. The locations should be well known and centrally situated for all volunteers.

- *Participant safety* – Each type of event should have a contingency of security personnel for the safety of the actual event. Whether contracted through a private security company or utilizing a community police force, there should be a feeling of safety. Additionally, because these types of activities are physical in makeup, emergency medical staff should be on-site. For walk-a-thons, plenty of water stations should be positioned along the route and the event should be conducted as early as possible in the day to reduce any heat-related issues. For swim-a-thons, medical personnel as well as certified life guards should be present for the duration of the fundraiser.

7. The planning aspect of the event should outline the post-event pledge collection procedures. Post-collection procedures (based on participants' accomplishments) should be through the following process:

Step 1: Volunteers collect pledges directly from their sponsors.

Step 2: If pledges are still uncollected at the completion of Step 1, the fundraising team bills the program supporters for their obligations through a well-written letter.

Step 3: After Step 2's collection cycle is concluded, any outstanding accounts will receive courtesy calls.

At the end of this three step process, the fundraising team will need to determine whether a fourth contact is beneficial/necessary.

8. The development of strategic alliances, not only to underwrite costs but to augment the event, should be prioritized.

9. The vital operational elements of the event should include:
   - a pre-published event-day schedule and program;
   - the timely starting and finishing of all activities;
   - the organized facilitation and traffic flow of participants;
   - the uninterrupted expediting of participants through activities (avoiding bottlenecks);
   - an enjoyable and encouraging environment;
   - a safety-first posture;
   - warm-up and cool-down activities; and
   - an appreciation for all participants/volunteers.

10. The marketing communication tactics for the event can consist of:
    - targeting the best workable date on the community calendar;
    - public relations announcements from local radio and TV; and
    - word-of-mouth promotions and personal selling by all athletic organization stakeholders.

Skills Contests

Another way for an athletic program to involve community members in the fundraising program, as well as raise funds and support, is to have sport-specific skills contests. Obviously, the athletic organization's sport(s) will be the foundation of the proficiency challenge. The contest/skills tests could be used with other fundraising events and activities or in concert with the athletic program's competition. The value and quantity of prizes can fluctuate with the level and costs incurred by the fundraising program. If the program elects to award considerable prizes, insurance can be purchased to

Fundraising Tip

All fundraising events in which volunteers are a functioning component should have appropriate insurance coverage, which should be examined along with the event's format by legal counsel to determine suitability.

guarantee and secure prizes (e.g., million dollar hole-in-one). A per-attempt fee can be charged and novelty prizes can be presented to maintain interest. These rewards can be donated by local vendors and retailers in exchange for name promotion at the event. Skills contests could include:

Golf – hole-in-one contest

Baseball/softball – throwing through a target or hitting a homerun

Basketball – half-court shot

Volleyball/Tennis – serving into a target

Football – punt, pass, or kick skills

Hockey/soccer/lacrosse – shot on goal contest

Bowling – three strikes contest

A fundraising administrator must balance contest creativity, supporter appeal, and achievability in constructing a skills contest.

Fundraising Tip

Skills contests can be categorized as indirect fundraisers. If the contests are open to a general audience at a sporting event, fees will not typically be charged. However, if the activity is popular and publicized well, attendance at the event could be increased which, in turn, will augment the athletic organization's revenue.

SUMMARY

The significance of fundraising activities and events as a core component of an athletic organization's fundraising program cannot be emphasized enough. Because all events and activities have far-reaching participative involvement from the community, they go well beyond endeavors to raise money. They are a way for the athletic organization to foster a relationship with its external stakeholders that will provide long-standing benefits such as visibility and brand recognition, increased attendance and community energy, and a strong public relations foundation. No matter which event or activity the athletic organization chooses, each should be developed, structured, and implemented with these elements in mind.

REVIEW AND DISCUSSION QUESTIONS

1. What are some of the 'out of pocket' costs associated with a golf tournament fundraiser?

2. What are the key areas to spotlight in the golf tournament fundraising plan?

3. What are some of the central fundraising factors to consider for luncheons/dinners/banquets?

4. What are some breakdown protocols for a banquet fundraiser?

5. What are some noteworthy points to reflect upon when considering the adoption of celebrity signing fundraisers?

6. Name the possible fundraising positions/human resource requirement for a celebrity signing.

7. What are four possible goals for a dream auction fundraiser?

8. What is the difference between an open format and blind format in a dream auction?

9. What are the three areas that should be emphasized when planning an entertainment fundraiser?

10. What is an overriding factor in the acquisition of a venue for an entertainment fundraiser?

11. What are some of the game-day activities an athletic organization can utilize?

12. Why are game-day fundraisers considered "piggybacking" events?

13. What are consignment sales?

14. Name the five pre-activity procedures for a product and holiday sale fundraiser.

15. What are some critical event-day elements for a car wash fundraiser?

16. For pledged fundraisers, why should there be a ceiling and minimum pledge?

17. What are some vital operational elements for a pledge fundraising event?

CHAPTER

9

Fundraising Programs

INTRODUCTION

This chapter provides detailed descriptions of popular long-term/perpetual fundraising programs that can be adopted by a variety of athletic organizations. Much like the model followed in Chapter 8, the programs described in this chapter will include a representation to be followed from the inception of the idea to the culmination and termination of the program. Types of fundraising programs discussed include booster programs, construction dedications, promotional sales programs, and other fundraising programs, such as deferred gifts and corporate sponsorship programs.

It is important to note that if an organization is managing multiple fundraising events/activities (see Chapter 8) as well as long-term programs concurrently, a carefully constructed fundraising calendar should be created and maintained. The monthly calendar format should:

- define start and completion dates of all events, activities, and programs;
- be a visual depiction that puts time into perspective rather than an unspecified list of things to do;
- be structured in a master calendar format along with each event, activity, and program's individual calendars;
- be a foundational component of the overall athletic organization's fundraising plan; and
- be utilized by all fundraising program stakeholders.

BOOSTER PROGRAMS

A booster program can produce enormous financial resources for an athletic organization. In some large athletic organizations (principally in an educational situation), the booster club is the cornerstone of the entire fundraising program. The appeal to maintaining a booster program is that the fundraising model is germane and applicable to all sizes and levels of athletic organization. Additionally, it enlists a variety of supporters while developing a foundational membership base that has a family atmosphere. This sentiment can and will create a community-wide vested interest in the athletic organization. Not only will direct financial backing increase from a booster club operation, but ticket sales, merchandise sales, and participation in other fundraising programs will be strengthened.

The dimensions of an athletic organization's booster club operation can range in scope from a small, in-house undertaking completely managed by internal fundraising personnel to a mega-booster program with board members, intricate hierarchical structure, multiple divisions, and a substantial pool of volunteers and paid personnel. A mega-booster club is characteristically its own not-for-profit incorporated venture that, while a separate entity, is classified as a direct contribution program for the specific athletic organization. However, mega-booster programs should function cooperatively with the internal athletic organization's fundraising program on other events, activities and programs.

Booster club promotion, development, and expansion can take considerable time and energy. A new booster club's status will predictably correlate with the current popularity of the athletic organization. As the club matures, numerous diverse divisions can emerge. Booster club branches such as a former athletic alumni category (also known universally as a varsity booster club), a business division for local, regional or national corporations, and a current student division are all possible. Additionally, as the booster club expands, so will its revenue sources. Revenue sources can encompass general and special membership fees, named endowments, booster events, activities and programs, bequests and wills, corporate sponsorship and other miscellaneous philanthropic contributions.

No matter what the extent of the booster club or its time in existence, it is imperative to acquire legal and accounting services and consultations. Lawyers and CPAs will assist in:

- formation and monitoring of the booster club statutes and bylaws, internal polices, and operating procedures;
- development and preservation of financial recording and reporting services;
- creation of tax-exempt status for the booster club; and
- construction and implementation of a booster club code of ethics.

Fundraising Tip

Booster clubs and members should have no ulterior motives. Booster club members' opinions should be heard and respected. However, they should have no control over internal operations, especially personnel and coaching decisions.

Planning, Organizing, and Staffing

Booster Club Mission Statement

The central purpose for a booster fundraising program is straightforward—to bestow needed financial assistance (whether it be for scholarships, new equipment and facilities, operating costs, or additional personnel) for the athletic organization. The wide-ranging mission of a booster fundraising program can encompass:

- inciting alumni involvement (individual, community, business);
- presenting existing students (in an educational background) booster opportunities;
- enhancing all public relations aspects of an athletic organization;
- amplifying athletic organization traditions, which then augment financial support; and
- possessing an inclusionary philosophy which underscores the attitude that anyone and everyone, no matter his/her financial situation, should have the opportunity to get involved and become a member of the booster club.

While booster fundraising programs are distinctive in their configuration and processes, the strategic long-term and short-term goals will have a level of commonality universal to all athletic organizations.

Long-Term Objectives

The long-term significance of a booster program will have an undeniable correlation with its current and future resource commitment. If the booster club is deemed to be a foundational element of a fundraising program's operation, then the designation of athletic organization resources will be noteworthy. Money, while being the most conspicuous organizational resource, is not the only ingredient that a booster program will need for long-term expansion. The promise of personnel as well as tangible assets (facilities, equipment, supplies, etc.) will also be critical aspects for the long-term achievements of the booster program.

Once the long-term resource obligation to the booster program is defined, the fundraising program will need to institute (or reinstate) targeted objectives for enlargement and success. These long-term objectives should be concentrated on membership development and subsequent financial growth. The two objectives go hand-in-hand—the more energetic and functional a booster program's membership, the better the chance the program will reach its financial goals. Does this imply that membership numbers should take precedence over large (and often substantial) philanthropic booster contributions? No. However, from base members to legacy contributors, all individuals and groups are essential in reaching long-term objectives.

The configuration of a cohesive booster infrastructure will be influential in the program's long-term accomplishments or, alternatively, its breakdown. Once again, if the booster club is an independent entity and categorized as a direct contribution organization, the organization should incorporate executive-level positions which

Fundraising Tip

Base-level members can mature into lifetime supporters throughout the years. Never forget that every booster can be vital to the financial success and traditions of the program.

should be filled by notable and devoted community and business members. Considerable booster programs could have management committees, sub-committee chairs, event administrators, and administrative employees. Smaller athletic organizations that have the booster program as an in-house department need to appoint a knowledgeable, adept fundraiser to head up booster interaction and development.

Either way, no matter the dimension of the athletic organization and its projected or current booster program, the hierarchical infrastructure must match anticipated strategic long-term goals. A mismatch between structure and strategy will unquestionably spell disaster for the booster club. Authoritative job descriptions, operational manuals, and a code of ethics are just a few of the structural mechanisms that need to be incorporated into a booster program.

The creation of booster contribution levels is a decisive long-term action that must be developed with great care and deliberation. Once donation/support levels are instituted, boosters will mentally 'lock in' perceptions on rates and benefits. Can level amounts and fees be modified and increased? Absolutely, but only increased incrementally. Indiscriminate changes to fee structures are not recommended. A possible fee structure template and the possible incentives that correspond to the different levels are delineated in Table 9.1.

Table 9.1. Fee Structure Template for Booster Programs

Individual Memberships

Level 1 – Student Boosters $25

Level 2 – General Boosters $50

Level 3 – Bronze Boosters $100

Level 4 – Silver Boosters $250

Level 5 – Gold Boosters $500

Level 6 – Platinum Boosters $1,000

Level 7 – Legacy Boosters $2,500

Level 8 – Lifetime Boosters $5,000+

Business and Corporate Memberships

General Business Membership $1,000

Gold Booster Membership $5,000

Lifetime Booster Membership $25,000

**Each level can be tied into the athletic organization's identity (e.g., name, nickname, mascot).

**Each level will have the previous level's incentives and benefits. Rewards will progressively accumulate with higher contribution amounts.

Individual and Group Booster Club Incentives

Individual Incentives

- Publications (newsletters, brochures, e-publications, sports-specific media guides)
- Priority Parking at Athletic Organization Competitions and Events
- Athletic Organization and/or Booster Club Merchandise
- Season Tickets (or Priority to Purchase Season Tickets) to Select Athletic Organization Competitions
- License Plates and Window Decals
- Plaques and Certificates of Contribution
- Rings, Jewelry, Pins, and Pendants
- Invitations to Athletic Organization Events and Miscellaneous Fundraisers

Group Incentives

- Socials and Mixers
- Meet-and-Greet with High Profile Coaches and Athletes
- Booster Travel to Select Away Games
- Pre- and Post-Game Functions
- Alumni/Booster Weekends

A concluding long-term booster goal could be to cultivate a business/corporate in-kind gift plan. The in-kind gift program is where businesses (both local and national) donate products to the athletic organization through the booster club. Business in-kind contributions would warrant membership in the booster club as well as the capability to promote products at booster program and athletic organization functions. In athletics, an example would be car dealerships donating courtesy car usage to athletic administrators and coaches.

Short-Term Goals

Short-term objectives and actions during the inception and advancement of a booster program can entail the following elements:

Development of booster club literature and publications – Either monthly, quarterly, semi-annually, or annually, a booster program should assemble and distribute newsletter-type documents. This periodical should be forwarded to all boosters and athletic organization stakeholders (either through electronic methods or hardcopy mail). A singular and knowledgeable individual, group, or committee should be empowered with and accountable for its production and circulation. As with all fundraising documents for external consumption, they should be (1) mistake free, (2) focused on pertinent information for the reader, and (3) as engaging and imaginative as possible. Facets of the newsletter could include a communication from the Booster President/Chief Operating Officer, a calendar/schedule of booster events and activities, a 'spot-light corner' article of an prominent booster, a booster club contribution and membership pull-out, and a broad-spectrum section for booster member news and accomplishments. Other publications that can be produced by the booster program can be annual athletic organization booster reports, brochures and membership literature, and noteworthy booster event pamphlets and guides.

Calendar of booster events – Booster programs, to be valuable and effective, need to be dynamic and active. Booster calendars should be 'sprinkled' with booster functions and promotions. These events should be an assortment of blocked activities (for booster members only) and open events that aim for increasing community awareness, goodwill, and membership. The variety of functions available is only constrained by the resources on hand and the commitment of the booster program to designing, organizing, and executing them. The feasible events, activities, and programs available to booster clubs are illustrated throughout this text.

Booster club personnel – As discussed, a booster program's operations are people-driven. For the booster program's success, high energy people who unconditionally commit themselves to the athletic organization and booster club's mission are essential. An ongoing endeavor that must be attended to is the recruitment and retention of a formidable booster club board of directors. With stability in the board of directors, booster program operational administration and staff should have elevated retention and permanence.

Booster club systems – For any operation to be successful, systems development and management is compulsory. The two operating systems that should be employed by all booster program are the financial system and database management.

The financial system is concerned with accounting methodologies utilized by the booster program. Accuracy in budgeting, transaction processing (income sources and expenditures), and fiscal reporting are among the sub-systems that should be constructed for error free operations. As with all professional areas of expertise, the initial development of accounting systems should be supervised by a certified public accountant (CPA). Additionally, CPAs should instruct bookkeepers and recording staff on prescribed accounting processes while periodically monitoring all financial activities.

An accurate, comprehensive membership database is the clerical foundation of a booster program. Database systems should have all-inclusive records of membership demographics, residences, contacts, and donation information. The system should be user friendly and accessible to a limited number of staff members.

Human Resource Requirements

As described previously, the personnel requirements for a booster program can range from a small, in-house staff to a large multi-divisional external program. Such an operation would need an extensive hierarchical structure and detailed job descriptions. However, in an educational setting (college or university level), a source of talented booster program workers could be through a cooperative internship program. The collaborative program with a college or university business/marketing/management department would have student workers (for course credit) augmenting booster club executives, administration, and staff members in many ways.

Marketing Communication

While the marketing communication mix elements articulated in Chapter 6 all pertain to the promotion of a booster program, the two core methods used by a predominate number of booster clubs in reaching existing and prospective supporters are direct mail and phone campaigns. Once again, while these marketing communication strategies are the most obvious methods in booster club promotion and membership drives, tactics such as advertising, public relations, sales promotions, and personal selling should be exploited to supplement direct mail and phone campaigns.

Direct Mail
Direct mail is an exceptional mechanism for 'laying the groundwork' for a booster fundraising program. However, because of the (on average) nominal response rate associated with its operation, it should not be regarded as the booster program's only marketing mechanism. The primary justifications for its adoption and overall objectives are as follows:

1. The principal rationale for a direct mail campaign for a booster program is to indoctrinate and enlighten alumni, community members,

and businesses about the athletic organization's successes as well as fundraising requirements and goals of the booster club. The solicitation of sizeable funds from a direct mailing can be somewhat limited, even with extensive volume mailing. Revenue generated from direct mailing is contingent upon the reputation and perceived worth of the athletic organization in the community and the targeted boosters on which the direct mailing instrument is focused.

2. Each distinctive direct mailing must undergo a cost-benefit analysis to uncover its effectiveness in relation to its substantive costs. The expense elements of a direct mailing are becoming a chief consideration in deciding whether to utilize this fundraising tool. Because of the escalating costs of postage, print work, and creative design, the booster program must forecast the realizable impact and earnings of the mailer and evaluate if the costs merit its inclusion in the marketing communication plan.

3. Products and materials for a bulk mailing must be engineered to be community-significant, successful at communicating the value of the booster program, straightforward and logical, astutely appealing, and easy to respond to.

4. To decrease costs while retaining a high contact concentration, a booster program can make use of email contacts as well as web-based technology to enhance hard-copy mailings. Utilizing technology for direct booster contacts is instantaneous and considerably more economical per unit than traditional methods. However, emails and websites employed by a booster program must uphold the same quality expectations as other booster communications.

> **Fundraising Tip**
>
> Because of the volume of direct mail received by existing and potential boosters, direct mail undertakings must be as unique and engaging as possible. Quality writing, artwork, and presentation is the optimum way to differentiate the booster program's direct mail from other non-profit organizations' solicitations.

Direct mailers are normally time-consuming in their production and necessitate extensive mailing lists. Booster mailing lists, which can be from internal construction or from external purchased sources, are a serious component of the direct mailing. A centralized, applicable list can facilitate booster mailing success. An unsuitable and outdated list will lead to expensive resources' being wasted and booster program limitations.

The human resource commitment necessary to design, assemble, and deliver a booster program direct mailing depends upon the magnitude of the mailing and the complexity and number of the mailing components. For considerable bulk mailings with multiple pieces for each individual mailer, a large volunteer core will be required. An assembly line operation with rotating shifts and an ample mailing supply inventory will need to be planned. Volunteers can be internal stakeholders such as athletic organization personnel and athletes. External volunteers can be fundraising program volunteers, youth groups, and senior groups.

Figure 9.1. **Components to an All-Inclusive Booster Direct Mailing**

Cover Letter

- Establish the objectives of the entire mailer
- Immediately convey the purpose of the booster club and the appeal of the solicitation to the potential/current booster (emotional, rationale, nostalgic, etc.)
- Contain high-quality writing with succinct and direct language
- Ask for action – in a booster program, the action is joining the booster club and donating funds

Booster Program Brochure

- Focal component of the direct mailing
- High quality presentation that delineates:
- Overall athletic organization information
- Booster program history and importance
- A complete outline of support levels - designations, donation amounts, and benefits
- Booster program registration form

Supplementary Literature (if financially feasible)

- Booster club publication (annual)
- Newsletters (monthly/quarterly/semi-annually)
- Pictures of booster events
- Promotional items

© Wavebreakmedia Ltd | Dreamstime.com

Phone Campaigns for Booster Programs

As with direct mail campaigns, phone campaigns are, to some extent, confined as a direct fundraising activity owing to the sheer number of phone solicitations an individual could entertain daily. Add to this 'Do Not Call' governmental regulations, and phone campaign operations can be problematic. Additionally, 'cold calling' will have a much reduced success rate compared to phone solicitations to a targeted, vested booster group (or potential booster group). However, for creating awareness and an appreciation of the booster program, phone campaigns are a compelling marketing communication strategy.

Some phone campaign fundamentals and issues that need to be addressed for the promotion and acquisition of boosters can include the following items:

- *Setting up phone banks and call facilities* – From a logistical standpoint, this facet of phone campaigns can be the most difficult to coordinate. A few of the qualities that the room(s) must have include: proper sound acoustics (little or no reverberation), the appropriate number of phone lines, comfortable tables, chairs, and adequate spacing.

- *Booster program sales script* – The composition of the sales script used by volunteers should balance the booster program's information dispersal needs with extemporaneous flexibility. The danger with an excessively detailed script is the 'canned' aspect of the communication.

- *Call scheduling* – All call times to current and potential boosters should be as nonintrusive and, hopefully, non-irritating as possible. Calls to boosters' workplaces should be minimal, if not eliminated entirely. All home calls should be made between 10 a.m. and 9 p.m.

- *Call lists* – Each volunteer should have a thorough call list from which to work. The call list, besides contact information, should have a way to indicate whether:
  - a contact was made;
  - a membership was sold;
  - there was an interest in membership in the booster program;
  - there was no interest;
  - a message was left;
  - there was no answer;
  - it was a wrong number; and/or
  - it was an out of service number.

- *Volunteer management* – Each volunteer should have:
  - a rotation/break schedule;
  - time limits for call sessions;
  - hospitality table access;
  - an FAQ sheet to assist in question answering; and
  - the ability to solicit input and have questions answered by a supervisor.

- *Professionalism of operation* – The issue of professionalism is key in a booster program's phone campaign. Each and every fundraising administrator, staff member and volunteer engaged in the phone campaign must comprehend that this booster solicitation activity is a direct reflection on the athletic organization, fundraising program, and booster club.

Booster Program Kick-Off

If an athletic organization is launching a new booster program, a sequence of kick-off events and promotional activities should be initiated. Additionally, the events and promotional activities could be tiered for targeted supporter accentuation. Tier one events and promotional activities could be for key potential philanthropic contributors and businesses. Tier two events and promotional activities could be for athletic organization/educational institution alumni (both former athletes and general alumni). Tier three events and promotional activities (open to the public) could be focused on general community members.

Different tiers will have distinctive events. For example, tier one events and promotional activities will be more in accordance with formal, black tie affairs such as dinner parties and special VIP receptions. This select group must know that they are a select group. During these events, the booster club board of directors and executive

Fundraising Tip

In booster program fundraising, phone campaigns are classified as an active solicitation tactic. Phone communications can also be used passively to help promote an athletic organization's booster program. This can be accomplished by having all athletic organization phone messages and call waiting/on-hold messages communicate information about the booster club and how to get involved.

administrators should exercise personal selling tactics for acquiring memberships and contributions. Conversely, a tier three booster program event or promotional activity could feature community-wide activities such as carnivals or entertainment programs. During these events, mass marketing communication strategies (advertising, canvassing booster program literature, sales promotions and giveaways, etc.) could be employed.

CONSTRUCTION DEDICATIONS

For an athletic organization that is constructing (or has future aspirations to construct) new athletic facilities or refurbishing older buildings and grounds, a construction dedication fundraiser is an economical, high potential fundraising program. The operational specifications for the fundraising program are as follows.

For a predetermined set of prices, the fundraising committee as well as internal administrators and staff solicit contributions by selling bricks (and interrelated commemorative items) to the new/renovated facility. The fundraising program's primary selling feature is that each brick or commemorative object will have the donor's name (or tribute name) inscribed and will be a permanent, picturesque component of the structure. The unit cost per brick or commemorative item will depend on (1) the characteristics and dimensions of the dedication, (2) the outsource companies' etching and ancillary costs, and (3) profit margin desired. The fundraising program is feasible for athletic organizations constructing various facilities:

- Gymnasiums
- Walkways
- Schools
- Courtyards
- Pools/aquatic facilities
- Fields/stadiums

The program commencement and publicity kickoff should initially be concentrated on prominent philanthropic donors who will purchase extensive construction dedication sections at a time. For large purchases, the contributor should have the option to erect a facility plaque in a distinguished, high traffic area of the construction. For contributions that would be regarded as exceptional, specialty dedications are possible (i.e., the XYZ Family Walkway in decorative stone/boulder). After the preeminent sponsors have been exhausted, intermediate to general athletic organization supporters should be cultivated.

Because of the permanency and affordability of this fundraiser program, the central marketing communication tactics will be personal selling and an exponentially escalating word-of-mouth campaign. Other promotional strategies for the community-wide fundraising programs could include a public relations media campaign in targeted publications, radio and television advertisement, direct mailers, and personal selling by all athletic organization stakeholders. It is advisable to institute publicity, marketing communication, and sales plans two years prior to the ground breaking and construction of the athletic organization structure. Because of this extensive lead time, the fundraising program's organization and operational systems must be fundamentally sound. All transactions must be chronicled and accurately mapped for referencing by donors. These maps should be as straightforward as possible to pinpoint any and all dedications.

Resource Commitment

The resource obligation required for a construction dedication fundraising program relates primarily to two factors: marketing expenditures associated with the program, and the engraving company's services and costs.

From a marketing resource commitment standpoint, the tactics employed will connect the current and potential supporter bases with the project being developed. Hopefully, if the athletic organization's supporter base is passionate and motivated to participate in the fundraising program, the construction dedication will 'sell itself.' Once supporters are conscious of the program, they will seek out an opportunity to have a permanent stake (and memorial) in the athletic organization. If the athletic organization's supporter base is not considered a strong asset, marketing tactics (to be discussed later) and their subsequent expenses will need to be accounted for. These expenditures will have direct bottom-line ramifications on the profit of the fundraiser.

The second element that can have a direct impact on the resource commitment necessary for a construction dedication fundraiser is the engraving company used for the program. It must be recognized that not all engraving companies are comparable in terms of quality and price. The fundraising team, through thorough online and direct contact research, needs to determine which outsourced brick engraving fundraising company to contract. Items (that can influence resource commitment) that need to be investigated include, but are not limited to, the aspects detailed in Figure 9.2 (p. 192).

Fundraising Potential

The dimensions of capital funds generated from this category of fundraiser are immeasurable. For every new building, walkway, or renovation, a new construction dedication fundraising program could be launched. The keys are the product's permanency, cost controls, and the athletic organization's dedication to the program's promotion and personal selling. Construction dedication projects should be selected strategically to circumvent the potential of fundraising saturation, which could diminish their importance.

Pre-Program Planning, Organizing, and Staffing

Mission and Philosophy of the Fundraising Program

The mission and philosophy of a construction dedication should accentuate the following elements:

Fundraising Tip

A vital first step to the construction dedication fundraiser (prior to promotion and sales) is getting a definitive maximum number of bricks/commemorative units from the construction engineers that can be retailed. All public areas should be accurately measured and bricks/commemorative items to be used quantified. It would be a public relations catastrophe to oversell units beyond capacity.

Fundraising Tip

Brick and construction dedication fundraising programs can be linked with other fundraising events and activities such as banquets and receptions. For example, the opening of a contemporary core athletic facility that has a brick/commemorative fundraiser could merit a major function with receptions, food, and VIP speakers.

Figure 9.2. Research Points for a Brick Engraving Fundraising Company

Customer Support Services

Hours of operation; level of expertise; phone/direct contact support; online support; location of operation

Shipping

Free or fees per unit; shipping method and timeliness; product damage guarantees

Marketing Support

Brochures; order forms; press release templates; scripts for radio and TV advertising; auxiliary services

Engraving Charges

Standard per unit or by the number of words and lines; catalog or prices for products available; etching vs. laser cost differences

Quality Guarantees

Lifetime of facility/construction for a delineated timeframe; product guarantees; return policies

Contingency Sales

Upfront contractual guarantees or through risk-free contingency sales; order size (minimum and maximum); sales support

Construction Support

Customer service and experts (liaisons) available to support dedications; design manuals/literature for brick-laying assistance

Tech Support

Establishment of website for the athletic organization; online ordering direct; FAQ section on company's website

Types of Products

Bricks (clay and concrete); decorative engraved stones, benches, plaques, walkway signs, artwork and graphic capabilities; color coordination

Donor Recognition Program

Donor certificates; duplicate bricks; miscellaneous products direct to donor

Supplementary Items

Proofing and verification systems and services; locator mapping; speed of items to construction site

1. *Teamwork* – For the fundraiser to be profitable, a team attitude needs to be instilled in all participant stakeholders. The synergistic benefits to a cohesive team environment are the amplification of fundraising energy and the encouragement of effort from all individuals involved in the program. Individual commitment will lead to the fruition of fundraising sales goals.

2. *Organization* – The rational foundation of a construction dedication fundraiser should be centered on the program's structure and organization. A strong and organized operation exudes professionalism while a disorganized undertaking will make a profound statement of apathy and overwhelming indifference.

3. *Empowerment with accountability* – All individuals engaged in the construction dedication fundraising program (particularly during the sales process) need to be empowered to make decisions and control their own performance. With empowerment, the fundraising administration needs to highlight the concept of accountability. Each empowered individual involved with the fundraiser needs to completely understand his/her accountability expectations.

4. *Leadership* – Owing to the duration of the construction dedication fundraising program (which can often be years), a sound leadership core will need to be formed and retained. The retention of the leadership core (which could be an intermingled collection of board members, fundraising administrators, and staff) will supply the fundraiser with long-term direction that will guide and motivate individuals to reach sales goals.

Long-Term Fundraising Goals

The most prominent ambition of any fundraising program is the attainment of its financial objectives. While this statement seems conceptually logical, in its application it can often get lost. The fundraising team should never lose sight of the income produced by sales, the maintenance of a stable profit margin, and, most notably, the controlling of projected and extraneous costs. Cost controls must be through operational efficiency as well as a cost-conscious state of mind among all program stakeholders.

Another long-term goal associated with a construction dedication fundraiser concerns the periphery benefit of creating a new level of awareness for the athletic organization. This attentiveness can positively stimulate an athletic organization's ticket sales, sponsorships, donations, and in-kind exchanges. Additionally, the heightened consciousness from a construction dedication fundraiser can also help develop a robust volunteer core for future athletic organization fundraising events, activities and programs.

A final, definitive, long-term goal of the construction dedication is the aesthetic improvement to the athletic organization's facilities, grounds and overall location. Improvements to the athletic organization's ambiance can overtly influence recruiting, ticket sales, visibility in the community, and the overall reputation of the fundraising program.

Short-Term Goals

The high priority short-term goals, which more correctly should be labeled short-term actions, all relate to the amplification and execution of the construction dedication fundraiser. Immediate actions such as the following should take precedence:

- formation of an administrative configuration/structure;
- delineation and differentiation of job descriptions for administration, operational staff, and volunteers;
- establishment and recruitment of a volunteer core;
- development of realistic, tangible sales goals (for both individuals and the entire fundraising program);
- articulation and operation of a logical marketing communication plan;
- research and contractual agreements with a reliable engraving company;
- meetings and clarification of fundraising stipulations with architects and construction engineers;
- systemization of sales (revenue collection, sales records, customer service, distribution, etc.); and
- other fundraising program elements.

Human Resource Requirements

Construction dedications are, predictably, labor-intensive fundraisers. With that being said, a top-down progression of establishing the fundraiser's administrative/leadership team at the outset, then recruiting the volunteer sales core to follow is the most sound development of the fundraising program's human resources. The number of volunteers needed to accomplish fundraising program goals relates directly to the magnitude of the project being applied for the construction dedication. For example, a small walkway with a limited number of dedication spaces accessible may need an administrative structure of a single program manager, a lone staff member, and a narrow volunteer pool. Conversely, a prominent undertaking such as a building, stadium or plaza will need a wide-ranging administrative team made up of board members and internal fundraising program administrators, scores of fundraising program employees, and an enormous volunteer core for sales.

As with most fundraising events, activities and programs, the volunteer core is frequently the most decisive success factor of a fundraiser. It is even more so with a construction dedication. To put the human resource element of a construction dedication fundraiser into the appropriate perspective, the volunteer core is the essential sales staff in a sales intensive fundraiser. They are the ones who make the contacts, facilitate sales, record data, and meet program objectives. However, the sales force for a construction dedication should not only be from external volunteers but from all internal athletic organization personnel (executive level, coaches, administrative assistants, even athletes) and fundraising board members.

No matter who is integrated into the sales force, each individual must have (1) an unambiguous picture of the operation through training, (2) a quota for sales, (3) straightforward lines of communication with fundraising team administrators, and (4) a monitoring system for performance. Supplementary human resource factors that lead to increased performance and fundraising success are illustrated in the following points:

- Each sales force member must be adept at the sales system, whether it is through a 'paper-and-pencil' approach or through web-based technology. The individual's comfort level with the system can have an unequivocal impact on their bottom-line productivity.

- Each sales force member must have a thorough knowledge of his/her job responsibilities and tasks. To acquire an effective uniformity, rudimentary job descriptions can be utilized.

- Each sales force member must be skilled in the fundamentals of personal selling tactics. Each individual should be cross-examined on FAQs.

- Each sales force member should be acknowledged for his/her contributions to the program. For individuals who surpass expectations, unique incentives could be developed.

- Each sales force member should be, through open lines of communication, continuously encouraged and regularly motivated. By stressing their worth to the athletic organization and fundraiser, each individual will have a discernable sense of inclusion.

Marketing Mix

Product

The quality and attributes of the product should be synchronized with the architect and construction engineers building the construction. The characteristics of the tile/brick/miscellaneous dedication should match the facilities, building, and walkway quality. For example, if an athletic organization is building a multi-million dollar facility, it would not be appropriate to use a low grade tile/brick as a visual component of the construction.

From a sales viewpoint, the customer's assessment of quality must be met by the product being marketed and sold. If expectations are not being fulfilled, the fundraiser will likely disappoint and/or fail. Two factors that most customers will concentrate on will be appearance and durability of the dedication.

Price

In a majority of cases, the cost of the dedication item to the fundraising program as well as its suggested retail/donation price to the contributors is determined by the engraving company. However, any modification to the suggested selling price (up or down) should be based on the prospective customer for the dedication item and his/her willingness to subsidize the fundraiser and athletic organization.

Place

When discussing the distribution facet of a construction dedication fundraiser, two factors need to be emphasized—safety and speed. The safety aspect of distribution relates to the engraving company's ability to get the product etched correctly, packaged, and shipped without damaging it. One damaged shipment that has to be recalled could severely slow down (if not shut down) a construction project. The second distribution factor concerns the sales and distribution speed to the construction site. For maximum promptness, reliable time frames must exist for (1) sales processing, (2) internal procedures, (3) engraving company's processing, and (4) delivery times.

Promotion

Pre-sales marketing communication should converge on advertising tactics, direct mail campaigns, and a comprehensive public relations drive in all relevant media outlets. The ultimate ambition of pre-sales promotion should be to generate awareness for the construction dedication as well as to prospect for fundraising program supporters. A thriving pre-sales marketing communications undertaking is one that has embraced not only the aggregate supporter base but the entire community. Advertising, which is through paid communications, can utilize TV, radio, print publications and all other avenues financially available. The advertising blend used will depend greatly on budgetary constraints. A pre-sales public relations drive should canvass any and all viable media outlets with press releases, personal contacts, in-kind trade/support, etc. The direct mail campaign could be the linkage between pre-sales marketing communication and the personal selling operation. The strategic tool for a direct mail operation is an all-inclusive brochure which itemizes the benefits and specifications of the construction dedication. The brochure could also be a direct order form for supporters who want to 'lock in' their dedication memorials. A number of engraving companies have brochure templates to help an athletic organization compose their own specific literature.

Once a pre-sales consciousness has been developed, the fundraiser needs to immediately commence its personal selling plan through its trained sales force. The three targeted groups for personal selling are:

1. Existing stakeholders (boosters, season ticket holders, businesses in strategic alliance with athletic organization, etc.);

2. The community in which the athletic organization resides; and

3. The general public (both locally and nationally, if applicable).

Program Operations

If the construction dedication fundraiser is for a major athletic organization facility (building, plaza, fountain, etc.), a kickoff event is a recommended activity. The fanfare for the fundraiser's kickoff could encompass a groundbreaking ceremony in conjunction with a promotional reception. The promotional reception should invite and attract media representatives, community and business V.I.P.s, board members, athletic organization personnel, athletes and the volunteer sales force for the construction dedication. The scale of the kickoff event could range from an unadorned reception with drinks and 'finger food' to a full-fledged banquet. The objective of the kickoff event (or events) is to draw attention to the fundraising program's marketing communication and to energize the sales staff.

From a day-to-day operational outlook, construction dedications should highlight the following points:

- The configuration and implementation of a system for tracking and collecting sales. This system should encompass accumulating sales forms and engraving information, accounting for and depositing money receipts, and delivering information to the engraving company.

- Monitoring and appraising the sales force for a construction dedication. This could entail

  - periodic comparisons of individual and group sales projections to actual sales;

  - redistribution or elimination of low-sales volunteers;

  - tracking sales by region and population centers;

  - adding or moving productive sales volunteers to high potential areas; and

  - providing feedback to the sales force.

- Staying well-versed on the progression of the fundraiser and acting as a liaison between the engraving company and the construction engineers/builders. The facilitation of the information flow between these organizations could deal with delivery times and volume, product specifications, and distinct issues unique to the construction.

- Fortification of marketing communication tactics used in pre-planning. If the previous marketing communication strategies were successful in producing awareness for the fundraiser, then the operational marketing/promotional goal should be to remind prospective supporters about the program and keep it fresh in their minds.

- A possibly overlooked but essential day-to-day activity for a construction dedication is financial recording. Each sale should generate a complete customer profile, not only for dedication mapping, but for future fundraising endeavors. The database should be as extensive as possible.

Program Termination

To gauge the level of success for a construction dedication is comparatively uncomplicated. Success is measured by the question: What percentage of projected dedications did the fundraiser actually sell? Obviously, the ultimate goal is to achieve 100% of projected sales and maximum project capacity. However, quantity sold should not be the only post-fundraising program evaluation criterion. The questions listed below should also be answered to help determine the construction dedication's success:

- How much community enthusiasm was stimulated by the fundraiser?

- What was the defined value of our volunteer core?

- How were the fundraising program's cost controls and operational efficiencies?

- Who were the identifiable community leaders, businesses, and alumni who 'went to bat' for the athletic organization and fundraising program?

- How engaged was the fundraising program's board of directors during the construction dedication fundraiser?

- From where were the preeminent groups of supporters coming?

- Which dedication products were the best sellers and why?

- What was the overall impression of the fundraiser?

As with the kickoff promotion, the project completion should have a grand opening to which all stakeholders, no matter what level of support or involvement, should be invited. The grand opening of the construction dedication could have a ribbon-cutting ceremony, a reception/banquet, certificates for all contributors, and comprehensive dedication mappings available to all stakeholders.

The initial element to describe when discussing promotional sales programs is the differentiation between product/holiday sales fundraising activities and promotional sales programs. The principal disparity between the two distinct fundraisers deals with their categorization and duration. Product sales fundraising activities are characteristically for terminal time frames and are more in line with augmenting funds for short-term operational expenses (annual expenses). Promotional sales programs are perpetual in nature and provide a stable stream of revenue with which the athletic organization can supplement both short-term (annual) and long-term (capital) expenses. Product sales are geared toward individual supporter sales, while promotional sales are focused on business sales. The varieties of athletic organizational promotional products in which businesses can purchase assorted elements include:

- Publications (advertising space)
- Facility Signage
- Website Banners and Links
- Visitor Travel Guides

Types of Promotional Sales Programs

Publications – The diversity and volume of publications that an athletic organization can produce is extensive. Each team/program within the athletic organization can generate game-day programs, media guides, pre- and post- season guides, schedule cards and posters, and flyers. Within this vast quantity of publications and promotional materials lies the potential for hundreds (conceivably thousands) of advertising space sales.

Signage – For every athletic facility, signage sales are a conspicuous opportunity. Signage possibilities and promotional displays that businesses can purchase include (but are not limited to) the following:

- wall space in a gymnasium;
- wall space in an aquatics facility;
- outfield fencing for softball and baseball complexes;
- tennis court fencing;
- soccer field barriers and stands;
- track and field barriers and stands;
- football scoreboards and seating; and
- electronic scoreboards and arena signs.

Fundraising Tip

The governing body of the athletic organization (State HSAA, NJCAA, NCAA, NAIA, etc.) will have explicit bylaws and regulations for this type of fundraiser. Consult all pertinent literature related to this program and, if there are any uncertainties, contact the governing body's compliance office directly.

For a signage promotional sales program to be successful, the images of both the business and the athletic organization need to be preserved and protected. Primary visual placement as well as sizes, graphics, and color schemes necessitate thoughtful consideration.

Website banners and links – Informational websites that publicize the athletic organization can also have links and banners that publicize businesses. Banners and web links can have exceptional features that go beyond permanent publication and signage advertising. The promotional messages have the capability to be continuously rotated electronically, which, in turn, can maximize revenue potential. Video streaming links and banners is also a distinct possibility.

Visiting travel guides – The formation of a visitors/visiting team travel guide has extraordinary financial promise for an athletic organization's promotional sales program. Visiting travel guides are documents that are transmitted, either electronically or by hard copy, to each team and/or group traveling to the athletic organization's location. They catalog (for fees or in-kind trade) all hospitality businesses and regional attractions within the general geographic area of the athletic organization. The benefits for an individual business enterprise participating in this program is that their brand name will be seen by hundreds of traveling teams with thousands of athletes, coaches, administrators, and family members. Hospitality establishments such as restaurants, convenience/grocery stores, hotels and motels, and transportation services are just a handful of the likely businesses for the travel guide promotional sales program.

General Promotional Sales Program Information

Planning – Promotional sales programs necessitate well-defined and separate strategic plans to facilitate their current and future operations. These types of programs can employ the same planning components as the overall athletic organization fundraising plan (discussed in Chapter 2). Furthermore, the promotional sales program will be incorporated as a prominent ingredient in the overall athletic organization's fundraising plan. However, promotional sales program plans should underscore the following distinctive elements:

- isolating marketing mix elements which accentuate program benefits, features, and costs;
- explaining potential revenue sources and cost controls through factual quantitative measurements;
- demarcating targeted objectives such as promotional sales goals and capacity utilization; and
- enumerating sales strategies to embrace prospecting, sales presentations, and sales facilitation.

Program establishment – It is necessary to acknowledge that in developing these forms of fundraising programs from the ground up, it takes tremendous energy and time to (1) create a stable clientele base and (2) reach maximum potential. Furthermore, once the program is operational, the continuation of client relationships as well as the ongoing cultivation of new prospective clients is a full-time undertaking. Like most visual fundraisers, if the dedication to and effort toward its success is not 100%, it is better to omit this form of fundraising program than to incorporate it as a core component of the fundraising operation.

In-kind trade – It is noteworthy that in-kind trade is ideal for this category of fundraiser. Is cash preferable? Not necessarily. If in-kind products/services are bartered at wholesale prices, not only will the athletic organization avoid cash expenses for products that would normally be purchased, but those products would be acquired through exchanges at reduced, non-retail prices.

Contractual arrangements – This type of fundraising program should have straightforward sales contracts that are well-structured and understandable to all parties involved. All contracts and agreements should be scrutinized by athletic organization legal counsel. Additionally, accounts receivable policies and transaction recording procedures will need to be structured through systems established by CPAs.

Product specialists – It is imperative to synchronize the sales aspect of a promotional sales program with the product specialists who produce the promotional products. Product specialists are technical professionals with proficiency and knowledge in the construction and distribution of promotional products. It is vital that they receive definitive guidance on each individual sale. Specifications such as location/placement, dimensions, and graphics all require clear lines of communication. For example, in a college/university setting, the product specialists for athletic organization publications are sports information directors. As technical authorities, they have product-specific proficiency in the creation of the athletic organization's media documents and promotional materials (e.g., media guides, visitor handbooks, gameday programs). However, without coordination and consultation from the fundraiser's program coordinator and sales staff, they cannot produce the individual advertisements for the customers.

Promotional Sales Program Objectives

In some shape or manner, most athletic organizations will produce publications, signage, websites, and travel guides. These items, which are constructed by the athletic organization, can be developed into lucrative fundraisers. The development of long-term cooperative relationships is a foundational objective for the success of the promotional sales program. These associations, which should have mutually beneficial advantages for both organizations, must aim for renewals as well as original sales. With a foundation of businesses renewing on a regular basis, the promotional sales program's targeted growth goals will be more realistic.

Customer service is an indispensible objective of the promotional sales program. Each business must experience personalized service and have an impression that their promotional advertisement, sign, link/banner, or travel guide inclusion is of great consequence to the promotional sales program. While technology can help facilitate the program's operation, personal contacts (either face-to-face or by phone conversations) must be the main communication and sales method.

Another program objective should be the operational philosophy of targeting capacity utilization. Each category of promotional sales (publication, signage, web link/banner, and travel guide) will all have capacity limitations. There are only so many advertising spots in the athletic organization's publications, so many signage areas in the athletic organization's facilities, so many link and banner opportunities available on the athletic organization's website, and so many pages in the athletic organization's visitors guide for businesses to purchase promotional products. Prior to the inauguration of the promotional sales program, a listing of all vacant sales opportunities should be determined. That listing (in each different sales category) represents the capacity targets for the promotional sales program. The listing's fulfillment is the ultimate sales objective for the program.

Each business participating in the promotional sales program is going to ask the same question: What is the promotional exposure of our purchase? This question is much better answered with authoritative numbers rather than broad projections. Quantitative measures such as number of publications distributed, media and fan coverage for athletic competitions in the signage program, aggregate total of web hits and link/banner connections, and number of teams and individuals who will receive and use the athletic organization's travel guide all need to be a part of the sales pitch. Obviously, the more coverage and exposure a promotional product has, the more value and revenue it can generate. In addition to quantitative support for the promotional sales program, target market profiles on who will receive and see each promotional sale need to be delineated.

Selectivity in business solicitations should be taken into consideration as a foundational goal. Businesses targeted for promotional sales must complement the values of the athletic organization. A promotional connection with a controversial or inappropriate business venture could damage the athletic organization's reputation far beyond the financial gains of the promotional sale.

Marketing of the Promotional Sales Program

Product Elements

Once again, since the fundraising sales program is joined directly to the athletic organization's image, quality is an imperative element for the fundraiser. Some basic quality factors and product features that need defining for the promotional sales program are detailed in Table 9.2.

Before developing the sales program and marketing strategies, an exact listing of promotional products with their specifications and prices should be constructed.

Table 9.2. Quality and Features of Promotional Sales

Publication Advertisements

Print and font style; color scheme; graphics, image/logo/trademark considerations; wording; contact information; sizes; placement

Facility Signage

Print and font style (for readability at facility); color scheme (not to clash or distract from competition); wording; graphics; materials – metal, cloth, nylon; sizes; hanging attachments and safety considerations; placement

Web Links and Banners

Links and banner timing; print and font styles; wording; color scheme (not to clash with website information); interaction and video capabilities; scrolling speed; placement

Visitor Travel Guide

Print and font style; wording; consistency in presentation; comprehensive business information; locations; category breakdown for referencing – hotel/motel, restaurant, maps and mileage charts; placement

---

Table 9.3. Value Specific Consideration in Pricing Promotional Sales

Publication Advertisements

- ¼, ½, or full page
- Front or back cover (inside and outside)
- Distinct placement inside document
- Noticeable positioning and sizes on flyer, schedule poster, or schedule card

Signage

- Location and prominence of sign placement
- Facility for sign placement
- Media and fan exposure

Web Link/Banner

- Frequency and permanence
- Video streaming
- Site hits and visits per period

Visitor Guides/Team Travel Guides

- Placement and prominence in guidebook
- Business information details
- Distribution capabilities

Knowing all of the promotional product features available for a business to purchase is the first step in selling advertisement spaces, signage, web links, and guidebook inclusion. This listing can also be assembled for distribution to potential business clients as an advertising tool for the program. If this is the case, the promotional product's specifications sheet should be coherently structured and have complete listings of all product features for the entire promotional sales program product line. Any deviations from the listing specifications (i.e., different sizes, locations, placements) must be approved by all parties involved with the fundraising program.

Pricing Considerations

The pricing of products and services (as discussed in Chapter 6) can be by cost plus pricing, competition/market pricing, or value pricing. While cost and market pricing aspects can help determine pricing foundations, the promotional sales program pricing should be primarily determined by the value given to the customer. Value will be centered on quality and features, targeting capabilities, and exposure and sales generation of the promotional product. Value determination can be used in concert with distinct elements for each promotional product (detailed in Table 9.3)

All of the factors in Table 9.3 will have divergent values. For example, a promotional sign located at a baseball/softball complex's centerfield has a considerably more value than a sign placed on a lower visibility foul line. Another signage example could be the value difference between an electronic, continuously rotating arena sign in a high traffic area compared to a permanent sign in a low-use/low-traffic facility. Because of each athletic organization's unique circumstances, the fundraising team will need to take into account all of the situations when valuing and pricing promotional sales products.

Marketing Communication Tactics

The dominant marketing communication tactic for a promotional sales program is personal selling and relationship building. Other marketing communication mechanisms such as advertising, public relations, sales promotions, and direct mail can be employed to generate awareness for the fundraising program. The 'personal touch' associated with personal selling is the means to developing long-term business relationships. If starting the promotional sales program from scratch, prospecting strategies for contacting businesses will need to be utilized. Prospecting for new contacts can range from cold calling area businesses to elaborating promotional events tied into athletic organization competitions. Recruiting athletic organization stakeholders to help develop networking connections is a formidable prospecting technique. Each internal stakeholder could supply (either through requests or mandates) 10 promising business connections for the fundraising sales staff to contact. Another viable tactic to acquire business connections and produce subsequent sales is a business referral program.

REFERRAL PROGRAM OVERVIEW

A promotional sales referral program is a proactive way for the athletic organization's fundraising department to enhance business contacts and networking connections. The referral program will actively solicit recommendations from businesses currently participating in the promotional sales program for different incentives. The recommending business could receive:

- a finder's fee for each prospective business contacted;
- a full referral fee after the recommended business purchases a promotional product; and
- a periodic royalty fee every year the recommended business renews its promotional product purchase.

There are many advantages to the promotional sales referral program. From the athletic organization's perspective, the program will broaden its base of businesses connections while minimizing organizational resource expenditures. Current businesses are a strong selling resource for the promotional sales program. Referrals will generate positive word of mouth among local businesses, which will increase promotional program recognition and external sales. From the current participating businesses' standpoint, the program is an undemanding way to supplement income which can be used to increase their promotional purchase. Finally, from the fundraising program's standpoint, the referrals will generate new business promotional sales with no cost risks. Since the program is designed to be a compensation-based plan, only when funds have been received will complete remuneration be paid to referring businesses.

REFERRAL PROGRAM OPERATION

The operation of the program is clear-cut and unproblematic to implement:

- Generate interest in the program with an internally and externally focused promotional campaign. The bulk of this marketing effort should be concentrated on existing businesses that have purchased promotional products in the past. Techniques to be employed encompass:
  - Personal selling by program coordinators

- Phone and email contacts
- Enlistment of business associations
- Promotion through information forums

- The promotional sales program coordinator will act as the referral program's facilitator. All referrals will go through that individual (unless the volume warrants additional assistance).
- All full referral fees will be determined and paid after a promotional sales commitment (and payment) by the referred business.
- Continuous royalty fees will be distributed at the end of each additional year of promotional sales.

Remember: After (and only after) the new business has committed to a promotional product purchase will the fundraising program generate the compensation check for the recommending business.

Human Resource Requirements

The promotional sales program, while exploiting all internal stakeholders for the development of business connections, should have a principal sales staff that consists of selling professionals and an internal fundraising program administrator as the program's operational coordinator. The selling professionals can come from the fundraising staff (depending upon their qualifications and negotiation skills) or can be external commission-based sales experts. The sales staff's responsibility is to prospect for new businesses, make primary contacts, and to generate final sales. The program coordinator's primary function is to take the information from the final sales and to coordinate the final promotional product with the specialist. Additionally, other administrative tasks that could be a component of the promotional sales program coordinator's duties could include database development, tracking sales and placements, billing and accounts receivable management, notifying clients on renewal information, and overseeing the sales staff.

DEFERRED GIFTS, WILLS, AND BEQUESTS

Deferred gifts and endowments are more comparable to planned gifts rather than special events and activities. The program's goal is to transfer monetary gifts and pledged assets to an athletic organization through fiduciary trusts, wills and endowments, and insurance policies and annuities. While this concept might seem somewhat radical for a small athletic organization, the long-term benefits of such solicitations are tremendously alluring. For example, endowed scholarships are directly related to an athletic program's wins and losses. They provide the scholarships the athletic team/program needs to compete.

For a deferred gift, will, or request fundraising program, legal counsel/lawyers are a compulsory component of the operation. Lawyers:

- assist in the generation of the fundraising program's planning, structure and staff necessities;

- construct technical processes which demarcate the step-by-step guidance for the program;

- are involved with all deferred gifts, wills and bequests in conjunction with the contributor's legal counsel/lawyers; and

- certify that all documentation is in proper legal format and in compliance with all state and federal laws and tax regulations.

In essence, lawyers are the controlling management of this category of fundraising program. An athletic organization can have these individuals on staff, on retainer, or as associates in the booster/fundraising program's board of directors. Some fundamental deferred gift, will and bequest programs can include the following:

Deferred payment gift annuities – In basic language, this type of program is equivalent to a retirement plan. Instead of an individual making stipulated payments throughout his/her life to a pension fund, the donor makes payments to the athletic organization with a guaranteed income, depending on the revenue put in and time frames to retirement, at the time of retirement. Additionally, instead of stipulated payments throughout one's life, a one-time cash gift (or multiple unscheduled cash gifts) can be donated and applied as retirement annuities.

Annuity trusts – These are the donations, investments, or assets/money given to an athletic organization with the assurance of fixed annuities immediately for the donor and/or designated beneficiary. The institution expropriates possession of the pledged asset at the time of the donor's death.

Charitable lead trusts – These are external trust funds authorized to compensate the athletic organization with fixed annuities. At the time of death, the principle funds are designated to an identifiable recipient or the athletic organization.

Donation of property – This is either the contribution of property at the time of death or the bestowing of property during one's lifetime, but retaining operational use until death. Property can go beyond traditional land and/or facilities to include all forms of assets.

CORPORATE AND BUSINESS FUNDRAISING PROGRAMS

In-Kind Gift Program

An in-kind gift program is predicated on an exchange of goods/services. The athletic organization obtains products and services in exchange for exposure/marketing communication opportunities for the business' products and services. This program is ideal for businesses with an earnest desire to support the athletic organization but without the monetary means. In the simplest terms, a business' products and services are more conducive for donations than actual cash. For the in-kind gift program to be beneficial, all stakeholders must have the outlook that in-kind product and service donations are the same as cash. Cash conserved is cash earned.

Any product or service used by an athletic organization has the potential for an in-kind fundraising program exchange. Prior to initiating an in-kind program, fundraising administrators will need to (in collaboration with the athletic organization's administration, coaches, and staff) compose a list of all assets and services used by the athletic organization. This inventory will be the foundation for solicitations.

Internal athletic organization networking as well as external community associations with current business supporters are critical factors in developing in-kind donation contacts. Internal networking should include everyone involved in the athletic organization (administration, staff, sales, maintenance, athletes). External connections can be developed through existing business contacts or through networking opportunities at area business events (e.g., Chamber of Commerce, business associations, local clubs).

The fundraising program should appoint one in-house fundraising administrator and a board of directors member as program coordinators. The internal fundraising administrator should have extensive selling qualifications as well as strong negotiation skills and aptitude. The external board of directors member should have multifarious business connections and an unassailable reputation in the community. Additional staff assistance for the program will depend on the work level and significance of the program to the athletic organization.

The sales program (which can be initiated by any athletic organization stakeholder) should be assertive and active. Through personal selling tactics, the accentuation on mutually beneficial transactions should be stressed. Businesses can piggyback on athletic organization advertising, acquire positive public relations advantages, have productive quid pro quo tradeoffs, and considerable tax benefits from contributing to the athletic organization's in-kind fundraising program. Additionally, promotional giveaways can be utilized to 'sweeten the deal' with business owners/operators.

Comprehensive contribution documentation detailing all donations should be submitted immediately to the owners/contributors. Dates, quantities, and values are among some of the documentation elements. As with all tax and legal forms, the donation templates should be evaluated and endorsed by tax and legal professionals.

Not only can brand-new products be requested, but any business that has a surplus of used products (in suitable condition) should be targeted. The key to this type of exchange is that the product be in safe, usable order. While an in-kind gift program seems perfect for tangible products, do not overlook the value of donated services. Services such as legal, accounting, website construction/maintenance, marketing and advertising, and maintenance are just a few of the possible service options. As with products, make a register of all services used by athletic organization. That listing could be an addition to targeted products inventory.

Corporate Sponsorship Program

In today's corporate world, businesses are struggling to balance their genuine desire for corporate citizenship and social responsibility with uncertain and difficult

Fundraising Tip

When soliciting in-kind gifts/trades, underscore the fact that all in-kind gifts/trades are valued at retail but cost the donating organization the purchased value. Also, highlight the possibility of substantial tax implications of retailed value gifts.

economic times. A corporate sponsorship fundraising program with an athletic organization could provide an opportunity for a business entity to contribute to a viable non-profit organization while getting perceptible value for their donations. In other words, a corporate sponsorship arrangement is a win-win for both organizations.

Corporate Vantage

From a corporate standpoint, sponsorship of an athletic organization can be a core ingredient of the operation's strategic marketing plan. The advantage to utilizing sponsorship as a foundational element in a business' strategic marketing plan is through identifying relevant strategic fit factors/criteria with the athletic organization that can benefit both operations. Strategic fit elements between the athletic organizations and businesses relate to the following factors:

- An interconnected and balanced image match between the two entities. The key is the balance between both organizations. One organization's image cannot drastically supersede another's for a mutually beneficial, strategic fit.

- A distinct and measurable customer crossover base between both operations. This customer crossover base can be dissected by demographic (characteristics), psychographics (lifestyles), geographic (location) and behavioral (action) factors.

- A synergistic advantage from both organizations working together. This, in turn, will provide a competition advantage and a new level of awareness for both operations.

- A reciprocal marketing communication/promotional relationship in which joint promotional campaign will increase exposure and decrease costs for both operations.

A corporation can attain internal benefits from sponsoring a non-profit athletic organization as well, the most evident benefit being the development of a socially responsible atmosphere inside the business operation. By developing a vested interest in a fun and constructive non-profit organization, employees can understand organizational values, which can increase productivity and retention. Additionally, the athletic organization can sponsor corporate-only events and activities. Employees exhibiting positive behavior and productivity could receive prime seating (in the corporate block section) at an athletic organization's competition(s) as an extrinsic reward.

Athletic Organization Vantage

The initial element that must be explained when discussing corporate sponsorship for athletic organizations is that they differ from in-kind fundraising programs. In-kind programs, while also targeting businesses, are concentrated on the acquisition of products and services. Corporate sponsorship programs are centered on monetary transfers. This is not to promote one program over the other. Both are critical value-added fundraisers. It is to state that the focal point is different when money is a primary target.

The accentuation on money for corporate sponsorships (often dealing with considerable dollar amounts) makes it imperative that the athletic organization's top executives and fundraising board members take the lead in solicitations. Corporate sponsorship programs are a one-on-one personal selling endeavor that must be performed by the highest level representatives of the athletic organization. While connections can be made by all possible stakeholders, contacts and the actual 'wine and dine' fundraising must be done by top, visible executives. The ultimate goal of this executive-level relationship building is the development of long-term associations that benefit both the corporate enterprise and the athletic organization.

The scope of corporate sponsorships can range from being basic contributors at a fundraising event all the way to being signature sponsors on a facility/field/building. If a business wants to get involved with small-scale contributions, then the donations should be gratefully received and acknowledged. Optimistically, small sponsors, with continuous interaction and tangible benefits, can become significant signature sponsors in the future.

Credit Card Strategic Alliances

© iStockphoto.com/hidesy

A credit card strategic alliance is not the same as a credit card commission sales program. A credit card commission-based sales program is comparable to a product sales fundraising activity. For every valid application collected, the athletic organization receives a one-time sales commission. A credit card strategic alliance fundraising program (also identified as an affinity credit card fundraising program) is one in which perpetual revenue/kickbacks are given based on the percentage of purchases for all cards distributed in the name of the athletic organization. These programs can also feature commissions for applications collected (and credit acceptances) in addition to continuous revenue generations.

Every type of athletic organization can use this program. However, the conventional adopters of this fundraiser have been sizeable athletic organizations inside well-known educational institutions. The obvious advantage of a credit card strategic alliance is that, if developed and executed correctly, it generates a continuous stream of revenue for the athletic organization. The obvious disadvantage (which often precludes small to mid-sized athletic organizations from the program) is receiving an ample amount of credit cards issued in the athletic organization's name to make the fundraiser worthwhile.

The overall mission of the credit card strategic alliance program is to determine (1) the targeted goal in number of cards issued on the athletic organization's behalf and (2) the expected incremental revenue generated by those issued credit cards. To reach this objective, an aggressive marketing communication campaign should be developed. This campaign should convince athletic organization supporters to sacrifice points and personal rewards from other credit cards for the benefit of the athletic organization. It should be noted that a person participating in the fundraiser has no upfront costs.

However, there is a loss of personal gains/incentives from other possible credit card reward programs (cash back, travel and frequent flier miles, free or reduced merchandise, etc.). Marketing promotional tactics could encompass the following items:

- Bulk mailing of credit card fundraising program literature and applications. The mailing should have a personalized cover letter and/or brochure which explain the fundraising program's purpose and its significance to the athletic organization. The literature should 'strike a chord' with the potential supporter and appeal to his/her sense of commitment to the athletic organization. The application (from the financial institution issuing credit cards) should be exclusive to the athletic organization and have an illustration of the issued credit cards with logos, mascots, and pictures.

- Piggybacking on other athletic organization marketing promotions. Whenever possible, credit card literature and applications should be integrated into other fundraising events, activities and programs. Whether it is an addition to another athletic organization mailer, distribution at a fundraising event, or having credit card information available at competitions, the canvassing of credit card applications should be a primary selling approach of the fundraiser.

- Other credit card promotional activities could include the following:
  - Within the entire institution (not only the athletic division) have an interdepartmental competition for the most participation and sales in the credit card program. The department that accumulates the most valid applications will win a noteworthy and desired promotional prize as well as institution-wide recognition.
  - The development of promotional activities geared toward alumni should be strategically highlighted in the marketing communication campaign for a credit card strategic alliance program. Credit card applications completed by alumni could entitle them to free tickets, reduced parking, merchandise, etc. The alumni should have a sense of inclusion and personal investment in the athletic organization with their participation in the fundraising program.
  - The credit card strategic alliance program should have an independent promotional approach for businesses (especially with financial ties to the athletic organization). The financial institution can issue business-only credit cards under the same premise as individual credit cards. The primary sales tactic for this division of the fundraiser should be through personal contacts and appeals.

> **Fundraising Tip**
>
> With advances in technology, the graphics and details for credit card designs are limitless. The program's fundraising administrator should select various logos and pictures for the supporters' cards that will increase the athletic organization's brand awareness and recognition. Providing credit card supporters a choice of cards with different graphics is a small but effective addition to the fundraiser.

The human resource administrative factor for this type of fundraiser is minimal. The program would need an in-house fundraising administrator to be designated as the liaison with the financial institution, as well as a volunteer coordinator to manage all of the marketing communication activities. Additionally, legal counsel will need to stay abreast of all subsequent laws and regulations associated with credit card strategic alliances. Conversely, the human resource staff and volunteer factor for a credit card strategic alliance could be extensive. Constructing and distributing bulk mailings, collecting and recording data on participants, monitoring sales, and controlling promotional activities all take considerable labor forces.

SUMMARY

No matter what the level or size of one's athletic organization, a foundational component of any fundraising strategic plan is its long-term, perpetual fundraising programs. Whether it is a booster club, construction dedication, sales promotion, or countless other fundraising programs, athletic organizations should purposefully measure, develop, and implement these fundraising elements as core components of their operation. Not only can these programs nurture a substantial and often permanent base of funds, they can also cultivate a sense of community with the athletic organization and its external stakeholders. While they can be difficult to construct, the zealous interest generated by long-term fundraising programs can have a profound impact on short-term revenue sources (e.g. attendance at athletic organization events, merchandise sales, annual fundraising activities) as well as team performance and athlete recruiting.

REVIEW AND DISCUSSION QUESTIONS

1. What are some of the benefits of developing a booster program?

2. What are the benefits of a cohesive booster program infrastructure?

3. For a booster program kick-off, why should different tiers have different events and promotional activities?

4. What are the operational specifications for a construction dedication?

5. What are the research points for a brick engraving company?

6. Which factors should be used when examining and monitoring a construction dedication sales force?

7. What is the difference between a product/holiday sales fundraising activity and a promotional sales program?

8. What are the possible types of publications and promotional material that can be used by an athletic organization during a promotional sales program?

9. What are the advantages of a promotional sales referral program?

10. What is the primary goal of a deferred gift, will, and bequest fundraising program?

11. What are the exchange elements in an in-kind gift program?

12. What are the four strategic fit elements for a corporate sponsorship fundraising program?

10

Summer Instructional Sports Camp Fundraisers

INTRODUCTION

From a sports-exclusive perspective, a lucrative and popular fundraising enterprise is found in instructional sports camps and clinics. Typically, these ventures are conducted during summer months and are fundamentally different from recreational summer camps. Recreational camps are more aligned with an extensive range of entertaining but independent activities in a child care environment. Instructional camps (in this case athletic instructional ventures) are sports-explicit and highly structured programs. "Sports are a natural fit for theme camps with many children seeking to improve athletic skills in the off-season. In the past, summer instructional sport programs were often limited to private clubs, but community centers and parks and recreation departments offering sports programs have opened up this type of program to a diverse population" (Culpepper, 2007, p. 58). The opportunity for generating fundraising revenue from summer sports camps is considerable.

The net revenue from a summer sports camp fundraiser can be used by coaches and athletic personnel to fund sports specific items such as:

- salaries;
- travel—team and recruiting;
- uniforms and equipment;
- operating and administrative expenses;
- recruiting costs; and
- marketing communication and promotional costs.

Additionally, the funds raised by a summer instructional camp can be applied to the overall athletic organization's expenditures. The proceeds from these prominently profiled, sports-specific fundraisers should be designated in advance to circumvent any possible misunderstandings and conflicts.

If a summer sports camp is to be developed and implemented through a distinct athletic organization's sport and coaching staff, it is imperative that all of the camp operations be absolutely separated and autonomous from one's coaching position and athletic program administration. To integrate a camp venture with a sport's normal administrative operations could be at best confusing and at worst destructive. Even though the proceeds from the camp can fund an individual sport's operations, the camp fundraiser should be treated as an entrepreneurial venture disconnected from the sport and overall athletic organization.

Sport instructional camps can have the auxiliary benefit (beyond raising immediate operational funds and training individual campers) of bringing parents into the athletic organization and team. In other words, "not only do summer camps generate extra revenue, they help develop relationships with parents—you know, the people with the money...the best way to impress parents is to put together a camp that uses children's time productively" (Janda, 2000, p. 28). Obviously, the more superior the quality of instruction and experiences generated by the camp (memories and camaraderie), the more likely the parent and other family members will contribute and support the athletic organization and its future fundraising endeavors.

FEASIBILITY STUDY

If constructing a new camp venture from the ground up, doing competitive research (local and regional) on other similar summer instructional camps is a necessary first step in a feasibility study. Each comparable camp should be investigated for the following:

- S.W.O.T. analysis components (strengths, weaknesses, opportunities, and threats)
- Current customer base loyalty
- Traditions in the community
- Resources and administrative capabilities
- Features that distinguish the camp from other operations
- Marketing mix elements such as
    - value and characteristics of its product and services;
    - pricing structure;
    - location and facility advantages; and
    - promotional communication tactics
- Human resource elements such as signature clinicians, camp instructor's backgrounds and expertise, and administrative qualifications
- Other competition-specific items

Fundraising Tip

A summer camp partnership program involves all sports-specific operations in the athletic organization functioning under one administrative summer instructional camp 'roof.' The advantages to this tactic are: pooling resources, maximizing capacity, and realizing economies of scale benefits.

If, after performing an analysis of relevant competitors, a fundraising or sports-specific program administrator judges that there is an opportunity and the market can sustain an additional summer instructional sports camp venture, an internal examination for viability must be conducted. Questions to be asked about an athletic organization's or sport's competencies and skills include (but are not limited to) the following:

- Does the athletic organization or sport program have the resources to take on a fundraising undertaking of this magnitude?

- Does the athletic organization or sports program have the upfront capital to start a summer camp fundraiser?

- Are facilities available for the projected summer camp operation?

- Does the athletic organization or sports program have the proficiency (both administratively and instructionally) to operate a summer sports instructional camp?

- Is there sufficient time available for the development of a camp plan, structuring the operation, marketing and promoting the camp, and organizing and administering an enterprise of this depth?

If, after both internal and external research proves the feasibility of a summer sports camp, an inclusive operational theme and strategy must be determined.

THEME AND OPERATIONAL STRATEGY

Thompson, Strickland, and Gamble describe five distinct operational themes and overall competitive strategies that must be examined by any business operation. They are:

1. *A low-cost provider strategy* – striving to achieve lower overall costs than rivals and appealing to a broad spectrum of customers, usually by under-pricing rivals.

2. *A broad differentiation strategy* – seeking to differentiate the company's product offering from rivals' in ways that appeal to a broad spectrum of buyers.

3. *A best-cost provider strategy* – giving customers more value for the money by incorporating good-to-excellent product attributes at a lower cost than rivals; the target is to have the lowest (best) costs and prices compared to rivals offering products with comparable attributes.

4. *A focused (or market niche) strategy based on low costs* – concentrating on a narrow buyer segment and outcompeting rivals by having lower costs than rivals and this being able to serve niche members at a lower price.

5. *A focused (or market niche) strategy based on differentiation* – concentrating on a narrow buyer segment and outcompeting rivals by offering niche members customized attributes that meet their tastes and requirements better than rivals' products. (Thompson, Strickland, & Gamble, 2010, p. 140)

Fundraising Tip

The fundraising team or sports-specific coaching/program staff must critically examine both the internal and external environments prior to the decision to launch a summer instructional camp. It is better to not to run a summer instructional sports camp at all than to operate a camp that is doomed to fail.

The selection of one of these far-reaching summer sports camp themes/competitive strategies should not be settled on hastily. It is the foundational aspect of the operation from which all other strategies stem. Once the summer instructional camp's overall strategy is chosen (and one must be definitively selected), a summer camp's operation will be indentified and often 'locked-in' with that strategic perception in the customer's mind.

No matter what operational premise and inclusive competitive strategy the summer instructional camp adopts, understand that "most summer camps share a common goal: to bring together new faces, offer new activities, and provide a home-away-from-home experience that helps kids build confidence" (Howard & Moore, 2008, p. 1). While the goal of sports-exclusive instruction and profitability are the paramount objectives of a summer instructional camp, the intangible experiences gained by the participants are just as important for the fundraiser's future growth and fruition.

COMMITMENT TO TOTAL QUALITY MANAGEMENT

It is well documented throughout hundreds of managerial textbooks and writing that one of the most important philosophies in today's business world relates to leadership's and management's commitment to the concept of Total Quality Management (TQM). In beginning a discussion of fundraising (summer sport instructional camps especially), dedication to quality should be a primary consideration. This concept, which can be adapted to athletics and summer sports camps, emphasizes that every action in the operation (administrative, instructional, customer service, etc.) should have quality as its primary objective.

What precisely is TQM, and how can summer instructional sports camp administrators, instructors, and staff utilize these principles? Deming, who was one of the most influential business figures of the 20th century, created a 14-point philosophy on quality management that is universal to all businesses, including summer sport camps. The following is a summation of his philosophies:

1. *Create constancy of purpose* – strive for long-term improvements rather than short-term profits.

2. *Adopt the new philosophy* – don't tolerate delays and mistakes.

3. *Cease dependence on mass inspection* – build quality into the process on the front end.

4. *End the practice of awarding business on the price tag alone* – build long-term relationships.

5. *Improve constantly and forever the system of production and service* – at each stage.

6. *Institute training and retraining* – continually update methods and thinking.

7. *Institute leadership* – provide resources needed for effectiveness.

8. *Drive out fear* – people must believe it is safe to report problems or ask for help.

9. *Break down barriers among departments* – promote teamwork.

10. *Eliminate slogans, exhortations, and arbitrary targets* – supply methods, not buzzwords.

11. *Eliminate numerical quotas* – they are contrary to the idea of continuous improvement.

12. *Remove barriers to pride in workmanship* – allow autonomy and spontaneity.

13. *Institute a vigorous program of education and retraining* – people are assets, not commodities.

14. *Take action to accomplish the transformation* – provide a structure that enables quality. (Bateman & Snell, 2011, pp. 321-322)

If a fundraising administrator or clinician can cultivate a summer instructional sports camp environment where there is an unconditional focus on and commitment to operational quality, the positive outcomes can considerably outweigh the time and effort required to implement these philosophies.

While summer sports camps are exclusive to the particular sport for which the participants are being trained, there are some recognizable, universal keys that transcend all sports camps and clinics. The following sections (Pre-Camp Administration, Summer Camp Operation, and Post-Camp Evaluation) and their conceptualizations can be focused on one's particular sport and its explicit operational methodology.

PRE-CAMP ADMINISTRATION: GENERAL ADMINISTRATION

Fundraising Plan

A summer instructional sports camp is frequently a central (if not solitary) component of an individual sport's and athletic organization's revenue stream. A summer camp plan should be employed to focus and systematize the camp's operations. The summer instructional sports camp plan is not of the same depth and complexity as the all-inclusive athletic program fundraising plan (outlined in Chapter 2); however, the formation of an abbreviated version that utilizes select modules of the athletic fundraising program plan, as well as original and camp-specific items, is indispensable. Figure 10.1 outlines the sectional breakdown of a summer instructional sports camp fundraising plan. The development of Sections 1-3 and 5-8 are featured throughout Chapter 2. However, Section 4—Operational Plan and Structure—necessitates singular delineation.

Summer instructional sports camp operations and structural determinates can incorporate the following elements:

1. *Category of instructional sports camp* – Are the camps going to be:

   - day camps with athletes being transported daily to and from camp?
   - overnight camps where participants stay in pre-arranged housing and have synchronized food plans?
   - team camps with tournament competition?
   - specialty sessions for singular, precise skill development?
   - coach's clinics in conjunction with other camp operations?

2. *Location decisions* – Is the facility (or facilities):

   - centrally positioned for maximum sales and customer accessibility?
   - suitable for the type of camp being presented?
   - cost prohibitive or reasonably priced?
   - safe, secure, and clean?
   - projecting the image the sport, fundraising program, and athletic organization want to exhibit?

3. *Governing body rules and stipulations* – Who is the athletic organization's principal governing body (NCAA, NJCAA, NAIA, high school athletic organizations, Junior Olympic, etc.)? What are their provisos/requisites on summer instructional sports camps' composition and operations?

4. *Equipment needs* – Planning questions should be posed, such as:

   - What are the targeted equipment requirements for the anticipated camps?
   - Do the athletic organization and sport have the appropriate equipment presently to facilitate camp operations?
   - What is the condition of the existing equipment? Is it in proper and safe condition?
   - If the athletic organization and sport have deficiencies in relation to equipment and the proposed summer instructional sports camp, are funds available to purchase the appropriate equipment?
   - Is the equipment summer sports-specific or can it be utilized by the athletic organization and sport after the summer camp is over?

Figure 10.1. **Summer Instructional Sports Camp Fundraising Plan**

Section 1: Summer Sports Camp Overview

Section 2: Mission and Long-Term Objectives

Section 3: S.W.O.T. Analysis

Section 4: Operational Plan and Structure

Section 5: Human Resource Systems

Section 6: Marketing and Promotional Communication Tactics

Section 7: Budgets and Financial Information

Section 8: Policies and Procedures

5. *Utilization of technology* – What form of technology will be required for the summer sports camp? Will it:
    - be user-friendly and accessible?
    - have a minimal or elevated learning curve?
    - be relevant to the camp's operations?
    - be affordable?
    - have a shelf-life and usefulness beyond the actual camp?

6. *Financial practices and budgeting* – Financial areas to delineate and construct could include:
    - accounts receivable policies and procedures;
    - accounts payable policies and procedures;
    - payroll systems (Will the staff be paid as independent contractors through I-9 regulations, or will they be classified as athletic organization employees and paid through the regular payroll process?);
    - break-even point analysis;
    - pre-camp budgeting;
    - post-camp financial statements and recording; and
    - other financial requirements as influenced by the athletic organization and its governing body.

7. *Strategic alliances* – Is having reciprocally advantageous relationships with local, regional, or national companies a pre-camp administrative consideration? Anything that can be utilized and/or consumed in camp (merchandise, equipment, food, the actual facility, etc.) can be explored for a potential strategic alliance with a company. The company obtains exposure with summer sports camp participants for its products/services. The summer camp fundraiser receives free or reduced products/services, which strengthen the bottom-line profitability of the fundraiser.

8. *Safety* – Summer sports camp safety should by no means be disregarded during the planning and structuring phase of pre-camp administration. Safety elements to reflect upon include:
    - insurance requirements (for athletes, staff, and facility);
    - medical staff and trainers;
    - facility safety (along with equipment safety);
    - location and area safety;
    - staff and personnel safety;
    - activity safety (based on daily instructional plans); and
    - other common safety elements specific to the sport and camp operations.

Fundraising Tip

All safety factors for a summer instructional sports camp should be collectively dissected by all parties involved with the operation. No concerns should be ignored and all voices should be heard.

Fundraising Tip

If a summer instructional sports camp is going to be independent of a controlling athletic organization, it is recommended that the camp be incorporated (LLC). Incorporation establishes a distinct, disconnected business entity. The core advantage for the fundraiser's administrator(s) is that personal liability is limited to the corporation and excludes his/her personal assets. Consult with a CPA and lawyer about the implications (as well as limitations) of the camp's incorporation.

9. *Auxiliary activities* – Will the camp make supplementary activities available outside sports-specific instruction? If so, some basic questions associated with these activities encompass the following:

- What activity or activities will be offered?
- What hazards (if any) does the activity pose?
- Who will be accountable for the activity? Will the responsible parties be in-camp staff members/clinicians or outsourced professionals trained in the activity?
- How many staff members/clinicians will be needed for the activity?
- Where will the activity be held (at camp or in an exclusive facility)?
- Does the activity warrant parental permission?
- How regularly will the activity be held?
- Will the activity cut into instructional sessions or will it be strictly for downtime?

Registration Systems

Having a well thought-out, systematized registration process in place is an obligatory element when discussing pre-camp administrative functions for a summer instructional sports camp fundraiser. Registration should be considered more than merely paperwork. Behind the paperwork are children. Their treatment throughout the registration procedures should be as stress-free, informative, and orderly as possible. Figure 10.2 is a general registration template that can be utilized by all summer sports camps.

Stage 1: Receipt and Acceptance of Registration

The receipt and acceptance of registration forms (through traditional mail or web-based technology) should be comprised of the following components. A camp deposit, centered on a time schedule, should be included to 'hold a spot' for participating athletes. A deposit/payment timetable could entail the following dates:

> **Figure 10.2. General Registration Template for Summer Sports Camps**
>
> **Stage 1**
> Receipt and Acceptance of Registration
>
> **Stage 2**
> Participant Documentation
>
> **Stage 3**
> Scheduled Reminders
>
> **Stage 4**
> Event-Day Registration

6 months to 3 months prior to camp – 50% deposit

3 months to 1 month prior to camp – 75% deposit

1 month to camp date – 100% paid in full

A deposit schedule should also be accompanied by a definitive refund policy. A workable refund policy on deposits and payments could parallel the above timetable with the following criteria:

6 months to 3 months prior to camp – 100% refund

3 months to 1 month prior to camp – 75% refund

> 1 month to 2 weeks prior to camp – 50% refund
>
> 2 weeks to camp date – 0% refund

Because summer instructional sports camps often have limited space, a camper who cancels two weeks or less before the camp date should lose all deposits because fixed and most variable costs cannot be recaptured from that point forward.

Once registrations are received, designation of athletes into identifiable camp sessions and rosters should be completed. If camp sessions are filled, an immediate contact with the parents or guardians should be made to either re-channel the participant into another session(s) or cancel the registration and send back deposits/payments.

The next step in the initial registration stage should be to record and calculate all payments and balances (if any) remaining on the account. The camp administrators and staff should establish an accounts receivable folio for each participant, either through a computerized accounting software package or through a manual ledger system. Finally, the administrators and staff should generate a hard copy folder for each athlete participating in the summer instructional sports camp. The hard copy dossier will be the primary reference for all financial documentation as well as athlete-specific information.

Stage 2: Participant Documentation

Immediately after receiving registration forms and deposits, dispatch (through either traditional mail or email/web access) all compulsory athlete documentation. Documentation could include:

- a confirmation sheet that verifies and delineates camps, sessions, levels, etc.;
- a medical questionnaire;
- a medical release form;
- camp insurance documentation;
- an emergency contact questionnaire; and
- all other camp-specific documentation.

To accelerate the return of documentation from participants and their parents, a pre-addressed, stamped envelope should be included in conventional mailings, and scanning instructions for email submission should be communicated. Documentation requirements should be evaluated by legal counsel as well as medical staff prior to the registration process commencing. A participant checklist should be assembled and maintained to record all completed forms returned and missing.

Special Note: Under no conditions or circumstances should a sports camp allow an athlete to participate in any camp activities without a complete file that has all of the above documentation. The liability exposure and ramifications to the athletic organization, fundraising program, camp administration and staff could be catastrophic. All returned medical forms should be reviewed by the camp's medical staff (certified

Fundraising Tip

An option for maintenance of an in-house paper registration system is through outsourced web-based technology. If your summer camp's size warrants, third-party technology companies can construct an electronic registration system tailored toward your particular camp's operation. Additionally, all of the registration procedures and forms (in the sections below) can be electronically created, scanned, and preserved through most popular software systems.

Fundraising Tip

For security, perpetually gather and lock up all payments made to the summer camp. Payment and check safeguards should be organized and tenable. Periodic bank deposits should be supervised by at least two camp staff members. All camp deposits should have bank confirmations.

athletic trainers) prior to the beginning of any and all camp sessions. Medical staff apprehensions and concerns should be discussed immediately with all administrators, clinicians and instructors.

Stage 3: Scheduled Reminders

Periodic planned reminders (email or post cards) should be sent to all parents and athletes. The reminder cards are used to reiterate camps being attended, dates, locations, and items due (forms and money).

Stage 4: Event-Day Registration

Registration on the first day of camp should include:

- having a centrally located and well-publicized registration area;
- staffing the registration area fully with competent personnel;
- having an inclusive inventory of supplies and blank forms;
- setting up a distribution area for camp items and promotional giveaways;
- having not only laptops but hard-copy files available to check in athletes; and
- facilitating traffic flow from the registration area to sports-specific instructional areas.

A standard rule for the final stage of a summer instructional sports camp registration process must be that all athletes go through a check-in progression (even if their files and payments are complete). Once registration is complete, final reviewed rosters should be copied to all clinicians and instructors.

PRE-CAMP ADMINISTRATION: HUMAN RESOURCE COMMITMENTS

Clarifying staffing needs for an established, ongoing camp fundraiser is problematic. It is even more challenging for new summer camp ventures. The key is to institute a baseline operational strategy by examining the camp's capacity and the targeted ratio of instructors to participants. For example, if the maximum number of campers that can be instructed safely and effectively in a facility is 100, and the strategic philosophy of the camp operation is to have an instructor to participant ratio of 10 to 1 (while preserving quality expectations), then the highest number of clinicians would be 10. From there, determine actual hires on projections, always knowing that the camp will not require more than 10 clinicians/instructors at any one time.

Compensation

The most valuable asset in a summer sports camp is its instructors and clinicians. To cultivate a premier quality camp atmosphere, hire the most competent staff and instructors. Their compensation should correspond to and (if the resources and camp revenues allow) surpass their expectations. Supply camp staff and instructors with supplementary perks to help retain them for future camp fundraisers. Perks can include:

- travel to and from camp (per diem or through direct reimbursement);

- on- or off-campus lodging (if being on campus is a responsibility of overnight camper supervision, additional compensation should be included);

- camp merchandise such as camp logo shirts, shoes, promotional materials, etc.;

- a hospitality table for pre-camp breakfast, during camp breaks and for post-camp meals;

- comprehensive insurance coverage for the duration of camp sessions (in most cases, this should be a mandate rather than a perk);

- recreational activities and accessibility to workout facilities; and

- camp meal/banquet at the end of all sessions.

Compensation arrangements for individual contractual employees should be as uncomplicated and comprehensive as possible. Letters of agreement/contracts must itemize identifiable responsibilities, time schedules, camp monetary compensation, benefits, payment schedules, and housing and food provisions (if applicable). All letters of agreement/contracts must be agreed to and signed while being permanently retained in summer camp files. In addition to letters of agreement/contracts, all-inclusive job descriptions should also be endorsed and signed.

Special Note: While it may be impractical to have legal counsel review each and every camp letter of agreement/contract, a detailed review of a letter of agreement/contract template and I-9 documentation is a must.

Human Resource Background Check

Due to the composition of summer sports camps, all camp administrators, clinicians and instructors who directly interact with youth participants should submit to comprehensive background checks. The process is as follows:

1. A preliminary offer of employment is made and an all-inclusive consent form is completed by the prospective employee. At this point, it should be made clear that all employment offers are contingent upon successful completion of a background check.

2. The consent form, which features all pertinent information for a background check, is transmitted (either electronically or by traditional mail) to an independent, authorized third party. At this point, fingerprint checks are also a prudent recommended action.

3. The prospective employee submits to a drug screening test through an independent, authorized third party. Any anomalies in screening results must be explicated and have a doctor's supporting documentation.

4. Camp administrators make reference calls to verify a prospective employee's information and character.

Fundraising Tip

The welfare of summer camp employees should be prioritized when developing an operational structure. Proactive safety issues should be collectively examined by all camp personnel, and all concerns should be addressed immediately. All camp personnel should have the option to purchase (or to be supplied free) summer camp insurance.

Under no circumstances should an individual be allowed to work at a summer instructional sports camp until their employment file and background check obligations have been fulfilled. A general time frame for turnaround for background checks and drug screening by independent agencies is characteristically between 48-72 hours. All background check practices should be examined by the athletic organization's human resources professionals and legal counsel.

Miscellaneous Human Resource Elements

The training for contracted, instructional personnel is extremely different from training a full-time fundraising or sports program employee. The training often consists of an orientation that reviews all facilities, outlines time sessions, discusses practice and instructional plans, and provides a general synopsis of principal operational elements. Due to restricted resources and time, instructional personnel must be equipped to instantly assume sport camp duties. They must already have sports-specific expertise and teaching abilities prior to arriving and working the camp fundraiser.

Courtesy of U.S. Army

The most significant instructional position in a summer sports camp is the head clinician. This individual is accountable for the following camp elements:

- All instructional sessions to include:
  - pre-camp lesson plans;
  - demonstration teaching;
  - drills and practice activities;
  - breaks and rest periods;
  - cross training activities (if appropriate); and
  - warm-up and cool down routines.

- staff assignments and supervision;

- medical staff assignments and supervision;

- participant safety during instructional activities; and

- all activities related to instruction.

PRE-CAMP ADMINISTRATION: MARKETING

While the theory of marketing for fundraising programs is thoroughly covered in Chapter 6 of this text, there are some pre-camp applications that require elaboration:

- Marketing Research for Summer Sports Camps

- Marketing Mix for Summer Sports Camps (which includes the communication and promotional mix for summer sports camps)

Fundraising Tip

Most summer camps within an athletic organization utilize the sport's head coach or assistant coach to be the head clinician. If contracting an external head clinician, he/she must be extremely knowledgeable, competent, and experienced.

Marketing Research

In most summer sports camp circumstances, marketing research, while of great consequence for decision making, is limited due to time constraints. Operating under this premise, marketing research must be as focused and proficient as possible to maximize the time available. The two areas on which most summer sports camps should concentrate their marketing research efforts are competition and potential customers. Competitive research should center on (but not be limited to) the following questions:

- Who is the competition—both direct with other sports camps and indirect with general recreation camps?

- What is the size and history of our competitors' camp operations?

- What are the inclusive competitive strategies of our competitors (low cost, differentiations, best value, or niche)?

- What do our competitors' S.W.O.T. analyses look like? Do they have a practicable advantage?

- What is the configuration of their operations?

- Where do their summer sports camps operate? What are the location advantages associated with these locales?

- What is the model/blueprint of the competitors' instructional sessions?

- What are the competitors principal intentions for running a summer sports camp?

- Who is their target market? What is the target market's assessment of the competitors' camps?

- Do the competitors have strategic alliances?

When researching customers for a summer sport camp, the following questions (and others) should be investigated:

- From the instructional camps being offered, what is the target market's customer profile like? What is the target market's discretionary income level?

- How great is the overall potential market for the summer sports camp in the operational area?

- Who are the participants? Who is the decision maker who will purchase/pay for camp?

- What are is the participant's motive for attending a summer sports camp?

- What association and exchange does the participant have with the sport and its governing body?

- Are there customer groups (teams, clubs, and educational institutions) that should be targeted?

Fundraising Tip

Due to time restrictions, primary research studies are ordinarily impractical for summer sport camp fundraisers. Possible research tactics can include utilizing secondary data, observations, online research, casual conversations and overall community discussions.

Fundraising Tip

A complete customer profile is an invaluable document when formulating marketing and promotional strategies. Make sure that the four major components are delineated in the profile— demographics (characteristics), psychographics (lifestyles), behaviors (tangible actions), and geographics (locations).

The more information gathered about the competition and customer base, the better the marketing decisions for the camp fundraiser.

Marketing Mix for Summer Instructional Sports Camps

Once marketing research has been assembled and analyzed, marketing mix elements (product, price, place, promotions) should be the main concern of the pre-camp marketing plan. Because of the significance of these elements, an open discussion based on the marketing mix factors should be conducted with all stakeholders involved with the fundraiser. The following points, questions, and details can focus the marketing mix discussion.

Product

The customer does not purchase a product or service—they purchase the benefits that come from a product or service. What benefits will the summer camp provide the athlete participants? Can those benefits be articulated into a convincing, clear message?

Product quality for a summer sports camp cannot be sacrificed. Besides the loss of current and future participants, there are safety issues that mandate quality. How will the summer camp realize and surpass quality expectations? How will the fundraiser determine and quantify the intangible service quality associated with a summer instructional sports camp? What systems will be in place to guarantee quality control?

A summer sports camp is a service and it differs from tangible products in that it is:

- more people-oriented;
- perishable and consumed at the point of delivery;
- intangible (correction of mistakes is more difficult);
- unique from session to session; and
- based on an elevated level of customer (camper) involvement.

How will the summer camp assure consistency and superior characteristics of the intangible services? How can the summer sports camp maximize these distinct service elements to provide the best possible experience for participants?

All opportunities are not always right for all operations. Are these camp sessions right for the organization? What type of product line (camp instructional sessions) should the summer camp fundraiser offer to its present and future participants? The ultimate goal of product determination is brand name recognition. How can the sports camp develop its brand recognition? What product/service elements should be emphasized that will lead to strong branding?

Continuous improvement is a strategic ingredient to fight complacency. How can the summer sports camp enhance its already recognized product (camp session)? Are these improvements sound? Does the athletic organization and/or sports program have the resources to initiate these improvements?

Price

Pricing considerations for a new camp venture must be in accordance with the overall operational strategy of the fundraiser (low cost, differentiations, best value, niche). For example, if a low-cost strategy is employed, prices charged to participants and the subsequent profit margins are smaller than those of competitors that employ a differentiation or best-value strategy. With the current overall operational strategy, can the fundraiser meet its financial objectives? With prices established by the operational strategy, what would be the break-even point (in number of participants) to cover all costs (both fixed and variable)?

External environmental factors can have a major impact on pricing decisions. The foremost external factors that can affect pricing relate to the economy and purchasing power. How do economic conditions (locally, regionally and nationally) affect the summer sports camp pricing decisions? Is the summer camp's target market drastically affected by economic downturns? What pricing tactics can the fundraiser utilize to combat a sluggish economy? How will the summer camp operations be shaped by these extraneous elements? Will the camp fundraiser need to re-strategize its operational model to account for these factors?

As discussed in Chapter 6, price elasticity is the concept of price changes and their effect on demand. How much price elasticity will/does the summer camp venture have? At what point will the camp 'price itself out of the market'? What has been the price elasticity history of the operation? Under which situation can the camp maximize the fundraiser's profits (maximum price with anticipated demand)?

Other discussion points related to pricing a summer camp fundraiser encompass the following:

- Will discounting (for early/timely payments, quantity purchases, special promotions) be exploited by the summer sports camp?
- If pricing is set to capture market share from our competition, could a price war be created? If so, how well can the summer sports camp handle price competition?
- How notable is the market price of related summer camps when choosing the athletic organization pricing strategy?
- How do we determine our summer camp prices for all of the instructional sessions—standardized hourly pricing or by value given?

Place

As previously discussed, location and facility determinations are related directly to the third marketing mix element, place (or product/service distribution). Open discussions with the camp administration and staff should relate to the accessibility of the facility for camp participants; dimensions, capacity, and appropriateness of the building for the projected operations; state/condition of the facility (i.e., is the facility in disrepair); safety of structure as well as safety of the general location; and overall customer impressions of facility and locality. Other questions relating to the summer sports camp's location and facility that can be discussed include:

- Can the athletic organization's existing facility be modified and used for the fundraiser?

- Will the facility be vacant for the camp's projected dates and times (in-house or outsourced)?

- Will housing be necessary and, if so, will it be on campus or outsourced to proprietary establishments (hotels, motels, other educational institutions)?

- Are parking and traffic flow tactical considerations for the summer sports camp?

- Are there medical/training facilities at the location? If so, are they accessible to camp participants?

- If conditioning sessions (aerobic, plyometric, weight, etc.) are an ingredient of the instructional camp, does the facility have the capability to conduct them?

- Does the facility have storage areas for equipment and camp merchandise?

- Are there locker rooms on-hand, and are they suitable for camp operations?

- If summer camp instructional sessions are open to the public (parents, college recruiters, etc.), is there proper seating available that does not obstruct camp operations?

- Does the facility have good quality ventilation and air conditioning?

- Does the facility have an isolated staff area that can be designated for meetings, hospitality, and relaxation between sessions?

The more superior each of these facility and location items, the more a summer camp's product will be perceived as having exceptional quality. Additionally, better facilities can influence pricing as well as assist with promotional communication messages.

Promotion

The marketing communication objectives in Chapter 6 (create awareness, build positive images, identify prospects, build relationships, retain customers; Churchill, 1998, p. 445-446) pertain to all summer sports camp fundraisers. The communication strategies chosen during pre-camp marketing discussions will be centered on one or more of those goals. Goal selection will be influenced by where the camp stands in its life cycle (embryonic, introduction, growth, maturity or decline). For example, a new summer sports camp in the embryonic stage of development would most likely accentuate creation of awareness as its fundamental marketing communication and promotional goal. To create awareness in the potential participants' minds, the summer camp administration team may conclude that the best marketing communication and promotional tactic is to blanket the target market with direct mailings and concentrated advertising.

A significant topic for the sports camp administrators and staff to discuss is which resources will be dedicated (up front) for the camp's marketing communication campaign. The allotted funds will determine not only the marketing communication mix (advertising, public relations, personal selling, direct mail, sales promotions) but with what frequency these promotional mechanisms will be applied. To establish a budget from scratch or to adjust previous expenditures, researching the costs and exposure potential of definitive market communication tactics is a prudent first step.

Once budgets have been finalized, the formation of a salient marketing communication message is the next critical element. No matter what the message, it should stress creativity while highlighting the benefits of the summer sports camp. The marketing message must spotlight what the participant gets out of the camp rather than the technicalities of the operation.

Target market determination for a summer sports camp is considerably easier than target market determination for recreational camps. Because of the exclusive nature and direction of specialized summer instructional sports camps, market segmentation and targeting can be narrowed down by factors such as the following:

- *Demographics* – age, income, education

- *Psychographics* – lifestyle of an athlete and sport participant

- *Geographics* – if operating a day camp within a reasonable radius of the facility (if operating an overnight camp, the geographic area expands)

- *Behaviors* – athletes involved in club programs and school/educational teams

MARKETING COMMUNICATION TACTICS

The most essential and indispensable marketing communication tool for a summer instructional sports camp fundraiser is the development and distribution of an all-inclusive camp brochure. Figure 10.3 illustrates the possible sectional breakdown and explanation for a summer camp fundraiser.

In addition to utilizing a camp brochure for marketing communication, other promotional tools that could be employed by a summer sports camp are web-based technology, personal selling, direct mail, sales promotions, and advertising.

Web-based technology is an economical way to promote a summer sports camp. Not only can the entire contents of the camp brochure be included on the website, but an expanded and more in-depth description of the camp operations can be built in. A portfolio of camp pictures, camp structure and learning objectives, facility directions, participant requirements, and contact information can be included in the website's shell. Additionally, all camp forms (registration, medical, insurance, questionnaires, evaluations surveys, etc.) can be placed on the website as downloadable attachments. If the summer camp fundraiser accepts credit cards, a payment link could be incorporated.

Personal selling, as it relates to summer sports camps, is geared toward relationship cultivation and educating prospective participants about the athletic organization's/sport program's camp. Two areas of personal selling to control are (1) having knowledgeable associates selling the camp and (2) finding new customers to establish an interchange and affiliation. Anyone and everyone can assist in the personal selling

Fundraising Tip

There is a conspicuous difference in the marketing message for recreational camps and instructional sports camps. Recreational camps' marketing communication messages emphasize fun as a major component, with learning and skill development as secondary elements. Instructional camps have a more serious theme in which learning and skill development are accentuated within a fun, social environment.

Figure 10.3. Summer Camp Brochure Template

COVER

This component of a camp brochure should be as dynamic and eye catching as possible. Remember, the camp brochure is as much a marketing tool as it is an informational document.

BIOS

Biographies should be provided on all key clinicians/instructors. The biographies should promote the individual's sport-specific accomplishments and experience.

CAMP BREAKDOWN

This is the primary segment of the brochure. There should be a clean delineation of:

- Dates
- Times
- Locations
- Levels
- Session Learning Objectives
- Format and Costs

This component should be readable and as comprehensive as possible.

REGISTRATION FORM

On the inside back cover of the brochure there should be a complete registration form.

The registration form should incorporate:

- A section for participant information (name, address, phone, email, educational institution, etc.)
- Check-off list with prices for camp sessions that participants will attend.
- Payment information/schedules.
- Return address (or web address for signing up online)

MAILING SECTION

The brochure should be able to be mailed directly to potential participants. On the outside back cover, a return address and open mailing address section should be designed. When a request comes in for camp information, it should be easy to fill in the potential participant's address, place a stamp in the top right corner, staple and send.

Other tips for the construction of a brochure include:

- Whether it is a tri-fold, bi-fold, or 8 X 10 booklet, the design and professional presentation of the brochure should be a top priority. The brochure is an explicit reflection on the sport program, fundraising department and athletic organization.

- Prior to finalizing the brochure, the promotional document should be examined by the compliance officer of the athletic organization for any possible sport/athletic organization violations (NCAA, NAIA, High School Athletic Association, etc.). The brochure should be signed off on by this individual.

- If designing a summer camp brochure is outside one's expertise (and one is employed by or has access to a college/university athletic department), contracting a member of a sports information department is a viable alternative. These individuals have hands-on experience in drafting athletic program catalogues, which are much more complex than a summer camp brochure.

- Consistency is a crucial element in developing an appealing camp brochure. Format, fonts, spacing, colors, etc. should all be uniform and complementary.

- Triple check all final prints before circulating the summer camp brochure to the target market. Errors in grammar, spelling, and sentence structure show a lack of detail and concern.

---

of a summer sports camp venture as long as they have a thorough knowledge of the operation. To ensure this knowledge base, training and open communication should be employed.

In the article "Choosing a summer camp," Markarian sums up a parent's perspective on selecting a summer camp by stating:

It's crucial to match your child's interest and personality to the camp's programs and atmosphere. Equally important is choosing a camp that has a philosophy and value system you support. For instance, many camps emphasize competitive sports, but there are also camps that focus on non-competitive activities. Some camps are highly structured, keeping campers busy with a full slate of programmed activities throughout the day. (Markarian, 1995, p. 311)

Knowing your camp is a salient factor when selling it to parents. Being forthright on the summer sports camp's structure, philosophy, competitive environment and overall program is a requirement for customer satisfaction. It must be categorically stated that some summer sports instructional camps are not fitting for all potential participants. During the personal selling process (and in all marketing communication tactics) this fact should be accentuated.

To find new customers/campers, a marketing tactic known as prospecting must be applied. Prospecting is "a systematic process of continually looking for new customers…one of the most efficient prospecting techniques is obtaining personal referrals. Such referrals come from friends, customers and other businesses" (Longenelker, Moore, & Petty, 2003, p. 427).

To incentivize personal selling, a sales commission program could be employed. For every camp admission sold, a percentage or sale commission would be earned. Different sales would generate distinctive incentives. For example, the sale of a team for a team camp/tournament would generate a different commission than the sale of an admission to a singular specialty camp.

Direct mail canvassing can use technology (specifically emails) to generate tremendous marketing communication benefits for a summer sports camp. The concept of mass customization is defined as "the ability of a company to prepare on a mass basis individually designed products, services, programs and communications, to meet each customer's requirement" (Kotler, 2003, p. 282). The marketing communication model of mass customization is the production of large quantities (of marketing communication emails) but tailoring them for each individual customer. The key to utilizing this strategy is the acquisition of relevant email listings and the construction of an adaptable email template.

Sales promotions (if allowed by the athletic organization's governing body regulations) can consist of coupons, frequent buyer plans, giveaways, bulk discounts, etc. Their use for a summer camp should be controlled and not a component of the regular camp marketing. Sales promotions should be manipulated to stimulate demand, both general or session-specific, over limited periods. Their overuse could lead to customer dependency. If sale promotions are expected then they become a permanent component of a summer camp's pricing strategy rather than a promotional tool to increase sales. As discussed previously in marketing communication concepts, "advertising is defined as any paid form of non personal communication about an organization, product, service, or idea by an identified sponsor. The paid aspect of this definition reflects the fact that the space of time for an advertising message generally must be bought" (Belch & Belch, 2009, p. 18).

Fundraising Tip

Under no circumstances should misinformation be communicated to potential participants and their parents/guardians. Everyone involved with personal selling must be instructed that if they are asked a question that they are unsure how to answer, they must either (1) find out the answer and communicate it back to the potential participant or (2) refer the question and potential participant to a camp administrator.

Fundraising Tip

Never turn down (or fail to contact) a referral. No matter how improbable the referral is for the summer sports camp, it could lead to a number of potential participants.

Courtesy of U.S. Marine Corps

With that being understood, selecting the best media with which to advertise (within budget constraints) to reach the target market is critical. Some promising advertising strategies and media that could be utilized by a summer sports camp include (but are not limited to) the following:

- sports-specific journals (local, regional, national);
- local publications, such as newspaper's camp editions, city magazines, community newsletters, etc.;
- athletic organization game-day programs, media guides, alumni periodicals, etc.;
- TV and radio (possible piggybacking on athletic organization broadcasts as well as local targeted television and radio stations);
- signage (banners at athletic organization events and community activities that have a high percentage of targeted potential participants);
- posters and billboards; and
- flyers and pamphlets.

SUMMER CAMP OPERATION

Introduction

For current and future camp development, offering superior customer satisfaction to all attending the summer instructional sports camps is essential. To do this, provide the highest quality product one's resources can afford. This, in turn, will generate positive word of mouth and enhance future operations. Never forget: The customer is everything. One's camp aspirations and actions should always have this in mind.

The quality of a summer instructional sports camp's operation is often determined by the fundraising administration's and instructional staff's commitment to innovation and continuous improvement. Continuous improvement (which is directly in line with

TQM principles discussed earlier in the chapter) is defined as "an ongoing effort to make improvements in every part of the organization relative to all of its products and services…The idea here is that the quest for better quality and better service is never ending" (Rue & Byars, 2009, p. 440). From an administrative standpoint, benchmarking other camps' operational structures to keep up-to-date with instructional camp operations is just one of the ways to commit to continuous improvement. Instructionally, researching sport-specific teaching advancements, staying abreast of new policies and procedures, learning new competitive rules and observing other great sport clinicians are just a few elements that could contribute to continuous improvement.

Management

Safety Issues

The most crucial facet of a summer instructional sports camp's operation is safety. As a function of sports camps administration, safety walkthroughs should be organized and conducted prior to the start of the summer camp. Additionally, a valuable practice is to have a one-time walkthrough for all clinicians/instructors as well as periodic walkthroughs for each individual clinician or instructor in his/her designated area. When assessing the condition, layout, and safety of existing (or potential) facilities and equipment, it is advisable to set aside time prior to camp operations to evaluate the situation. Once a scheduled camp begins, an instructor's focus is on the instructional aspect of the operation. That is why facility/equipment walkthroughs should be completed in advance of activities—to circumvent any other distractions.

In reviewing conceivable facility and equipment risks, a clinician and camp administrator must first think of all the worst-case scenarios and of potential problems. The question that one must always ask is: What is the most catastrophic scenario? In other words, a clinician and camp administrator must be a reliable predictor of potential disasters. Facilities and equipment deal with the physical aspects of summer sports camps. They are tangible objects that one's senses (sight, hearing, touch and smell) can inspect and evaluate. For example, a day before commencing camp instruction, set up the gym, field, or facility according to the precise session requirements. With the camp's staff, do a safety walkthrough using the senses and consider factors such as:

- How does the ground (floor) feel? Is it clean or does it need more attention?
- Is the light adequate enough to conduct camp?
- What is the facility temperature? Is there proper circulation?
- Is there proper spacing around the participation areas? If not, are the walls or boundaries padded to avoid injury?
- What is the condition of the operational equipment? Is it in good working order?
- What is the condition of the locker rooms? Is there an unsanitary smell? Is the locker room's area secure?

- Does the current design of the field (court, gym) minimize the chance for injury?

- Where will the athletes obtain water? Could its placement and distribution cause a hazardous situation?

- Cognitively examine contingencies and unforeseen possibilities. Do all scenarios necessitate some type of safety plan?

- Have all staff and instructors been safety trained for sports-specific contingencies? Has staff attendance been stressed and/or mandated in formal certifications and sanctioned training seminars (i.e., CPR/First Aid)?

- Do all instructors and clinicians know where medical/training staff is at all times throughout camp activities? Minutes can be decisive in minimizing long-term ramifications of accidents/injuries.

- Is there a system in place to assure that non-approved individuals cannot participate in any of the camp's activities?

- Does the training and conditioning equipment have the comprehensive endorsement of the medical/training staff?

- Is there an all-encompassing safety procedural manual? Has it been circulated to all internal stakeholders?

- Has the instructional staff been properly trained to use the equipment? Ensure that equipment is used correctly, and under no circumstances improvise with equipment or use personally devised contraptions.

- Have all weather considerations been discussed and alternatives planned?

- Have the instructional staff and clinicians been trained in the most recent sports-specific exercise and teaching techniques?

- Is there a structured warm-up and cool-down plan? Never sacrifice warm-up time for the camp's athletes. The risk and endangerment to athletes is exponentially increased in these instances.

The number of questions to be asked will be based on the condition of the summer camp's equipment and facility and the administration and instructional staff's sensitivity to risk.

Another safety element of a summer sports camp that has justifiably received mass media attention is the possibility of skin infections due to sports related activities.

Because skin infections are preventable, a skin infection prevention plan should be in place at all facilities that host sports activities. Athletes should understand the plan and follow the precautions off the field as well. This plan should include:

1. Providing sinks and liquid, antibacterial soap for washing hands and arms before and after practices and games; if a sink is not available, providing antibacterial gel or wipes that contain chlorhexidine gluconate (CHG) in order to provide long-term protection from bacteria;

2. Providing clean and available showers for athletes, if at all possible;

3. Ensuring sports equipment is cleaned and dried between practices and games;

4. Assuring all wounds be covered with clean, dry bandages and checked by a physician if inflamed or painful;

5. Eliminating the ability of athletes to share towels or other personal items; and

6. Encouraging soiled clothing and towels to be taken home in separate bags for cleaning (not put back in lockers or bags with clean clothes). ("Back to School Means Back to Sports," 2010)

Fundraising Tip
Have top-skilled training and medical personnel on staff to assist in all medical, safety, and insurance considerations.

Prior to the commencement of camp operations, an official meeting (or meetings) should be conducted with all maintenance and set-up/breakdown crews. These meetings should unmistakably confirm expectations concerning set-up criteria, maintenance and cleaning, and camp breakdown. Walkthroughs with maintenance crews, in conjunction with meetings, should be conducted to visualize the requirements of camp operations. In addition to this process, it is advisable to construct standardized checklists and time schedules to reinforce the importance of auxiliary items and to certify each task's completion.

General Management Elements

A summer instructional sports camp should maintain a beneficial, straightforward recordkeeping system. Utilizing any number of computer software programs for precise accounting is an administrative must. Administrators should plan on the camp being audited. This mindset will intensify the camp's accounting system integrity. If one is not detail oriented, outsource this administration function to someone who is. Medical records, insurance forms, emergency contact information, employment contacts, and specialized sports-specific information are all detail-oriented materials that need compulsory upkeep.

Special Note: By no means consent to a child or clinic member participating in any event or activity without his or her entire set of records being on file. This could be construed as gross negligence and may be a cause for loss of protection under the camp's insurance carrier.

An administration and instructional conundrum can transpire when discussing the balancing of participant numbers and volume with personalized teaching goals. From an administrative perspective, the fundraiser will want to capitalize on capacity limits for maximum financial returns. From an instructional standpoint, clinicians/ instructors will want somewhat smaller sessions to accentuate individualized attention. If open communication and cooperative planning are utilized, both objectives can be accomplished in the camp's operations. Fundraising administrators need to appreciate quality instructional limitations, and instructors/clinicians need to recognize the importance of reaching financial objectives.

Once the administrative accounting/record-keeping and safety inspections are completed, the focus of the operation should be on the most important instructional position during the summer sports camp, the head clinician. The head clinician could be categorized as the director of all camp activities and instruction. For the success of a head clinician, the following points illustrate critical managerial concepts that should be adopted. An effective head clinician:

- always remembers that he/she is in a position of leadership and control;
- encourages empowerment with accountability among the summer camp's instructors;
- does not act as though he/she is 'above the law' and operational policies and procedures do not apply to him/her;
- is willing to 'roll up his/her sleeves' and assist camp instructors in any way possible;
- is adept at conflict resolution and mediations;
- encourages innovation in instruction and camp tactics with his/her instructors;
- ensures that ethical standards are being maintained;
- eliminates or minimizes environmental distractions to provide the best teaching and learning atmosphere;
- is adaptable and can 'think on the fly' when it comes to adjusting instructional objectives;
- insists on inclusion for all participants regardless of skill level;
- shows profound commitment to pre-established instructional goals.
- is a dynamic and charismatic ambassador for the summer sports camp;
- promotes teamwork in staff and participants; and
- is skilled in the use of his/her formal authority.

There are other generic summer camp elements that are universally beneficial to all summer instructional sports camp fundraisers. They are described in the following paragraphs.

Maintain high positive energy and encouragement. The environment set by the instructional staff and clinicians involved in a summer sports camp is crucial to the participants' learning and enjoyment. Summer camps can be a new experience for young athletes and therefore trigger some tension and fear. From the moment a participant arrives, the registration process, facilitation into groups, instruction, and post-camp activities must all be encouraging and friendly. Typically, the most trepidation for participants will come during the actual instruction and participation in activities and drills. Clinicians/instructors should at all times be as affable, personable, and as supportive as possible (maintaining a professional manner) while helping the athlete develop, correct, or enhance his/her talents.

Provide activity breaks and rest periods. In conjunction with the summer sports camp's training/medical staff, appropriate breaks should be scheduled in all instructional sessions. These rest periods become of greater consequence in summer sports camps that are outdoors or in poorly air-conditioned facilities. There should be ample hydrating stations with water and prescribed sports drinks. Trainers (who should always be in attendance) can stop any camp session to allow for breaks. The summer sport camp training/medical staff is unconditionally in charge of the participants' health and safety. Their recommendations should be deemed absolute without discussion.

Be hands-on and visible while maintaining a structured, controlled camp atmosphere. Even if one is not acting as a clinician, walk the facility and communicate with the participants. Show an allegiance and commitment to the product. A well-run camp will convey professionalism as well as lessen campers' anxieties. Post schedules at instructional sites whenever possible. Additionally, have pre-camp staff conferences to dissect schedules, locations, activities, and job responsibilities. The more systematic the camp operation, the better flow and more constructive atmosphere the camp will have.

Instructional Fundamentals

Prior to placing athletes into camp groups, the instructional staff will need to determine the level of participants' skills and competitive abilities. A pre-instruction questionnaire (which can be distributed during the registration process or during inaugural camp activities) should be considered. Quantitative factors such as age, grade, number of years involved in the sport, and a breakdown of progression levels could be definitive elements used to verify a participant's placement into summer camp groups. Subjective questions based on specific skills (on a numerical scale of 1-5) could be asked to allow participants to elaborate on areas of strength and deficiency. Once groupings are determined, in-camp assessments (through empirical observations by instructional staff) should be used to move participants 'up or down' to the suitable skill grouping.

Special Note: To avoid any possible embarrassment, any camp athlete being moved down into a lower skill group needs to be tactfully informed and moved as promptly and as quietly as possible. Recommendations on moving an athlete up into an advanced skill group should take into account emotional maturity as well as skill level.

Depending on the sport for the summer camp fundraiser, a pre-instruction fitness assessment of all participants could be a necessity. The physical fitness evaluation, which should be administered by the camp's athletic trainers/medical staff, should be directed at aerobic, strength, and flexibility elements that are inherent in that specific sport. Instrumentation and documentation should be used. All results should be discussed with participants and made a permanent component of the athlete's camp file.

The head clinician should organize and conduct, before every session, an exhaustive review of the instructional plan. The review should consist of:

- all new and innovative learning goals—all activities and drills should have these learning goals in mind;
- demonstration cues to teach skills and activities;

Fundraising Tip

The idea of fun should be intermingled into as many summer sports camp functions as possible while still achieving instructional goals. The assortment and design of participant activities should be done with both objectives in mind. This philosophy of fun is relevant for all participants, whether novice or elite.

- delineation of who will demonstrate skills and who will instruct;
- an all-inclusive elaboration and clarification of drills (from concept to application);
- time frames for particular activities and break schedules; and
- all other relevant elements of the instructional plan.

The more thorough and prepared these meetings are, the more enhanced the camp quality and impression of professionalism. It will also amplify the speed and flow between activities which, in turn, will increase the amount of instruction necessary.

If considering a team camp concept as a summer instructional sports camp fundraiser, there are specific decisions (administrative and instructional) that need to be determined:

Will the team camp be a combination of team instruction and tournament play or will the camp be structured as a competitive tournament only? If a combination is employed, what percentage of camp time will be designated for instruction and what percentage of camp time will be for competition?

Will teams be constructed randomly from a general pool of campers or will teams be constructed prior to camp (junior/senior high, junior Olympic, etc.)? If the teams are assembled from a broad-spectrum pool of participants, what will be the decisive factors for grouping athletes into teams?

For the competitive component of a team sport camp, what will be the layout of tournament play? Will the competition be single elimination, double elimination, multi-level, round-robin, or head-to-head? Who and which factors will govern the seating and team placements? Does the competitive configuration coincide with the facility and time constraints of the camp?

Who will coach each team? Since most athletic associations, whether educational or national (AAU, JO's, etc.), have specified regulations about off-season contact by regular team coaches, what will be the instructional staff needs? What will be the coaching structure of each team (head coach, assistants, and managers)?

If instruction is an ingredient of a summer team sports camp, how will the instruction be delivered? Will it be by definite assessments of each team's capabilities and then tailoring instruction based on that evaluation? Will it be a generic instructional plan that is used by all teams in the camp?

After all sessions are over (instructional and competitive) and athletes have finished drills and activities, a fun and educational pastime is to have a culminating competition utilizing willing instructors as participants. Depending on the sport, the purpose of such an in-camp event is to reinforce all of the skills learned by participants through observing high-level play/competition. As with participants, all safety factors should be followed for instructors (camp insurance, warm-up, equipment, etc.). Under no circumstances should an instructor be forced to take part in such activities.

Fundraising Tip

A foundational feature of the camp that should be stressed to all individuals involved is the development of a sense of citizenship and community in the camp environment. While competition might occur in drills and game situations, sportsmanship should always be highlighted. Non-compliance with these imperatives should immediately be addressed and corrected.

Camper Surveys

At the conclusion of each camp, surveying the campers (either informally through walk-around discussions or through formal survey techniques) is a sound, continuous improvement application. Ask campers about their experiences at camp and what other services and training they may want in the future. If the parents are involved, solicit their assessments. Additionally, enlist the camp staff through a recap session and get their input. Feedback is the key to improving quality in the future. A camp survey template is provided in Appendix 10.1.

Miscellaneous Post-Camp Administrative Elements

- *Precision of financial reporting* – When closing down a summer sports camp operation, financial statements should be constructed which accurately represent the entire summer camp program. These financial statements should be disseminated to all relevant stakeholders.

- *Preservation of a permanent filing system* – The archiving of e-files and hard copy files should be a post-camp priority. For easy access, these files should be securely stored and disconnected from other athletic organization files.

- *Discontinuation or suspending of bank accounts* – An athletic organization fundraising program or sports program should close or suspend its summer sports camp bank account immediately after all camp distributions and receipts have been accounted for. For the integrity and financial safety of all who are involved with a summer camp, it is important to empty the account, halt all transactions, and document bank account closure.

- *Brand recognition* – Just because the summer sports camp fundraiser is concluded does not mean that there are no opportunities to cultivate the camp's brand awareness. Continually communicate with camp alumni and their families throughout the year. These informative communications can enlarge positive word of mouth advertising and provide a summer sports camp with a competitive advantage through a devoted clientele base.

- *Solicitation of feedback from camp administration and instructional staff* – If financially feasible, have a final camp get-together that merges social interaction with information gathering. Within the goal of gathering feedback, ask direct questions related to the improvement of camp operations, the increasing of value given to athletic campers, and the potential for enlarging the operation.

Fundraising Tip

Clinicians, instructors, and administrative personnel are an excellent resource for continuous improvement and feedback. The information they provide could be through casual conversations or through formal instrumentation such as surveys or focus groups assessments.

SUMMARY

The importance of a summer instructional sports camp as a fundraising mechanism cannot be overstated. A well-organized camp operation can provide essential revenue as well as enhance positive impressions and goodwill for the athletic organization in the community.

The elements of pre-camp operation can encompass elements such as planning, human resource development, marketing and promotional communication. Actual camp operations can include safety considerations, accounting procedures, and job responsibilities. Post-camp administration should scrutinize techniques and instrumentation for acquiring feedback, which is an essential component of continuous improvement. Within each of these factors, the emphasis on fun and developing strong sportsmanlike behavior is an underlying principle that all summer instructional sports camps should adopt.

REVIEW AND DISCUSSION QUESTIONS

1. What are the eight components of a summer instructional sports camp fundraising plan?

2. What are some fundamental safety items to consider for a summer instructional sports camp?

3. What are the four major stages of a summer instructional sports camp registration system?

4. What are some possible participant documentation requirements for a summer instructional sports camp?

5. Name and describe some post-camp administrative elements.

References

Aberle, K. B. (2009). Everything I need to know about volunteer management. *Associations Now, 5*(12), 14.

Anthony, R. N., & Govindarajan, V. (2007). *Management control systems* (12th ed.). New York, NY: McGraw-Hill/Irwin.

Anthony, W. P., Perrewe, P. L., & Kacmar, K. M. (1993). *Strategic human resource management.* Fort Worth, TX: Dryden Press.

Back to school means back to sports: Prepare for and prevent common sports injuries. (2010). *PR Newswire.* Retrieved from http://www.prnewswire.com/news-release.

Bateman, T. S., & Snell, S. A. (2004). *Management: The new competitive landscape* (6th ed.). New York, NY: McGraw-Hill/Irwin.

Bateman, T. S., & Snell, S. A. (2010). *Management: Leading and collaborating in a competitive world.* New York, NY: McGraw-Hill/Irwin.

Beckwith, S. (2003). *Complete publicity plans: How to create publicity that will spark media exposure and excitement.* Avon, MA: Media Corp/Streetwise Publishing.

Bedeian, A. G. (1993). *Management* (3rd ed.). Fort Worth, TX: Dryden Press.

Belch, M., & Belch, G. (2009). *Advertising and promotion: An integrated marketing communication perspective* (8th ed.). New York, NY: McGraw Hill/Irwin.

Black, J. S., & Porter, L. W. (2000). *Management: Meeting new challenges.* Upper Saddle River, NJ: Prentice Hall.

Blackwell, R. D., Miniard, P. W., & Engel, J. F. (2001). *Consumer behavior* (9th ed.). Orlando, FL: Hardcourt College Publishers.

Bohlander, G., & Snell, S. (2007). *Managing human resources* (14th ed.). Mason, OH: South-Western.

Bohlander, G., Snell, S., & Sherman, A. (2001). *Managing human resources.* Cincinnati, OH: South-Western.

Boone, L. E., & Kurtz, D. L. (2006). *Contemporary business 2006.* Mason, OH: Thompson South-Western.

Branham, L. (2001). *Keeping the people who keep you in business.* New York, NY: AMACOM.

Byars, L. L., & Rue, L. W. (2008). *Human resource management* (9th ed.). New York, NY: McGraw-Hill/Irwin.

Carrison, D. (2010). The benefits of corporate volunteerism. *Industrial Management, 52*(2), 6.

Carson, M. (2006). Saying like it isn't: The pros and cons of 360-degree feedback. *Business Horizons, 49*(5), 395-402.

Certo, S. (2008). *Supervision: Concepts and skill building* (6th ed.). New York, NY: McGraw-Hill/Irwin.

Churchill, G. A., & Peter, J. P. (1998). *Marketing: Creating value for customers.* Boston, MA: Irwin-McGraw Hill.

Ciconte, B. L., & Jacob, J. G. (2005). *Fundraising basics: A complete guide* (2nd edition). Sudbury, MA: Jones and Bartlett.

Ciulla, J. B. (2004). *Ethics, the heart of leadership* (2nd ed.). Westport, CT: Praeger.

Byl, J. (1999). *Organizing successful tournaments* (2nd ed.). Champaign, IL: Human Kinetics.

Clow, K. E., & Baack, D. (2002). *Integrated advertising, promotion, and marketing communications.* Upper Saddle River, NJ: Prentice Hall.

Craig, R. L. (1996). *The ASTD training and development handbook.* New York, NY: McGraw-Hill.

Culpepper, J. (2007). How to revamp your camp. *Parks and Recreation, 42*(2), 56-61.

Curzon, S. C. (1996). *Managing the interview.* New York, NY: Neal-Schuman.

Cutlip, S. M., Center, A. H., & Broom, G. M. (2000). *Effective public relations* (8th ed.). Upper Saddle River, NJ: Prentice Hall.

Daft, R. L., & Marcic, D. (2006). *Understanding management* (5th ed.). Mason, OH: Thompson South-Western.

Dienhart, J. W. (2000). *Business, institutions, and ethics: A text with cases and readings.* New York, NY: Oxford University Press.

DeNisi, A., & Griffin, R. W. (2001). *Human resource management.* Boston, MA: Houghton Mifflin.

Dibble, S. (1999). *Keeping your valuable employees.* New York, NY: John Wiley and Sons.

DiMauro, L., & Grant, T. (2006). *Ethics: Opposing viewpoints.* Farmington Hills, MI: Greenhaven Press.

Dove, K. E. (2001). *Conducting a successful fundraising program: A comprehensive guide and resource.* San Francisco, CA: Jossey Bass.

DuBrin, A. J. (2003). *Essentials of management* (6th ed.). Mason, OH: Thompson South-Western.

DuBrin, A. J. (2006). *Essentials of management* (7th ed.). Mason, OH: Thompson South-Western.

Edmonds, T. P., Tsay, B., & Olds, P. R. (2008). *Fundamental managerial accounting concepts* (4th ed.). New York, NY: McGraw-Hill/Irwin.

Ellis, S. J. (2003). Do volunteers deserve the board's attention? *Nonprofit World, 21*(1), 19-21.

Filing—like the beat—goes on…and on. (2001). *Journal of Accountancy, 192*(5), 24.

Flanagan, J. (1993). *Successful fundraising: A complete handbook for volunteers and professionals.* Lincolnwood, IL: Contemporary Publishing.

Frels, M. (2006). Motivating volunteers. *Associations Now, 2*(12), 15.

Garrison, R. H., & Noreen, E. W. (2003). *Managerial accounting* (10th ed.). New York, NY: McGraw-Hill/Irwin.

Gazley, B., & Dignam, M. (2008). Are you in or out? *Associations Now, 4*(9), 89-95.

Getha-Taylor, H. (2003). Including young people on nonprofit boards of directors. *PA Times, 26*(6), 4.

Griffey, D. C., & Houser, L. D. (2007). *Designing effective instructional tasks for physical education and sports.* Champaign, IL: Human Kinetics.

Griffin, R. W., & Ebert, R. J. (2004). *Business* (7th ed.). Upper Saddle River, NJ: Prentice Hall.

Hall, W. D. (1993). *Making right decisions: Ethics for managers.* New York, NY: John Wiley and Sons.

Hartman, L. P., & DesJardins, J. (2008). *Business ethics: Decision-making for personal integrity and social responsibility.* New York, NY: McGraw-Hill/Irwin.

Hiebing, R. G., & Cooper, S. W. (1997). *The successful marketing plan: A disciplined and comprehensive approach* (2nd ed.). Chicago, IL: NTC Business Books.

Hill, C. W. L., & Jones, G. R. (2004). *Strategic management: An integrated approach* (6th edition). Boston, MA: Houghton Mifflin.

Honaman, J. (2005). How can we boost our board from good to great? *Association Management, 57*(1), 83-84.

Hopkins, B. R. (2005). *650 essential nonprofit law questions answered.* Hoboken, NJ: John Wiley and Sons.

Howard, A. W., & Moore, C. J. (2008). Nonprofit summer camps offer kids much more than S'mores. *The Chronicle of Philanthropy, 20*(20), 1.

Iecovich, E. (2004). Responsibilities and roles of boards in nonprofit organizations: The Israeli case. *Nonprofit Management & Leadership, 15*(1), 5-24.

Janda, J. (2000). Happy campers. *Club Industry Magazine, 16*(2), 28-30.

Jones, G. R., & George, J. M. (2004) *Essentials of contemporary management.* New York, NY: McGraw-Hill/Irwin.

Jones, G. R., & George, J. M. (2006). *Contemporary management* (4th edition). New York, NY: McGraw-Hill/Irwin.

Jones, G. R., & George, J. M. (2006). *Contemporary management.* New York, NY: McGraw-Hill/Irwin.

Kendall, R. (1996). *Public relation campaign strategies: Planning for implementation* (2nd ed.). New York, NY: Harper Collins.

Keown, A. J., Martin, J. D., Petty, J. W., & Scott, D. F. (2001). *Foundations of finance: The logic and practice of financial management* (3rd ed.). Upper Saddle River, NJ: Prentice Hall.

Kinicki, A., & Williams, B. K. (2003). *Management: A practical introduction.* New York, NY: McGraw-Hill/Irwin.

Korngold, A. (2005). *Leveraging goodwill: Strengthening nonprofits by engaging businesses.* San Francisco, CA: Jossey-Bass.

Kotler, P. (2003). *Marketing management* (11th ed.). Upper Saddle River, NJ: Prentice Hall.

Kouzes, J. M., & Posner, B. Z. (1997). *The leadership challenge* (2nd ed.). San Francisco, CA: Jossey Bass.

Kreitner, R., & Kinicki, A. (2008). *Organizational behavior* (8th ed.). New York, NY: McGraw-Hill/Irwin.

Ladner, S., & Zimny, S. (1995). Fundraising with your board: Making it work. *Nonprofit World, 13*(5), 12-14.

Lal, R., Quelch, J. A., & Kasturi, R. V. (2005). *Marketing management.* New York, NY: McGraw-Hill/Irwin.

Lamb, C. W., Hair, J. F., & McDaniel, C. (2003). *Essentials of marketing* (3rd ed.). Mason, OH: Thompson South-Western.

Lazer, W., & Layton, R. A. (1999). *Marketing of hospitality services.* Lansing, MI: Educational Institute of the American Hotel and Motel Association.

Lindberg, J. (2007). Feedback without fear. *Associations Now, 3*(3), 34-38.

Longenecker, J. G., Moore, C. W., & Petty, J. W. (2003). *Small business management: An entrepreneurial emphasis* (12th ed.). Mason, OH: Thompson South-Western.

Lussier, R. N. (2006). *Management fundamentals: Concepts, applications, skill development* (3rd ed.). Mason, OH: Thompson South-Western.

Lussier, R. N., & Achua, C. F. (2007). *Leadership: Theory, application, and skill development* (3rd ed.). Mason, OH: Thompson South-Western.

Lysakowski, L. (2005). Getting board members to ante up. *Associations Now, 1*(2), 25.

Madura, J. (2007). *Introduction to business* (4th ed.). Mason, OH: Thompson, South-Western.

Markarian, M. (1995). Choosing a summer camp. *Black Enterprise, 25,* 310-313.

Marks, R. B. (1997). *Personal selling: A relationship approach* (6th ed.). Upper Saddle River, NJ: Prentice Hall.

Maslow, A. (1954). *Motivation and personality.* New York, NY: Harpers Row.

Mathis, R. L., & Jackson, J. H. (1982). *Personnel: Contemporary perspectives and applications.* St. Paul, MN: West Publishing.

McLaughlin, P. (2007). Giving good feedback. *Supervision, 68*(2), 7-8.

Megginson, L. C., Byrd, M. J., & Megginson, W. L. (2006). *Small business management: An entrepreneur's guidebook.* New York, NY: McGraw-Hill/Irwin.

Merriam-Webster Online Dictionary. (n.d.). Retrieved from http://www.merriam-webster.com/dictionary/fundraiser

Mitchell, S. A., Oslin, J. L., & Griffin, L. L. (2006). *Teaching sport concepts and skills* (2nd ed.). Champaign, IL: Human Kinetics.

Mutz, J., & Murray, K. (2000). *Fundraising for dummies*. Foster City, CA: IDG Books Worldwide.

Nilson, C. (1990). *Training for non-trainers*. New York, NY: AMACOM.

Northcraft, G. B., & Neale, M. A. (1994). *Organizational behavior: A management challenge* (2nd ed.). Fort Worth, TX: Dryden Press.

Paley, N. (2000). *How to develop a strategic marketing plan: A step-by-step guide*. Boca Raton, FL: St. Lucie Press.

Perreault, W. D., & McCarthy, E. J. (2006). *Essentials of marketing: A global-managerial approach* (10th ed.). New York, NY: McGraw-Hill/Irwin.

Perreault, W. D., Cannon, J. P., & McCarthy, E. J. (2010). *Essentials of marketing* (12th ed.). New York, NY: McGraw-Hill/Irwin.

Porter, M. E. (1998). *On competition*. Boston, MA: Harvard Business Review Books.

Pride, W. M., Hughes, R. J., & Kapoor, J. R. (2002). *Business* (7th ed.). Boston, MA: Houghton Mifflin.

Ross, S. D. (2007). Segmenting sports fans using brand association: A cluster analysis. *Sports Marketing Quarterly, 16*(1), 15-24.

Rue, L. W., & Byars, L. L. (2009). *Management: Skills and applications* (13th ed.). New York, NY: McGraw-Hill/Irwin.

Schoell, W. F., & Guiltman, J. P. (1990). *Marketing: Contemporary concepts and practices* (4th ed.). Boston, MA: Allyn and Bacon.

Shank, M. D. (2005). *Sports marketing: A strategic perspective* (3rd ed.). Upper Saddle River, NJ: Prentice Hall.

Shim, J. K. (2006). *Dictionary of business terms*. Mason, OH: Thompson.

Thompson, A. A., Strickland, A. J., & Gamble, J. E. (2010). *Crafting and executing strategy: The quest for competitive advantage* (17th ed.). Boston, MA: McGraw-Hill/Irwin.

Walsh, J. A. (2002). Nonprofit boards: Eight leadership development stories. *Nonprofit World, 20*(1), 11-17.

Warren, C. S., Reeve, J. M., & Fess, P. E. (2002). *Accounting* (20th ed.). Mason, OH: Thompson South-Western.

Weaver M. C. (1998). Staffing fundraising in small organizations. *New Directions for Philanthropic Fundraising, 1998*(20), 45-56.

Weisman, C. (2002). Getting comfortable with the F word: Fundraising and the nonprofit board member. *Nonprofit World, 20*(4), 10-15.

Wendroff, A. L. (1999). *Special events: Proven strategies for nonprofit fundraising*. New York, NY: John Wiley and Sons.

Wilcox, D. L., Ault, P. H., Agee, W. K., & Cameron, G. T. (2000). *Public relations: Strategies and tactics* (6th ed.). New York, NY: Longman/Addison Wessler.

Williams, C. (2000). *Management*. Cincinnati, OH: South-Western.

Wright, P., Kroll, M. J., & Parnell, J. A. (1996). *Strategic management: Concepts and cases* (3rd ed.). Upper Saddle River, NJ: Prentice Hall.

Yow, D. A., Migliore, R. H., Bowden, W. W., Stevens, R. E., & Loudon, D. L. (2007). *Strategic planning for collegiate athletics*. Binghamton, NY: Haworth Half-Court Press.

Zikmund, W. G. (2000). *Business research methods* (6th ed.). Fort Worth, TX: Dryden/Hardcourt College.

Zikmund, W. G. (2003). *Essentials of marketing research* (2nd ed.). Mason, OH: Thompson South-Western.

Appendices

APPENDIX 2.1

Fundraising Program Plan Outline

The following is a detailed sectional outline of a fundraising program plan that can be adopted by any athletic organization. Note: There is no single standard format for a fundraising plan. General sections are consistent, but order and format are not.

Fundraising Plan Outline

  I. Title Page
- Athletic Organization Name (school, university, club)
- Operational Address, Phone Numbers, Emails, Website
- Athletic Organization Logo
- Page Title – Fundraising Program Plan
- Date of Plan
- Fundraising Administrators and Team Members
- Completion/Distribution Date
- Copy Numbers (for tracking)

    (Unpretentious creativity is a plus.)

  II. Table of Contents
- Major Sections
- Sub-Sections
- Page Numbers

  III. Fundraising Plan Summation
- One Page Synopsis of:
  - Overall Fundraising Program
  - Products and Services
  - Marketing Strategies
  - Operational Systems
  - Management Team
  - Financial Status and Need

  IV. Fundraising Program Vision and Mission Statement
- An All-Encompassing Statement of Fundraising Philosophy, Future Vision, and Major Operational Goal

  V. Athletic Organization and Fundraising Program History
- A Synopsis of:
  - Athletic Organization History

- Past Fundraising Efforts
- Past Fundraising Achievements

VI. Long-Term Fundraising Goals (3-5 years)
    – Four to Five Total Long-Term Goals of the Fundraising Program.
    – Broad and Quantitative (if possible)

VII. Short-Term Fundraising Goals (1-2 years)
    – For Each Long-Term Goal, Have Specific Actions (this year or next) to Reach Goal.
    – Precise and Measurable
    – Accountability
    – Time Frames

VIII. Fundraising S.W.O.T. Analysis
    – Strengths, Weaknesses, Opportunities, and Threats
    – Scenario Analysis

IX. Fundraising Policies, Procedures, and Ethical Obligations
    – Breakdown of the Fundraising Program's Policies (rules)
    – Breakdown of the Fundraising Program's Procedures (critical fundraising functions)
    – Ethical Guidelines
        • Ethical Code of Conduct

X. Fundraising Program Human Resource Management
    – Fundraising Team's Job Descriptions
    – BOD Job Description
    – Staff Job Descriptions
    – Net Human Resource Requirements and Action Plan
    – Selection and Hiring Procedures
    – I.T. System
    – Orientation and Training
    – Performance Appraisals
    – Compensation and Benefits
    – Disciplinary System
    – Safety and Health Issues

XI. Fundraising Marketing and Promotions
    – Fundraising Marketing Mix (product, price, place, promotion)
    – Brand Development
    – Target Audience
    – Marketing Communication Mix

XII. Fundraising Program Financial Projections and Financial Statements
    – Expenditure and Revenue Projections for the Fundraising Plan

XIII. Appendix
    – Event Itineraries
    – Training Program Agendas
    – Timetables and Schedules
    – Booster Club Criteria
    – Legal Documentation

APPENDIX 4.1

Fundraising Program's Executive Administrator

For a fundraising program to prosper, a critical, prominent ingredient is the executive fundraising program administrator. The selection of an individual to fill this position must correspond with the fundraising program's aspirations, principles, and atmosphere. The decisive factors that make up a proficient fundraising executive are immeasurable. The indispensible prerequisites of an affluent, consummate athletic organization executive fundraising administrator include, but are not restricted to:

- formidable cognitive abilities;
- ability to recognize and manage change;
- empathetic, employee-centered personality;
- strong and dynamic interpersonal communication skills;
- ability to inspire, encourage, and develop subordinates;
- proficient conflict resolution and negotiating capabilities;
- capacity to utilize and apply sound business practices;
- authoritative decision-making abilities; and
- willingness to empower and hold subordinates accountable.

Three of these characteristics are particularly germane for an executive fundraising administrator. The first and most integral element for any fundraising administrator is having resolute decision-making abilities. Fundraising administrators must be willing to accept the challenges that go along with their determinations and understand the consequences of their actions.

The second attribute that directly relates to a successful executive fundraising administrator is his/her adeptness in inspiring, encouraging, and developing subordinates. To motivate subordinates, a fundraising administrator must:

- continually communicate the athletic organization's and fundraising program's message and mission;
- maintain an emotionally stable environment;
- establish unambiguous expectations in explicit language for subordinates to abide by;
- objectively critique a fundraising program staff/team member's performance and impart corrective feedback when necessary;
- develop an adept use of program incentives to 'steer' subordinates toward pre-established fundraising goals;
- have a constructive, 'hands-on' management style;

- assist (whenever possible) in career planning and development with subordinates; and

- show an unconditional commitment to the fundraising goals, program, and entire athletic organization.

Finally, the third element that contributes to an executive fundraising administrator's achievement is his/her ability to communicate. Can the fundraising administrator:

- foster relationships through persuasive interpersonal communication?

- engage and inspire people through his/her communication style?

- divulge information competently to all athletic organization stakeholders?

- develop a professional persona from his/her skills as a communicator?

- analyze his/her audience and select a communication strategy that is suitable for them?

- listen to others (encoding messages) and apply that information to decision making?

- interpret non-verbal behaviors/gestures/mannerisms accurately?

The selection of a talented, gifted executive fundraising administrator is the first step in obtaining targeted program objectives. Unfortunately, the selection of the wrong individual could set the program back in financial acquisitions, cause lost opportunity costs, and damage public relations.

APPENDIX 6.1

Marketing Plan Outline

The marketing plan is a micro-design of the athletic organization's fundraising program plan (Chapter 2)—it is a plan within a plan. Its mission, objectives, and strategies all emanate from the comprehensive fundraising program plan. It principally focuses on the marketing aspect of the fundraising program and how it will help accomplish the program's overall goals and mission.

The following is an outline of the marketing planning process. Note the close resemblance between marketing planning and organizational/program planning.

Marketing Planning Process

Step 1: Business review

Step 2: Problems/opportunities

Step 3: Sales objectives

Step 4: Target market and marketing Objectives

Step 5: Plan strategies

Step 6: Communication goal

Step 7: Tactical marketing mix tools

Step 8: Marketing plan budget and calendar

Step 9: Execution

Step 10: Evaluation

(adapted from Hiebing & Cooper, 1999, p. xxvii)

APPENDIX 6.2

Internet Technology and Fundraising Program Marketing Communication

The following lists illuminate the magnitude and importance of Internet technology, the marketing communication applications for fundraising programs, and the possible dangers associated with Internet operation.

Importance of the Internet Medium

- Accessibility to the Internet is commonplace. From a fundraising program vantage, this ease of use can affect image, productivity, and support.

- Internet/website technology is informative beyond all other marketing communication techniques. A well-designed website can be the centerpiece of a fundraising program's marketing communication. Internet technology can assimilate all promotional mix elements (advertising, sales promotion, public relations, personal selling).

- Costs associated with Internet use 'levels the playing field' between smaller athletic programs and sizeable athletic programs because the medium is affordable to all athletic organizations.
- The scope of the Internet is global. No other marketing communication technique has this much wide-spread impact on a fundraising program's operations.

Internet Marketing Communication Uses for Fundraising Programs
- With the newest hardware and software improvements, fundraising program websites can make profound and dynamic statements about the fundraising program's quality.
- Websites have become a key recruiting tool for fundraising program personnel.
- Internet technology has mass customization and direct marketing capabilities at a fraction of the cost of other techniques. The Internet furnishes fundraising programs with the capability to contact unlimited individual supporters while tailoring the message for each.
- Websites for fundraising can be constructed for an extensive variety of informational capabilities.
- Internet technology has the internal ability to measure (quantitatively) its own effectiveness.
- If a fundraising program has tangible products, they can be sold and distributed directly to supporters.
- A fundraising program's incorporation of its website into powerful search engines can increase exposure tremendously.
- With future technological advances, creativity options for website design are unlimited.

Dangers
- Failing to update and revise a fundraising program's website can adversely affect marketing communication.
- Websites are carefully scrutinized by external stakeholders. Fundraising programs are now being compared based on website appeal.
- The most important danger in dealing with Internet technology and websites for fundraising programs is the risk of underestimating their exponentially increasing importance in the athletic industry.

APPENDIX 10.1

Summer Sports Instructional Camp
Survey Template

On a 1 to 5 Scale with

1 = Poor   2 = Below Average   3 = Average   4 = Above Average   5 = Excellent

Rate the following aspects of XYZ's Summer Camp and your experience. Circle one answer only.

1) How would you rate the registration process?

Poor   Below Avg.   Avg.   Above Avg.   Excellent
1   2   3   4   5

What could be done to improve XYZ's Summer Camp Registration process?

2) How would you rate the camp facilities?

Poor   Below Avg.   Avg.   Above Avg.   Excellent
1   2   3   4   5

What facility features would you like to see for next year's summer camp?

3) Rate the following camp instruction elements:

Element	Poor	Below Avg.	Avg.	Above Avg.	Excellent
New learning from instruction	1	2	3	4	5
Quality of drills	1	2	3	4	5
Quality of competition	1	2	3	4	5
Instructor's knowledge	1	2	3	4	5
Instructor's helpfulness	1	2	3	4	5
Individual attention	1	2	3	4	5
Demonstrations	1	2	3	4	5

From the above instructional elements, what suggestions would you make:_____

How would you rate XYZ's medical/training staff?

Poor   Below Avg.   Avg.   Above Avg.   Excellent
1   2   3   4   5

What medical treatments did you receive?

What is your overall opinion of XYZ's Summer Sports Camp?

Poor   Below Avg.   Avg.   Above Avg.   Excellent
1   2   3   4   5

How did you hear about XYZ's camp? Circle all that apply

TV   Radio   Newspaper   Flyers   Brochure   Signs/Posters

Coach's Recommendation_____   Other Players _____   Other _____

What camp session(s) did you attend?_____

Other comments: _____

*If the summer instructional camp is an overnight camp, questions relating to auxiliary activities, quality of accommodations and food program should be added.

*For the best survey accuracy, response rate is critical. Make the survey a compulsory final component of the camp.

Index

About the Author

Dr. Richard Leonard's professional knowledge and experience in sports administration is in the tangible, real-world development and operation of NCAA athletic programs. For six seasons, he was the head women's volleyball coach at Georgia State University in Atlanta, Georgia. Under his leadership as a head coach and his guidance as a program administrator, he led the team to a record of 144-69. His GSU team still holds the best winning percentage in school history at .676. He was named Trans American Coach of the Year in 2000 and the Atlantic Sun Conference Coach of the Year in 2001 and 2003. The GSU program won five different conference titles during that period as well as a multitude of post-season individual awards.

Prior to Georgia State, Leonard spent four seasons as associate head coach at Saint Louis University. During his tenure, the Billikens compiled a 91-59 mark, including a 29-10 record and a trip to the Volleyball National Invitational Tournament.

Leonard's first coaching position was at the University of North Florida. The UNF Ospreys went to the NAIA National Championship in the first two years of intercollegiate competition. In the team's first season as an NCAA Division II member, UNF gained a top 15 national ranking and a number one ranking in the Southeastern United States Region.

In addition to his coaching duties, Leonard has served as an adjunct and assistant professor of business for numerous colleges and universities. He has taught classes in entrepreneurship and all levels of management, as well as a range of marketing classes. He is currently an associate professor and chair of the Department of Business Administration and Accounting at Flagler College in Tallahassee, Florida. Additionally, Leonard is an adjunct professor of sports management at the United States Sports Academy, teaching human resource management, marketing, and fundraising at the graduate level, as well as strategic management at the doctoral level.

Leonard was a member and player in the United States Volleyball Association from 1980 to 1997 and was AA rated. He was on four USVB regional championship teams and seven USVB semifinalist and finalists. During his playing career, his teams have won more than 125 tournaments and league championships. Additionally, Leonard served as a USVBA Regional Tournament Director and Regional Marketing Director. He is US Volleyball CAP Level II certified and US Volleyball Critical Thinking Seminar certified. He also has his ACEP certification.

Leonard has written numerous articles in the field of sports administration. These articles (published by the American Volleyball Coaches Association—the governing body of the sport) encompass every aspect of sport management including planning, organization, human resource management, and strategic management. His main focus over the past four years has been publishing textbooks. Leonard's second textbook, *The Administrative Side of Coaching: Applying Business Concepts to Athletic Program Administration and Coaching* (2nd ed., 2008), is published by Fitness Information Technology. He (in collaboration with two colleagues) presented a paper to the Society for the Advancement of Management's (SAM) International Conference entitled *Employee generated separation: A new attitude.* The article was published in the SAM's quarterly journal in 2009.

As the program coordinator for the Jewish Community Center in Pinellas County, Florida, Leonard was involved in far-reaching fundraising activities. Due to the not-for-profit status of the organization, fundraising was a continuous and imperative activity. The diversity of fundraising activities with which Leonard was involved in his five years at the J.C.C. are too numerous to list. As a collegiate coach in a non-revenue classified Olympic sport, Leonard continued operating wide-ranging fundraising programs, including his proprietary summer camp operation, which in a four-year period experienced over 400% growth.

Leonard has a bachelor's degree in accounting from Robert Morris University, an MBA in management from Florida Metropolitan University—Tampa College, and a PhD in administration and management from Walden University. He has certifications in strategic management and leadership from the American Management Association as well as certifications in professional learning, collaborative learning, and classroom management.